Stability a in Marriage:

Between discerning marriage vocation and together in Heaven

Rev. Joseph Kabali, Ph.D.
LMFT, STL.

ISBN: 978-1-953837-03-5

Book Reviews

Having been married for over 50 years and overcoming many challenges, I realized how helpful the book would have guided us. With very little preparation for married life, our love, respect and Catholic teachings enabled us to face our problems. At one time when my elderly parent needed us, through our love, faith and values, we agreed on a solution. Here I found guidelines which would have eliminated troublesome situations. Maintaining stability in marriage, raising and educating children became an act of compromise.

When retirement comes, the education of your children and assisting in the care of grandchildren no longer exists, your lifestyle changes. Facing these changes mentally, physically and financially is also advised herein. This is a very informative, positive and faith in God guide book, encompassing the many joys, successes, trials and tribulations of married life.

Florence Capriatti
Edison, NJ.

As a married man, civil attorney and a canon lawyer serving in Tribunal ministry, I often encounter instances where persons may be mature chronologically, but perhaps have not yet reached that level of inner maturity that is crucial in adequately assesses and appraising the object and obligations of marriage. Indeed, marriage is not only for the procreative aspect but also the intimate partnership for life and love. Father Kabali's work assists in evaluating whether a degree of maturity proportionate to the nature, purpose and obligations were undertaken in entering into marriage. His work also assists in seeing whether a couple undertook the marital obligations to enter into a partnership of the whole of life with one another ordered to their good as well as to the procreation and education of children. Sadly, sometimes a couple entering into marriage ignores those aspects of one another's character which they found troubling when they undertook the obligations of marriage.

Father Kabali assists as to whether the evaluative faculty was present, as well as whether the couple somehow lacked the internal and/or external freedom to act on the significance of their marriage as evaluated. For myself, Study Session: "Physical and mental health sensitivity before marriage and after" in Father Kabali's work is just one example of where this may be seen.

As a doctor in family psychology and a licensed marriage and family therapist, Father Kabali's expertise and compassion make this an important book for those engaged in that life-long marital formation process or for those who assist others in that formation.

Christopher J. Fusco, JCL, Esq.
Attorney-at-Law; Tribunal Judge
Metuchen, New Jersey

I am a Catholic female, married for 37 years. This book made me reflect on those 37 years. My husband and I were married when I was just 18 years old. Back then, pre-Cana was not yet offered at our church, so for these past 37 years we have been navigating through a lot of similar problems and situations mentioned by the participants, ALL on our own. How we got through the problems is outlined in the book, for example: commitment to the relationship, Faith and forgiveness.

I feel this book is a great teaching tool for couples contemplating marriage or remarriage. This book offers many scenarios in which couples can discuss and explore with each other, especially before they take their vows. Great pre-Cana teaching tool!

Ana Jorge, RN
Edison, NJ

Reading this book has empowered me to affirm that my vocation in life is marriage. All other interests and professional careers resolve around my being a married woman. My first marriage was not successful due to multiple expressions of domestic violence which I suffered from my ex-husband; and after three years of marriage, we divorced. I could not however give up on my vocation of married life. As stated in this book, I sought therapy for my own healing from my wounds of divorce. I also used the wisdom gained from my family of origin and past experiences to discern well a better partner for me. After meeting him, we had and still have honest communication about most of the topics discussed in this book. We established a special bond of committed love with one another.

Truth be told, when some of his family members knew that I had been divorced, and given that he had never been married, some of them immediately rejected me. They claimed that, like himself, he should marry a woman who had never been married before. It was very painful for both of us, but as emphasized in this book, we realized that in today's society it is becoming a common practice for someone with a previous marriage experience to get married to someone who is getting married for the first time. The committed love we had developed between us helped us to withstand those external pressures. Progressively, they realized that we were committed to one another and they started to accept me as a suitable partner for him. We have been together for over twenty-years, and we are committed to another for life. Therefore, based on my personal experiences, I find this book very helpful to people who find themselves in almost a similar situation like mine and/or that of my husband.

Alicia
Bogota, Columbia

I am a 27-year-old South Asian (Indian) male, who has never been married. Honestly, my past dating experience was not successful, partly because of seeking instantaneous gratification and my lack of what to focus on during courtship. Fortunately, reading this book has provided real life stories and experiences of people regarding discernment of the vocation to marriage, how they met their partners, subsequent communications, to being stable and happily married. The participants in this book narrated what it takes to make a marriage long lasting, stable, successful and fulfilling. Both my parents have been happily married for 30+ years and I have always idealized their marriage as a marriage I would like to have in the future. Reading this book, has provided me with direct experiences from married and remarried spouses regarding what has led to their success, stability and happiness in their marriages.

Along with my parents' stable and happy marriage, this book has allowed me to understand, develop and be thoughtful while searching for my life partner, as well as the type of questions and discussions I will have during my courtship/dating phase. I would highly recommend this book to unmarried and single individuals who are looking to find a long-term partner to help identify a suitable life-partner, how to prepare together for stable and satisfactory marriage, especially by having meaningful discussions during the courtship and there-after.

Kevinn Eddy, Ph.D.
Cellular and Molecular Pharmacology Program
Rutgers, The State University of New Jersey

———————————◆◆◆◆◆◆———————————

I am a widow as a result of the death of my husband with whom we had a stable and happy marriage. Reading this book, especially the chapter referring to the widowed spouse, reminded me about my own story and experience after the death of my husband, leaving me at a young age with five children. I was forced out of the house by the family members of my late husband. It makes me cry to think about the sufferings and injustices I experienced as widow and single mother when my deceased spouse was no longer there to defend me and my children. Above all, this book has helped me to realize that spouses need to write their Wills together, considering the wellbeing of one another in the event one of them dies. I was touched by the experience of the widow in this book because being cared for financially is very empowering to the widowed spouse. I encourage the family members of the deceased to realize that the widowed spouse should be cared for. I found myself identifying with her and realized that stability and satisfaction in marriage goes beyond the death of a spouse.

Gertrude Nasanga
Kampala, Uganda

Reading this book taught me a lot about couples and how they deal with their relationships. It made me see how everyone handles the situation... if you want your relationship to work, there's a lot of compromising. When you enter into a marriage you should be all in and be willing to put the work into it to make it successful.

Phyllis Maffucci, married for 28 years, wife and mother, in a dual career marriage

I learned many things from this book especially the usefulness of communication, committed love and spirituality. I am a man of few words, but I enjoyed reading and reflecting about the experiences of the participants. I was touched by their honesty, stories, experiences, forgiving spirit, reconciliation, perseverance and efforts to find solutions in difficult times, rather than walking away from the marriage. In a special way, I realized that my grandparents didn't have most of the challenges in their marriage in comparison to the ones influenced by the improper use of technology today. I emphasize this point because one of the participants mentioned how he struggled to overcome his addiction to pornography because he was at a point of losing his marriage. He admitted that he had lost a lot of sexual interest in his wife and found sexual intimacy with her to be a chore. Her frustrations made her wonder what to do until she decided to confront him about his addiction.

Likewise, I am grateful that my wife confronted me, even if I felt so much shame and humiliation. Otherwise, I was at the point of losing my marriage. Instead of retaliating or arguing with her, I admitted that I had an addiction to pornography and I sought help. She was very supportive of my recovery process which was not easy. Even if I had moments of relapse, I didn't give up. In retrospect, I realized the amount of time I had wasted and what I could have used it for. All this gave me the motivation to save my marriage. I have to admit, I also spent a lot of money on this addiction. I advise others who find themselves in this situation or feel inclined to start it not to follow through. As the adage goes: "Curiosity killed the cat!" I am grateful to my wife for that confrontation and support because now we are happily married and our sexual life has improved for the better.

Frank
New York, NY

————————————◆◆◆◆◆◆◆◆————————————

Opening quotation from the Bible:

"1 Happy the husband of a good wife;

the number of his days will be doubled.

2 A loyal wife brings joy to her husband,

and he will finish his years in peace.

3 A good wife is a generous gift

bestowed upon him who fears the Lord.

4 Whether rich or poor, his heart is content,

a smile ever on his face.

13 A gracious wife delights her husband;

her thoughtfulness puts flesh on his bones.

15 A modest wife is a supreme blessing;

no scales can weigh the worth of her chastity.

16 The sun rising in the Lord's heavens—

the beauty of a good wife in her well-ordered home."

(Sirach 26:1-4,13,15-16)

I pray therefore, that those with the vocation to heterosexual marriage life may find the right companion with whom to walk the journey of marriage to Heaven. [Author]

Dedication

This book is dedicated to my parents, relatives, friends, teachers, physicians, benefactors for your support in different ways and to God who brought each one of you into my life. God bless you.

Acknowledgments

Thanks to all the individuals who responded to the questions I asked you and for sharing such profound insights based on your marriage-related experiences. Without you, this book would not be what it is. Deep within my heart, I consider all of you as the co-authors. In fact, I have honored your experiences and insights by using most of the exact words you used to express them. I pray that many people may find something beneficial in this book in order to embrace stability and satisfaction in their marriage and for the well-being of their loved ones, the church and society at large. Peace and God's blessings to you all.

On Feb 23, 2019, one the participants, fictitiously identified in this book as Ted, wrote to the author: "Thanks for the opportunity to put in writing what we know is in our hearts."

Table of Contents

Preface

I was inspired to write this book by one of my close friends who is in her first marriage. After the first publication of my book entitled *Embracing Remarriage Stability and Satisfaction (2017),* I showed her a copy of the book. Surprisingly, though usually soft spoken, on that day, while holding my book, she raised her voice and asked me: "Joseph, are you telling me that I should leave my current marriage and embrace remarriage?" I tried to explain to her why I had written about remarriage, but she still insisted: "This book was designed to focus on remarriage not on first marriages." Every effort I made to clarify was in vain.

Consequently, I changed the topic by asking her: *"Are you happy in your marriage?"* Without responding in words, she immediately sat on the floor and broke into tears. I tried to calm her down as much as I could. After some minutes of sobbing, she looked me in the eye and asked me: "Then, why don't you write about embracing stability and satisfaction in first marriages?" As she calmed down, I listened attentively and non-judgmentally to her story. She spoke at length about her marriage. She described it as "unhappy and at the risk of ending in divorce."

After that historical day with my friend, I took her cited question to heart. I formulated an informal questionnaire to be responded to individually by various participants in their first marriages. I also interviewed two widows and two widowers to get their retrospective experiences of marriage stability and satisfaction as well as some descriptions of their lives after the death of their spouses. Each volunteer contributed with profound insights and grounded responses to this book. Additionally, after reflecting on the conversation with the aforementioned close friend, I decided to edit and reprint my first book with a modification to the title and some changes. Instead of *"Embracing Remarriage…,"* it is entitled: *"Stability and Satisfaction in Remarriage"* (2024).

Another historical day is February 18, 2019. That is when I started writing the first draft of this book. On that day, I overheard someone on a radio station say: "Compassion without wisdom can be dangerous."

Based on that insight, I realized that as much as I feel compassionate about helping couples, it was time to start writing the participants' words of wisdom. I felt empowered to start writing this book because I realized that the responses received from the life experiences of the participants were like fountains of wisdom. Therefore, with every participant's written consent, I started to put in writing this book in order to share them with other people, especially those who seek to embrace stability and satisfaction in their marriage.

On the other hand, although the primary focus in this book is designed to be on marriage, I am also interested in the strengthening of family life and society at large with the help of happy and stable couples. The participants who contributed to this book are also interested in helping children grow up in a home where they see their parents amicably interacting with one another. Therefore, one of the key ingredients in this book is to prevent divorce and help children to grow up in families with both caring parents. This starts by empowering individuals contemplating marriage and those already married to learn how to establish and maintain stability and satisfaction in marriage.

The author's intention is to narrate the participants' experiences as lived, and should not be understood as an endorsement or rejection of any of the participants' life choices or experiences.

Ideally, marriage is for life ("until death do us part"). However, given that some people remarry (once or more) after divorce and/or the death of a spouse, it is also important to clarify that in this book, the word "marriage" is used to refer to one's "first" marriage. Therefore, those who are planning to get married or already married to someone who has an experience of marrying for the first time, second time, or more, are encouraged to read this book and also the other one by the same author, titled: Stability and satisfaction in remarriage (2024). Likewise, those with previous marriage experience(s), if getting married or already married to someone marrying for the first time should read these books.

Introduction

Why another book on marriage?

Although many books and articles have been written and published
about marriage, I have written this book because it may be beneficial to
people interested in preparing themselves for monogamous and
heterosexual marriage and/or those who want to explore strategies of
how to reinforce their stability and satisfaction in marriage. As humans,
we prepare ourselves for many things and get training in different fields
(e.g., to become a teacher, athlete, doctor, mechanic, farmer, driver and
other vocations). However, many people tend to forget to prepare
themselves for the greatest vocation and role in society: MARRIAGE.
Based on the experiences and stories of many married people and those
who have experienced divorce, it seems that the marriage bond needs to
be nurtured, otherwise, it wears off and may disintegrate completely if
not reinvigorated. Within marriage, one becomes a husband or a wife.
Furthermore, with the presence of one child or more the partners become
parents, and later, possibly grandparents and successively, great-
grandparents.

In today's society, some people are still focused on getting married with
those of their kind ("tribe") in terms of culture, religion, socioeconomic
status, education, and other variables. On the other hand, many people
are open to going beyond those significant variables. However, in order
to have a framework, the author has focused more on the teachings of
the Catholic Church as a reference point about marriage. Therefore, non-
Catholic readers are encouraged to develop their respective frameworks
as they reflect on how the presented teachings may be integrated into
their religious backgrounds.

Based on the insights of the participants in this book, it is advisable that
partners interested in marriage stability and satisfaction should seriously
consider preparing for marriage instead of "practicing everything on

stage." Clinical findings also indicate that some spouses stay together as husband and wife for years, but they lack marital satisfaction (Gottman, 1993, 1994b; Johnson & Greenberg, 1994; Larson & Holman, 1994). On the other hand, some spouses experience temporary marital satisfaction with their spouses and then decide to separate (Russell-Chapin, Chapin & Sattler, 2001).

Such marital stabilities without satisfaction or marital instabilities with temporary satisfaction affect the spouses themselves. This, in turn, impacts all the significant people in their lives, especially the children. Children are profoundly affected by the levels of their parents' marital instability and lack of satisfaction (LeBey, 2004; Walsh, 1992). Therefore, each spouse has to learn to make marriage a success and persevere by doing his or her best.

The factors explored in the questionnaire in this book were for both stability and satisfaction in marriage. Stability in marriage refers to a spouse's responsibility to develop and maintain a permanent marital commitment with his or her spouse until biological death separates them (Berger, 1998; Champlin, 1997). Satisfaction in marriage refers to a spouse's responsibilities to establish a marriage, in which he/she perceives the relationship as generating happiness and meaning as well as providing a mutually life-giving structure with his or her spouse and children (Gottman, 1994b; Jacobson & Greenburg, 1994).

Therefore, this book is a preparation and an on-going resource for embracing both stability and satisfaction in marriage. In a search for how to prevent and respond to the increasing percentage of divorce after marriage and the challenges of serial monogamy (Gottman, 1993), partners contemplating marriage and married ones are invited to reflect upon some of the findings in this book and integrate them into their marriage.

This book is based on the feedback from participants in their first marriages. Some of the research findings I received while conducting my doctoral dissertation in regard to the factors for stability and satisfaction in remarriage, have been frequently reported by spouses in first marriage, while others are specifically applicable to remarriage. Therefore, in this book, I have republished some of the common insights from that dissertation as well as my reprinted book entitled: *"Embracing Stability and Satisfaction in Remarriage"*.

Additional resources and studies are cited in this book to help partners contemplating marriage or those already married, as well as to help the significant people in their lives. Such resources may help people to understand in greater depth the complexities in marriage. Various authors and researchers are cited in this book to reinforce and shed more light on the ideas presented. Some of the referenced resources may seem outdated just by looking at the years of their publication. However, given the words of wisdom contained in them, they are worthy of revisiting. They are a treasure which transcends time and geographical locations. They remind me of the words of wisdom which my grandmother used to graciously share with me till her death at the age of 99. (May she rest in peace.)

Why a book with questions?

The questions included in this book are intended to stimulate the reader's creative thinking and problem-solving skills and to make in-depth responses. The questions are also geared at serving as step-by-step exercises to help the reader master the main ideas within a given chapter. Whenever necessary, one should reread the session for greater comprehension in order to search for ways of applying these ideas to daily living. Various spaces for writing are provided at the end of each session. The organization of the book materials also provides the reader with an opportunity for introspective and insightful self-study.

Another reason for integrating some of the findings from my book on remarriage is the likelihood that someone in his or her first marriage may be married to a person who had a previous marriage experience(s) and/or to a single parent. Consequently, a knowledge and implementation of many of the unique factors applicable to remarriage may be beneficial to integrate into his/her preparation for marriage or current marriage.

Conceptualization of marriage and clarifications of some of the words and phrases used in this book

It is beyond the scope of this book to embrace the diverse, historical, traditional and contemporary descriptions of marriage. In this book, the word marriage will be limited to the following conceptualization, and it is intended for people who embrace such framework.

Marriage: The word marriage is presented in this book in reference to a monogamous life commitment between a man and a woman. Both voluntarily enter into marriage. Each man and woman has to discern first if he or she has the vocation to married life with another person of a different gender (woman or man), evaluate before marriage his or her motivations for getting married and communicate them in a timely manner to his or her prospective spouse. The two have to mutually agree to start their married life as husband and wife within a formal civil, religious or traditional/customary ceremony. Such a ceremony (wedding) serves as an official mark for the starting of their marriage, in the presence of a legitimate official and witnesses.

In other words, in this book marriage is conceptualized as a lasting bond between one man and one woman. It goes beyond a physical union to include other levels of connection and commitment (e.g., spiritual, emotional, moral, ethical, financial, cultural, ethnic, religious, mysterious, social, and psychological, as well as union with God). Marriage provides husband and wife with the opportunity to grow in unconditional and sacrificial love and selflessness as they serve one another. Marriage is also presented in this book as a significant ingredient of family and societal life. Therefore, unless age, health difficulties and /or complications do not permit, married couples should be open to welcome biological children, grandchildren and great-grandchildren.

Monogamy: In this book, monogamy refers to a form of marriage in which one man is married to one woman till death or divorce separates them. Therefore, this book is designed for those who want to embrace a life commitment to monogamous married life. This book is designed to reduce the risks of divorce and the practice of what Rutter (1998) referred to as "serial monogamy." Rutter used this phrase to refer to a situation where someone embraces monogamy for a period of time, then divorces and embraces monogamy again for a time. Then that marriage ends in divorce and one enters another monogamous marriage, and then a series of remarriages after each subsequent divorce.

Heterosexuality: In this book, those who decide to embrace a life commitment of monogamous marriage, should also be heterosexual. This means that one's sexual attraction has to be toward the person of the opposite gender.

In other words, a man who wants to enter into marriage should have a sexual attraction/orientation toward a woman and the woman must also have a sexual attraction/orientation toward a man. Consequently, it is beyond the scope of this book to include the commitments between individuals and partners having other sexual attractions and commitments. Such attractions include: homosexual [sexually attracted to same sex, term generally used for two men], bisexual [sexually attracted to both sexes], lesbian [homosexual relations between two women], transgender [involving a partial or full reversal of gender], transsexual [desirous of being, or completely identifying with, the opposite sex], transvestite [receiving sexual gratification from imitating the opposite, e.g., wearing clothing of the opposite sex], as well as other sexual attractions.

Stability in marriage: This phrase refers to a married person taking individual and mutual responsibility to develop and maintain a permanent marital commitment with his or her spouse until biological death separates them (Berger, 1998; Champlin, 1997). It has also been observed by other authors (e.g., Crowley, 2018; and Gold, 2019) that separation and/or divorce may occur even after many years of marriage or what Crowley refers to as "Gray Divorce." Therefore, to highlight the value of stability in marriage, the author of this book selected participants who described themselves as having a profound experience of security (stability and satisfaction) in their current and first marriages.

Satisfaction in marriage: This phrase refers to an individual spouse's responsibility to establish and maintain a marriage in which each spouse perceives the relationship as generating happiness and meaning through his or her interactions with his or her spouse. Each spouse learns to persevere by doing his or her best to make marriage a success. It requires each spouse to provide a mutually life-giving structure with his or her spouse (and their children) (Gottman, 1994b; Jacobson & Greenburg, 1994).

Gender, culture, Catholic teachings on marriage and ecumenical sensitivities in this book

The author wants to clarify that this book is primarily written for people who want to follow the teachings of the Roman Catholic Church in regard to marriage. This involves the understanding of marriage as a Sacrament and as only between a man and woman (cf. Beal, et al., 2000). Additionally, the author's experiences and interactions with people of different religions and cultures have helped him to understand that many people, regardless of religious and cultural differences, are interested in embracing stability and satisfaction in marriage.

Therefore, even if it is beyond the scope of this book to present a comprehensive study of how people of various religions and cultures can work together to embrace stability and satisfaction in marriage, the author thinks that people's gender, ethnic, cultural, religious and historical experiences seem to play a significant role in their marriages (cf. McGoldrick, et al., 2005; McGoldrick, 1998; Bishop & Darton, 1987).

Consequently, the author decided to use a problem-and-solution focused approach (Haley 1984, de Shazer, 1985) by interviewing Catholics and people of different religions and cultural/ethnic backgrounds. This approach was geared at exploring how people having different religions and cultures have addressed the problem of instability and lack of satisfaction in marriage. This book contains some of the solutions which have worked for the participants and their suggested words of wisdom to help others interested in establishing and maintaining stability and satisfaction in marriage.

Participants

The names and identifying data of the participants who responded to my informal questionnaire have been changed in this book. Any resemblance of name and/or other demographic data about anyone is a mere coincidence. However, with the permission of the participants, some of their original words, phrases and narratives have been directly cited.

The gender and sexual orientation of every spouse who responded to the questionnaire study were taken into consideration. All the participants who contributed to this book described themselves as living in committed monogamous marriages. Additionally, all identified themselves as heterosexual.

All participants attributed their stability (feeling of security) in their respective marriages to many factors included in this book, and also to the knowledge they had gained from resolving conflicts they had encountered in their current and first marriages. The author encourages reading about the diversity of the challenges, conflicts or problems that each of the participants encountered in marriage and how they were resolved. The lack of knowing how to resolve problems or how to develop coping strategies may result in many couples simply staying together, tolerating each other, but chronically unhappy together, or eventually separating/divorcing or dying.

The questionnaire was also designed for participants whose first marriage was between a man and a woman. Therefore, this book is based on findings the author received exclusively from heterosexual spouses who were in their first marriage, as well as findings from other heterosexual spouses who contributed to the author's previous book on remarriage. This book focuses on partners contemplating heterosexual marriage and/or currently living in a heterosexual marriage.

Consequently, this book may not reflect the key areas that are specific to committed partners of other sexual orientations. They are advised to consult other resources.

No monetary incentives or other benefits were given or promised to any of the participants. All of them volunteered to contribute to the questionnaire with the self-expressed desire to empower other people in romantic relationships toward stability and satisfaction in marriage.

I interviewed a number of participants to get a diversity of feedback that would be helpful to people of different backgrounds, in terms of age, formal education, economic status, ethnicity and culture, with the hope that readers with diverse backgrounds would benefit from the findings. This book is a fruit of in-depth words of wisdom from trusted friends, friends of friends and reviewed literature.

The participants included men and women between 26 to 85 years of age, each in his or her first monogamous and heterosexual marriage. Each participant was married either in a civil court or in a traditional or religious denomination. However, I decided to include one participant (fictitiously named Joana) to get a sense of why she decided to cohabitate with her boyfriend before marriage and to explore the strategies she is implementing with her boyfriend to empower them to feel more secure in their relationship so as to consider marriage.

After beginning to receive similar ideas, though expressed in different words. I stopped conducting interviews and sending out questionnaires. I identified the factors which permeated through all of the participants' responses, and developed themes based on factors influencing their stability and satisfaction, as well as their insights for other individuals and couples. Each of these factors is discussed in this book and some of the identified factors are followed by questions for personal reflection and an invitation to implement strategies that bring about a positive change.

Based on the feedback and responses from the participants in their first marriages, the author has realized that some of their experiences and insights are in some ways similar to those of the remarried participants who contributed to his previous book on remarriage, yet different in other ways. Therefore, whenever considered appropriate, the author has reprinted and integrated some of those similarities and other significant insights into this book. The reprints may be beneficial to those contemplating marriage, those already married, and interested others by stimulating their thinking, and inspiring them to take concrete actions to reinforce stability and satisfaction in marriage.

Part 1

Know yourself and your story

Everyone has a story and a history to tell. If there is no one to tell and/or to listen to your story, write it down and read it to yourself. Our stories have significant ways in which they can influence how we perceive ourselves, others and God. More often than not, we tend to project our past experiences into the future.

Becoming aware of your past and present, of unhealed wounds, dreams, failures, successes, joys, challenges and your innermost needs may help you in the future.

This demographic section was created by the author to help any person in a marriage situation make an in-depth exploration of one's contextual realities. Each person is encouraged to write down any dominant feelings, thoughts and/or memories that he/she may experience while filling-in the blank spaces or after the exercise. Fill in the gaps wherever applicable to you and to those related to you. (The term "first spouse" is used below to apply to a "prospective," as well as a "first" spouse.)

About us

My gender:

- o   Male

- o   Female

Date of birth: /   /

Age:

Religion:

Denomination:

- o   Nondenominational

- o   Atheist

My current attendance of religious services:

- o   Once or more times a week

- o   Once a month

- o   Less than five times a year

- o   Not attending

Gender of my prospective or first spouse:

- o   Male

- o   Female

Date of birth: /   /

Age:

His or Her Religion:

Denomination:

- Nondenominational
- Atheist

His or her current attendance of religious services:

- Once or more times a week
- Once a month
- Less than five times a year
- Not attending

His or Her Religion:

Denomination:

- Nondenominational
- Atheist

His or her current attendance of religious services:

- Once or more times a week
- Once a month
- Less than five times a year
- Not attending

Gender of my second spouse/cohabitating partner:

- Male
- Female

Date of birth: /   /

Age:

His or Her Religion:

Denomination:

- o Nondenominational
- o Atheist

His or her current attendance of religious services:

- o Once or more times a week
- o Once a month
- o Less than five times a year
- o Not attending

Cultural / ethnic background of my biological mother:

_____

Cultural / ethnic background of my biological father:

_____

Cultural / ethnic background with which I identify myself:

_____

Highest level of my formal education:

_____

My sexual orientation:

- o Heterosexual
- o Homosexual
- o Bisexual
- o Other

Cultural / ethnic background of my first spouse's mother:

_____

Cultural / ethnic background of my first spouse's father:

_____

Cultural / ethnic background with which my first spouse identified himself / herself:

_____

Highest level of formal education of my first spouse:

_____

Sexual orientation of my first spouse:

- o   Heterosexual

- o   Homosexual

- o   Bisexual

- o   Other

Cultural / ethnic background of my second spouse's (or cohabitating partner's) mother:

_____

Cultural / ethnic background of my second spouse's (or cohabitating partner's) father:

_____

Cultural / ethnic background with which my second spouse/cohabitating partner identifies himself / herself:

_____

Highest level of formal education of my second spouse / cohabitating partner:

Sexual orientation of my second spouse / cohabitating partner:

- o   Heterosexual

- o   Homosexual

- o   Bisexual

- o   Other

————————◆ • ◆ •◆• ◆ • ◆————————

Family of origin

(Fill in all the spaces below that apply)

My biological mother:

- o   Alive

- o   Deceased

- o   Married

- o   Divorced

- o   Remarried

- o   Remarried more than once

- o   Never lived together with my father

My biological father:

- o   Alive

- o   Deceased

- o   Married

- o   Divorced

- o   Remarried
- o   Remarried more than once
- o   Never lived together with my mother

Biological mother of my first spouse:

- o   Alive
- o   Deceased
- o   Married
- o   Divorced
- o   Remarried
- o   Remarried more than once
- o   Never lived together with my first spouse's father

Biological father of my first spouse:

- o   Alive
- o   Deceased
- o   Married
- o   Divorced
- o   Remarried
- o   Remarried more than once
- o   Never lived together with my first spouse's mother

Biological mother of my second spouse:

- o   Alive
- o   Deceased

- o Married

- o Divorced

- o Remarried

- o Remarried more than once

- o Never lived together with my second spouse's father

Biological father of my second spouse:

- o Alive

- o Deceased

- o Married

- o Divorced

- o Remarried

- o Remarried more than once

- o Never lived together with my second spouse's mother

Biological siblings: numbers, birth order and marital status

Number of my older brothers:

Number of my younger brothers:

Number of my older sisters:

Number of my younger sisters:

Number of my single brothers

(Over eighteen years of age and never married):

Number of my brothers in their first marriages:

Number of my currently divorced brothers:

Number of my currently remarried brothers:

Number of my single sisters

(Over eighteen years of age and never married):

Number of my sisters in their first marriages:

Number of my currently divorced sisters:

Number of my currently remarried sisters:

I grew up with:

- o Both biological parents
- o Single mother
- o Single father
- o Adoptive parent(s)
- o In a stepfamily
- o With a stepfather
- o With a stepmother
- o With another relative

Number of my first spouse's older brothers:

Number of younger brothers:

Number of older sisters:

Number of younger sisters:

Number of my first spouse's single brothers (over eighteen years of age and never married):

Number of brothers in their first marriages:

Number of currently divorced brothers:

Number of currently remarried brothers:

Number of my first spouse's single sisters

(Over eighteen years of age and never married):

Number of sisters in their first marriages:

Number of currently divorced sisters:

Number of currently remarried sisters:

My first spouse grew up with:

- o Both biological parents
- o Single mother
- o Single father
- o Adoptive parent(s)
- o In a stepfamily
- o With a stepfather
- o With a stepmother
- o With another relative

Number of my second spouse's older brothers:

Number of younger brothers:

Number of older sisters:

Number of younger sisters:

Number of my second spouse's single brothers (over eighteen years of age and never married):

Number of brothers in their first marriages:

Number of currently divorced brothers:

Number of currently remarried brothers:

Number of my second spouse's single sisters

(over eighteen years of age and never married):

Number of sisters in their first marriages:

Number of currently divorced sisters:

Number of currently remarried sisters:

My second spouse grew up with:

- o   Both biological parents

- o   Single mother

- o   Single father

- o   Adoptive parents

- o   In a stepfamily

- o   With a stepfather

- o   With a stepmother

- o   With another relative

Custodial parent's first marriage, divorce, and remarriage

My age at first marriage:

Duration of my first marriage:

Time between my first divorce and second marriage:

Duration since my second marriage to present day:

Number of my biological children in first marriage:

Age(s) of my biological child(ren) at time of second marriage:

Gender and current age of my biological children from my first marriage living or having lived with me in my second marriage

Females:

Males:

Number and ages of my biological children born in my second marriage:

Age of my ex-spouse at time of my first marriage:

Age of my current spouse at time of my remarriage:

Gender and current ages of my stepchildren (current spouse's children) living with me at present in my second marriage

Females:

Custodial parent's first spouse: Marriage, divorce, and remarriage

Age of my first spouse at his/her first marriage:

His or her number of prior marriages:

Duration of his or her prior marriage(s):

Time between his/her first divorce and second marriage:

Number of biological children in his or her prior marriage(s):

Age(s) of his or her biological child(ren) at time of his or her marriage to me:

Gender and current age of his or her biological children from prior marriages who lived with me in my first marriage

    Females:

    Males:

Age of my ex-spouse at time of his or her marriage with me:

Gender and current ages of his or her stepchildren who lived with me in my first marriage

    Females:

    Males:

Custodial parent's second spouse / partner: Marriage, divorce, and remarriage

Age of my second spouse at his / her first marriage:

His or her number of prior marriages:

Duration of his or her prior marriage(s):

Time between his / her first divorce and second marriage:

Number of biological children in his or her prior marriage(s):

Age(s) of his or her biological child(ren) at time of his or her marriage to me:

Gender and current age of his or her biological children from prior marriages living with me in my second marriage

    Females:

    Males:

Age of my current spouse at time of his or her marriage to me:

Gender and current ages of his or her stepchildren who lived with me in my second marriage

Females:

Males:

———————◆ • ◆ •◆• ◆ • ◆————————

Current marriage

Is there something unique about the structure of my future   or current marriage I think needs to be considered in my marriage?
Circle Yes or No.

If yes, identity it and describe it clearly as follows:

_____

_____

_____

_____

_____

_____

_____

_____

_____

_____

Part 2

Meet the Participants

Data was collected from married individuals, not couples, all in their first marriage. As mentioned before, for reasons of confidentiality, all the names of the participants have been changed, as well as some of the identities in the data. However, the stories presented are life experiences of people who volunteered to share about their lives and acquired wisdom regarding marriage and family life, with the goal of inspiring others to embrace stability and satisfaction in marriage. One of the most significant lessons the author learned from all the participants was that every participant had experienced, or was still experiencing, one or more stressful challenge(s), and yet decided to find ways of resolving it, or found alternative ways of coping with the identified challenge(s).

This solution-focused approach to the problem(s) experienced is one of the highlights in this section in the presentation of each participant. Most of the problems could have sparked a reason for separation or divorce because of resultant pain, doubts, humiliations and other risks, but the resolution to move forward is one of the greatest lessons each participant inspires as a model of hope, perseverance, love, faith and/or how to handle some of the problems in marriage and family life. The focus is geared to honoring every participant's experience, not to make comparisons of who faced a greater challenge than the other. Everybody's pain is pain, and we can all learn from it, as well as becoming more compassionate, less judgmental and supportive of one another.

Clarification: The word "challenges" is used in this book to refer primarily to the various difficulties or problems which the participants have experienced in their marriages and have volunteered to share. The challenges presented by each of the participants are in NO WAY intended to be conceptualized as *Immoral Behaviors, Personality Disorders, Sins against God's Commandments, nor Crimes against the Civil Laws.* Instead, the participants identified and described their challenges in marriage with the goal of helping other people to know how they resolved them or continued to cope more effectively with them in order to stay happily married.

Table 1. Demographics of the male participants

#	Name	Age	Spouse's Age	Participant's age at marriage	Duration of marriage by 2019 & number of children	Cultural/ ethnic background & religion	Spouse's cultural/ethnic background & religion	Highest level of education & spouse's highest level of education	Joint annual income in US dollars
1	George	62	63	28	34,8	German Am, Catholic	Italian Am, Catholic	CG,CG	120K
2	Matt	30	26	28	2,0	Indian, Catholic	Indian, Catholic	MA, MA	INM
3	Ted	71	67	21	46,(1)*	Italian Am, Catholic	Italian Am, Catholic	BA,BA	100K
4	Freddie	40	38	30	10,2	Irish, Catholic	Italian, Catholic	BA,RN	INM
5	Nelson	32	31	27	5,1	African Am, Baptist	African Am, Baptist	MA,BA	INM
6	Albert	49	47	28	21,2	Irish, Catholic	Polish, Catholic	MA,BA	250K
7	Antonio	84		27	57,3	Italian Am, Catholic	Brazilian Am, Catholic	No HS, BA	INM
8	Charles	78	75	26	53,1	Ugandan Am, Catholic	Ugandan Am, Catholic	MA,BA	INM
9	Miguel	41	33	33	9,2	Ecuadorian, Christian	Italian Am, Catholic	PhD, MA	INM
10	Lee	51	53	28	26,2	Chinese Am, Confucian	Chinese Am, Confucian	MA,BA	INM
11	Salvador	40	37	20	20,4	Peruvian Am, Catholic	Colombian Am, Catholic	BA,HS	INM
12	Andy	55	53	35	20,2	Irish Am, Catholic	Polish, Catholic	MS,BA	INM
13	Alfredo	42	38	27	15,2	Spanish Am, Catholic	Spaniard Am, Catholic	PhD, PhD	INM
14	Robert	55	50	25	30,3	Irish Am, Catholic	Italian Am, Catholic	BA,HS	INM
15	Ivan	70	68	24	46,(1)*	Haitian Am, Catholic	Haitian Am, Catholic	AD,HS	INM
16	Jimmie	64	62	28	20,2	Irish Am, Catholic (NP)	Irish Am, Catholic (NP)	AD,HS	INM
17	Mateo	49	49	18	31,4	Filipino Am, Catholic	Filipino Am, Catholic	BA,HS	INM
18	Erick	72	70	27	45,2	Polish Am, Catholic	Polish Am, Catholic	BA,HS	INM
19	Dave	45	44	30	15,2	British Am, Anglican	African Am, Baptist	Esq,MA	INM
20	Rowland	71	67	25	46,3	Irish Am, Catholic	Italian Am, Catholic	Ed.D,MA	170K
21	Andrew	35	33	15	15	Portuguese Am, Catholic	French Am, Catholic	BS, BA	INM
22	Lorenzo	43	42	27	16,3 (+1*)	Ecuadorian, Catholic	Ecuadorian, Catholic	HS, No HS	120K
23	Paul	77	75	24	53,6	Ugandan, Anglican	Ugandan, Anglican	HS, No HS	INM
24	Peter	72	69 (Decd)	20	50,4	Nigerian Am, Catholic	Nigerian Am, Catholic	MA,BA	INM
25	Stephen	62	60 (Decd)	28	34,5	Filipino Am, Catholic	Indian Am, Catholic	MA,RN	INM

Key: Am = American; RN = Registered Nurse, CG = College Graduate; AD = Associate Degree; ES = Elementary School; SH = High School; INM =Income Not Mentioned, Religion - NP = Nonpracticing; Decd = Deceased, (1)* = 1 adopted child; (+1*) Child from an extramarital affair 100,000

Note: Most of the participants in their first marriage preferred not to indicate their exact or approximate annual joint income. This was the direct opposite of all the participants in their remarriage who spoke about their annual joint income with ease and exactness.

Table 2. Demographics of the female participants

#	Name	Age	Spouse's Age	Participant's age at marriage	Duration of marriage by 2019 & number of children	Cultural/ethnic background & religion	Spouse's cultural/ethnic background & religion	Highest level of education & spouse's highest level of education	Joint annual income in US dollars
1	Anna	61	61	23	34,4	German Am, Catholic	German Am, Catholic	AD,MS	INM
2	Ellen	67	72	21	46,1	Irish Am, Catholic	Irish Am, Catholic	RN,MA	100K
3	Joyce	55	57	22	33,3	Ugandan Am, Anglican	Ugandan Am, Anglican	MD,MA	INM
4	Sarah	47	48	26	21,2	Polish Am, Catholic	Polish Am, Catholic	BA,BA	INM
5	Chen	53	54	25	28,2	Chinese Am, Buddhist	Chinese Am, Confucian	BA,BA	INM
6	Cynthia	45	47	23	22,2	Irish Am, Catholic	Irish Am, Catholic	MA,PhD	INM
7	Lea	26	27	24	2,0	Caucasian Am, Catholic (NP)	Italian Am, Catholic (NP)	BA,BA	INM
8	Teresa	56	57	23	33,4	Kenyan Am, Presbyterian	Kenyan, Methodist	BA,MS	104K
9	Jessica	66	69	27	29,2	Hungarian Am, Catholic	German Am, Lutheran	BA,MA	INM
10	Karen	66	70	19	47,2	Italian Am, Catholic	German Am, Lutheran	HS,BA	INM
11	Suzanna	45	50	25	20,1	So. Africa Am, Jehovah	So. Africa Am, Jehovah	AD,BA	INM
12	Linda	35	46	19	14,1	Chilean, Evangelical	Chilean, Evangelical	HS,HS	INM
13	Christine	28	32	23	5,0	Indian, Catholic	Indian, Catholic	MA,MA	INM
14	Marie	39	39	25	13,1	Ghanan, Catholic	Ghanan, Catholic	BA,BA	INM
15	Doris	69	71	23	46,3	Italian-Irish Am, Catholic	German Am, Catholic	PhD,PhD	170K
16	Joana	33	34	32, live together	Cohabitating, 1,1	Irish Am, Catholic	Italian Am, Catholic	CG,BA	INM
17	Raquel	35	40	23	12,3	Canadian Am, Catholic	Italian Am, Catholic	BA,MA	INM
18	Jean	73	75	22	51,1	Polish Am, Catholic	Irish Am, Catholic	HS,AD	100K
19	Lucy	65	67	24	41,2	So. Korea Am, Catholic	So. Korea Am, Catholic (NP)	BA,MA	INM
20	Sonia	34	41	27	7,3	Salvadorian Am, Catholic	India Am, Hindu	BA,MD	INM
21	Esperanza	34	35	27	7,1	Colombian, Catholic	Cuban Am, Catholic	MA,MA	INM
22	Maggie	48	52	22	26,1	African Am, Baptist	Egyptian Am, Baptist	MA,MS	150K
23	Sofia	34	41	27	7,3	Salvadorian Am, Catholic	Indian Am, Hindu	BA,MD	INM
24	Olivia	70	65 (Decd)	18	52,2	German Am, Catholic	Irish Am, Catholic	PhD,PhD	INM
25	Josephine	76	77 (Decd)	23	40,0	Polish Am, Catholic	Polish Am, Catholic	HS,AD	INM

Key: Am = American; RN = Registered Nurse, CG = College Graduate; AD = Associate Degree; ES = Elementary School; SH = High School; INM =Income Not Mentioned, Religion – NP = Nonpracticing; Decd = Deceased, (1)* = 1 adopted child

Meet each male participant

George

George is a 62-year-old man. His wife is 63 years old and they have been married for 34 years. He married at age 28, in 1983. His father was German-American and his mother was Swiss-American. He is a college graduate and described himself as German-American, Roman Catholic and a traditional husband who works hard to be a breadwinner. George and his wife met in college and got married immediately after their graduation. A few months after their wedding, the wife became pregnant. George promised his wife that he was going to work hard to be the sole breadwinner. George's wife is an Italian-American and has been a homemaker since the couple's wedding. His annual income is $120,000.00 and the couple has eight children, ages: 33, 32, 30, 29, 27, 25, 21 and 19.

Elaborating on some of the key factors which have empowered his marriage, George emphasized:

> Before we became engaged, both of us spent a lot of time talking and listening to one another. Inspired by the teachings of our Catholic Church, we both agreed that our ultimate goal and destination is to strive and support one another to go to Heaven. We decided to pull together in the same direction. We spent a good amount of time communicating back and forth. We strive to listen to each other, paying attention, wanting to understand and value what the other is saying, and not to come up with a counter-argument. It is more important for us to find the truth than for one of us to 'win' in making decisions.

> My wife agreed to stay home to care for the children, and so we live frugally on one salary. Almost every Friday is our date-night and we have fun together, enjoying each other's presence. We put caring for one another and our children ahead of 'getting ahead' financially. Self-sacrifice is an essential ingredient for manifesting love to each other, bearing a cost personally to benefit the other.

Matt

Matt is a 30-year-old man, born and raised in India in a Roman Catholic family. He came to the United States when he was 26 and lived with friends while he studied to establish himself in the United States. He is currently married for two years to a 26 -year-old woman and both of them have their master's degrees in information and technology.

Matt mentioned that one of the greatest difficulties that he has experienced was the loneliness he felt after leaving his family in India. Elaborating on loneliness Matt mentioned:

> I was so lonely, and even almost decided to go back home, which is a real contradiction to all the desires and effort I made to come to the United States. Many friends and family members in India whenever I talked with them, called me the 'lucky one' but there was no way I could convince them of the pain that I was feeling in my heart. This loneliness affected me so much that one day I was forced to call one of my best friends in the middle of the night to look for a Roman Catholic woman in India who I could marry.

> Four days later, very early in the morning, my friend called me back, and he said that he had good news for me. He had talked to one of his friends and she accepted to give it a try. Thanks to modern technology my friend put us in contact and we started talking and the rest is history. Now we are happily married together and we feel secure in our marriage even if we have only been married for two years. I encourage men and women to listen to their pain of loneliness. They should ask God to give them the grace and wisdom to transform it into true love and commitment to marriage.

Ted

Ted is a 71-year-old man, Roman Catholic, who currently attends religious services one or more times a week. His wife is 67, also a Roman Catholic, and she has always attended religious services one or more times a week throughout their marriage. His highest level of formal education was five years of college. His parents were both of Irish descent and he identifies himself as American Irish. He married in 1972, at the age of 21. The couple cohabited for one year. His wife is a registered nurse. They have been married for 46 years. The couple earns a combined annual income of $100,000 before paying taxes.

Elaborating on one of the greatest challenges to stability and satisfaction in his marriage, Ted mentioned:

> My wife and I greatly wanted to have a child but we realized that we could not. My wife had several operations in an attempt to get pregnant. It took us eight years before we were able to finally adopt a baby girl. We were under a lot of pressure due to family influences. My sister and brother each had six children all the while we were trying to have a baby. With each new pregnancy, they felt our pain more and more. It brought my wife and me closer together. We sort of adopted our nephews and nieces, because we have the financial ability to provide things for their kids that they couldn't. It became a running joke that when we came to visit my wife would take them all out to get new sneakers. They would be sure to wear their oldest sneakers when we arrived. It gave us great pleasure.

> Eventually, we adopted one girl when she was four days old. She is now 38 years old and we have both experienced many joyful as well as challenging experiences with her.

Freddie

Freddie is a 40-year-old business man. He has a very high paying job and he is financially stable. Freddie narrated in detail his decision to get married civilly before the church wedding as follows:

> As a young man, I dated many women, primarily for sex, before I met my wife in my thirties. She asked me to marry her. The request to marry her helped me to stop being promiscuous and ever since, I focused my attention on her alone. Forgive my language, but I think that one of the reasons I was not interested in marriage was the inner fear which overwhelmed me of being used by a woman who would get married to me and then divorce me to get alimony. I wanted to make sure that I was not getting into trouble with a person with a hidden agenda.
>
> Therefore, I arranged with my new fiancée to stay away from engaging into sexual relations before marriage. We did this so that we could know one another better. Two years later, we got married civilly because both of us had come to know one another more closely. After this two-year period of civil marriage, I was able to know her true colors and with no make-up.
> Four years later, it was then my turn to ask my civilly married wife to get married with her again in the Catholic Church. She agreed and we spoke to one of the most approachable priests I have ever known in my church. He listened to us and explained to us all that we had to do and needed to get married in the Catholic Church. He uttered the following phrase with a fancy word I had never heard before: '… given that both of you are already married civilly, what is needed is the co-validation of your marriage.'
>
> Being an easy person to speak with, I felt comfortable to ask him: 'Father, what does the word co-validation mean?' He (priest, whom we address with the title of 'Father') replied with a smile: 'Co-validation involves what we are talking

now. In simple words, it the process whereby the Catholic Church acknowledges and blesses the existing civil marriage between a man and a woman, after ascertaining that there are no impediments to that marriage. The ceremony of getting married with the same person is then performed in front of the Church's ordained minister and with two witnesses present. Consequently, the origin marriage is then considered co-validated and it becomes a Sacrament of Matrimony.'

Freddie added:

> After a few months of preparation with the same priest, our civil marriage was co-validated in a religious ceremony in the Catholic Church. My wife and I have been married in the Church for 10 years and our two children were both baptized in the same church. My wife is very active in the church, serves on a number of committees and serves as a Lector. I support her in all she does in our church and I am the director of the Rite of Christian Initiation for Adults (RCIA) in our parish.

Nelson

Nelson is a 32-year-old man, African American, born and raised in New Jersey by his single mother. He has been married for five years and Nelson emphasized:

> I have a lot of great respect for my mother because she did not take the option to abort me, due to the intense pressure she endured from some of her close relatives and friends. She has suffered so much for me and my young two half-siblings. She is a registered nurse and worked many hours at work as well as at home. She helped us with our school projects and taught us to do household chores. I guess that the values my mom 'implanted in me' so to speak, contributed a great deal to choose the woman of my dreams from our church. Mom used to take me to the Baptist Church every Sunday and she insisted that I join the Children's choir. As a result, I love singing and praising

the Lord for all the good things God has done and continues to do in our lives.

My wife is a registered nurse and we have been married for five years. Six months into the marriage, I became so concerned because I realized that she was making more money than me. I felt like less of a man and I tried to take on two full-time jobs and a weekend job, but immediately realized I was just doing it for the money, and to prove to my wife that I am a man by how much money I brought in. I stopped going to church in order to make money and that upset my mother so much. Thanks to God, one day I had a very difficult conversation with my wife. I told her why I had kind of abandoned her and our first baby son to work to prove to her that I am a man. At first, I think she thought I was kidding but soon realized that I was sincere and upset about my competition with her.

We went to our pastor and talked about the issue and by the end of the meeting, I had resolved to accept myself as a man, who has to work to support the family but not to compete with my wife. She was also very supportive of me. We decided to open a joint bank account, as well as each to be available in the raising of our son. I started going to church again that made my mom very happy. We started to live within our means, frugal, and we opened a savings joint account as well. I no longer measure my manhood by how much I make but by the kind of man God wants me to be for my wife, family, church and society.

Albert

Albert is a 49-year-old man, a Permanent Deacon in the Roman Catholic, completed graduate school, married at age 28 and has two children. Albert also has a secular job and together with his wife, they earn an annual income of about $250,000. He is very dedicated to his wife and both of them are involved in the raising of their children, as well as serving in their local church. When asked about one of the major challenges Albert has experienced in his marriage, he responded:

> Thank God, the problem is resolved, but my wife was very controlling at the beginning of our marriage. I kept silent for the sake of peace but it reached a time when I decided to address the issue directly with her.

Albert elaborated:

> One day, I was so hurt by her verbally expressed anger and sharp criticism of the tie I had put on while going to work. I did my best to control my anger and told her that we will sit down and talk after I returned from work. Off I went and she followed me out the door with some nasty comments. Upon my return, I took a shower, we ate together and then I asked her to have a conversation about whatever was bothering each one of us. Before our conversation we both agreed on the following ground rule:
>
> 1. both of us to sit, facing each other and be mutually respective of one another
>
> 2. one person to talk at time in a calm voice while the other is listening without interruptions
>
> 3. each person speaking, while using 'I' messages which are rooted in facts
>
> After taking our sitting positions within one of our rooms in the house, without any outside interruption, I was the first to talk using words more or less like these:
>
> 'My wife, I love you and I know that you love me and you care about me. I am grateful for all that. At the same time, I have been struggling since we got married to understand why I feel very controlled by you. I haven't been able to come up with any specific response. Above all, I feel so frustrated because of your constant inquisitiveness and kind of compulsive control of

almost every aspect of my life. For example, this morning, I don't understand why you became so critical of the tie I put on my way to work!

Albert recalled how his wife responded as follows:

> First of all, she took a deep pose and then tears started flowing from her eyes. Then, she said: 'I regret if that is how you perceive me to be controlling almost every aspect of your life. Now that you bring it to my attention, I am so sorry for having dumped on you the frustration and anger I accumulated against one my aunts who was my guardian when I was in high school. My parents sent me to stay with that aunt during my high school years; she was such a control freak. I later realized that the reason why my aunt was so controlling of me could have been related to her husband who was extremely controlling of her. He was an alcoholic, and he was very disrespectful of her. My aunt seemed to be very fearful of her husband, he was very manipulative, controlled the finances, criticized how my aunt was dressing, constantly threatened to divorce her and she had no courage to stand up to him. Instead, she turned to me and became very controlling of me. She refused to allow me to interact with my peers and cut me off from talking to my parents and siblings …

Albert also recalled some of the words his wife directed to him, especially her request for an apology and wake-up call as follows:

> I feel great remorse for what I have been doing to you. I am so sorry for projecting the control I felt from my aunt upon you and she seemed to do it to me because her husband was controlling her. I thank you in a special way for bringing my control of you to my attention. It is as if you have challenged me to stop this kind of control, which has become like a kind of transmitted disease, passed on from one person to another. I am glad you have pointed it out to me, so we can address it and put an end to it in our family.

Albert concluded:

> Based on my wife's disclosure and some of the controlling people I have come across in my life, I have realized that it helps to bring it to their attention, challenge them whenever possible, recommend them to work through their anger, resentments and for those who do it subconsciously to bring it to their awareness. On a personal note, being a person of faith who believes in a forgiving and merciful God, I decided to forgive my wife, reconciled with her and then we started a new chapter of our marriage. Hence, the adage: 'Charity begins a home.'

Antonio

Antonio is an 84-year-old man. He was born in Italy and he came to the United States at the age of 7. He received some education up to his first year of high school and then started working with his father as a barber. He shared the story of how he came to meet his wife through "unusual circumstances and by God's mysterious design."

Antonio elaborated:

> My father told me to go to cut the hair of one of our customers who was sick at his home. After cutting his hair, that customer informed me that the nurse who was caring for him is a very nice person. On my way out of the house, I greeted her and left.

> Three weeks later, my dad told me to go to cut that customer's hair again. This time, after cutting his hair, he told me: 'Your father is my friend and I imagine you are still single.' He added: 'I have never been a match maker but there is always a first time for everything. Why not stay for a light lunch with me and my nice nurse? I accepted the invitation to a free lunch, and during the meal, I learned a lot of things about his nurse. One of her wishes was to see some historical places in the State of Pennsylvania. I offered to take her to some of the ones I knew and she accepted. We chose a day and I went with her.

We traveled safely and we talked about many personal stories, which helped us to feel mutually connected. Just almost a mile to the end of our trip, I asked her if I could meet her parents. She accepted and in two months I asked her father for the permission to marry her. He granted it in words, which sounded like delivering a sermon to me. I still recall one of his phrases: 'Love and respect one another till death ...' He was right. Recalling that phrase in the midst of temptations and difficult moments has helped me to stay faithful to my wife and wedding vows.

Our 'match-maker' attended the wedding in a wheelchair and two months later he died with a smile on his face as he gazed into the eyes of my wife and mine at his death bed. I am a Catholic man, I believe in God and I think the greatest gift God has ever given me is my wife, with whom I have two sons, one daughter and twelve grandchildren. We have been married for 57 years. I am still a barber at 84 years of age, and my wife is still 'a very nice person.' I have very vivid memories of the first day I went to cut that man's hair at his home because he was sick and he told me about his nice nurse. That is how it all started. God works in mysterious ways!!!

Charles

Charles is a 78-year-old man born and raised in Uganda. He got married in Uganda and one year later he went away for further studies, leaving his wife alone for two years. Upon his return, he spent one month with his wife and then received a scholarship for advanced studies in the Unites States. Consequently, he left his wife again. Two years after he arrived in the United States he had a terrible accident, which left him paralyzed. His wife came to take care of him and given his long process of recuperation and permanent damage done to his body he was no longer able to be intimate with his wife. He suffered emotionally, spiritually, financially, and many other losses. Finally, he was able to obtain a job, which he could perform from his wheelchair. After many medical tests and with the help of medical doctors he was able to have a child with his wife at a very late age. When asked about one of the challenges he encountered in his married life and how it was resolved, he discussed the lack of being available to his wife as a husband. He elaborated:

> I suffered the loneliness of being away from my wife while taking advanced studies just a year after our wedding. I suffered more the pain of compassion for her because she was so caring and I kept feeling guilty for being away from her, even if I knew that my studies were for the good of our marriage and family. After the accident, I suffered the pain of knowing that I would never be able to share the love as a husband to my wife for the rest of my life. I am glad I am still alive and my faith is so strong after the accident. My wife has been very supportive of me and for that I am eternally grateful. I share the pain of many people whose lives are changed by circumstances beyond their control that bring about lasting consequences.

Charles mentioned that his wife's commitment to their wedding vows, remembering how God created Adam and Eve and commanded them to take care of each other until they died and their strong faith in the Passion and Resurrection of Christ as well as getting a child through extraordinary means have saved them as a couple. He encouraged all couples to take their marriage vows seriously.

Miguel

Miguel is a 41-year-old man born and raised in Ecuador. He migrated to the United States at the age of 25 and got married after eight years of courtship to a woman of Italian and Irish decent. He earned his doctorate in the Unites States in Marriage and Family Therapy. The couple has two children, a six-year- old and a one-year-old; they live in the inner city. They have been married for nine years and they are both practicing Christian Evangelicals. When asked about challenges the couple has experienced and how it was resolved, Miguel mentioned:

Cultural traditions and habits contributed to misunderstandings. As we improved our communication, we were able to identify the elements of our diverse cultures. Open communication, tolerance, and forgiveness have been instrumental in helping us to resolve our cultural differences and adapt to one another. In terms of communication, rather than keeping feelings bottled up, we have agreed to talk about an issue that produces disagreement or tension, no matter how hard it may be. Through tolerance, we have learned to accept each other with our virtues and our weaknesses, instead of trying to change each other. By means of forgiveness, we have overcome holding onto grudges towards each other because we want to live without resentment.

Lee

Lee is a Chinese man, 51 years old. He was born in China and moved with his parents to Holland when he was 5 years old. He did most of his education in Holland and moved to the United States when he was 24. He met his wife in the United States. She is also of Chinese background. They have been married for 26 years after four years of courtship. They have two children a son and a daughter, ages 24 and 20. They live in a suburban neighborhood in New Jersey. Lee works with his wife in the same company and in the same office. He is the director and his wife is the vice director. They have a very profound experience of their faith in Buddha and they believe in karma. When asked about one of the great challenges they experienced as a couple, Lee mentioned the complication his wife had during her second pregnancy. His wife was so sickly that Lee had to learn the hard way how to do house chores, to take care of his 4-year-old son and his wife, as well as provide for the family. According to Lee:

> This was one of the most difficult times in my life. I feared I would lose my wife to death. She was bleeding profusely and the life of our baby daughter was in danger also. Fortunately, though money does not buy everything, having it helped us a lot because I was able to provide the best medical care for my wife and our near-to-be-born daughter. Ever since, I resolved to work

54

hard, and to develop a financial plan in case of an emergency. Currently I am working with my wife to encourage people to buy life insurance and to take this insurance extremely seriously.

Elaborating on the notion of karma and marriage, Lee mentioned:

I believe whatever goes around comes around. I also believe that there are consequences to every action. Consequently, my wife and I have grown together in love within the same belief. We love each other, we care for each other, we trust each other, and we are very faithful to one another because we know that the contrary has its consequences. We therefore encourage other couples who seek informal counsel from us to know about karma and how it has empowered us in our marriage.

Salvador

Salvador is a 40-year-old man. He was born and raised in Ecuador. He married his high school sweetheart at the age of 20 and two years later, his wife gave birth to their first child. A year after the birth of their first child, Salvador's wife was again pregnant. He migrated alone to the United States, leaving behind his pregnant wife and their first child with the hope of earning some money to support his growing family. During his first two years in the United States, he lived with his brother in a two-bedroom apartment. He worked very hard and earned more money in one year than he had earned in five years in his native Ecuador.

When asked by the author about a significant challenge he has faced in his marriage and how it was resolved, Salvador identified the challenge of a "marital infidelity" and talked about it with significant details. He mentioned that he decided to talk about this particular challenge in order to help other people in similar situations to prevent it from happening or to learn from what his wife did for him to save their marriage. Salvador narrated:

During the first four years of my stay in the United States, I worked so hard and used to send money to my wife on a monthly basis to support her and our children. I spent money to pay rent for my separate apartment. During the first four years after leaving my wife and children in Ecuador, I was feeling so lonely. My wife was caring for the children alone. We missed each other so much but I had no plans of going back to Ecuador. Consequently, I made arrangements for them to come and stay with me in the United States. Thanks to God, they arrived safely. We got a bigger apartment and we were happy to be reconnected. I thank God that I was able to stay faithful to my marriage vows during those years of being apart.

Two years after my wife's arrival with our two children, my wife told me that her young sister was also interested in coming to the United States but was still concerned about the high costs of living, especially during the first year. I recalled how my brother helped me during the first month of my arrival. So, based on the size of our apartment, I told my wife that we could accommodate her sister until she could get on her feet in the United States. In two-months' time, her sister came and started living with us. She helped my wife with caring for our children and with a lot of household chores.

As soon as her sister came, my wife was offered a night shift job with more money and she accepted the offer. Though I was excited about the higher pay, which my wife started getting, the excitement almost cost me the loss of my marriage. Now, what follows, it is not something I take pride in, yet it is what made me honor my wife than ever before.

A few months after my wife started working the night shift, I started to feel a strong attraction toward my sister-in-law. I fought the temptation as much as I could but one night, I made a joke and both of us laughed so much and we started feeling very comfortable with one another. The next night, I shared a strong hug and by the time we came to our senses, we had gone too far. That went on for almost a month.

My wife started suspecting that something might be going on between me and her sister. One day, she confronted me about her suspicions and I admitted. I told her the truth. I was so scared. I cried and pleaded with her to forgive us. I cannot tell how my wife managed to forgive us!!! I felt so bad about my behavior. Although infidelity in all its forms is bad, I wished I had cheated on my spouse with a stranger but not with one of her closest relatives, her sister.

My wife's tears because of my betrayal brought me to my knees. I was so scared of my wife divorcing me and I felt so ashamed of myself. I asked God to give my wife a special grace to heal her bleeding heart. I recited the Serenity Prayer many times a day and Psalm 51 in the Bible. I asked my sister-in-law to move out of our apartment, and she started renting her own apartment. Then, I waited for my wife's decision regarding the fate our marriage and family.

A month after informing my wife of the truth of my actions, I asked her to forgive me, and she did. She told me that she was going to give me a chance to get my act together. I have done everything it takes to save my marriage. Based on personal experience with my wife, I pray that the people may learn to ask for forgiveness, stop the affair and that the offended party forgive so that spouses reconcile with one another. I am so grateful to my wife for forgiving me and for staying with me. I give thanks to God for sending us the graces we have received to be able to save our marriage and to be reconciled in Christ Jesus.

Andy

Andy is a 55-year-old man. He has been married to his wife for 20 years. By profession, he is a pilot and travels a lot nationally in the United States and internationally. He elaborated:

The first four years of our marriage were extremely wonderful. My wife would sometimes travel with me and we visited so many parts of the world together. We knew one another in high school and we kept in contact even when we went to different schools. After the birth of our first child, my wife stayed at home with the baby most of the time. I kept working as a pilot, but then the fun in our marriage started to fade away. I would come home, my wife was tired with a baby who would not sleep most to the time at night and that was the time, I kind of lost interest in coming home. Most of her attention was with the crying baby.

Looking back, I left all the caring for the baby to her and my excuse was she is the mother and my role is to be the provider. We started to distance ourselves, and with less communication and after the birth of the second child, she decided to invite her mother to help her with the children. Since I was frequently away from home, it seemed to me that she developed a stronger bond with the children than with me, and that she had more communication with her mother than with me. It is a difficult feeling to express, but I really started to feel as a stranger in my own home.

On one weekend, I was home and so lonely and frustrated with the feeling of being unloved by my wife. I was feeling angry at my wife and kind of resented the children who seemed to have taken their mother's full attention, and she consequently abandoned me. I had started to seriously think of divorcing her and by God's mysterious design, I found myself going to a Sunday Mass alone in one of the cities almost four thousand miles from home. For reasons best known to God, after Mass I stayed in the church as the people were leaving. I was the last to leave and then the priest greeted me as I was leaving the church. As he extended his hand to greet me with a big smile, I asked him: Reverend Father, do you have a minute, I would like to talk with you? He replied: "Yes."

He seemed easy to talk with, a genuine man of God and pastorally focused based on the way he delivered the homily. He invited me to go back into the church and we sat in one of the back pews where I felt comfortable to pour out my heart to him. I told him that I am a pilot and my marriage was falling apart due to my constantly being away from home, feeling lonely when I am away from home and even when I am at home. He asked me only one question, which stuck with me: 'Have you ever attended a marriage encounter weekend with your wife?' I replied no. He told me briefly about it and gave me a website to check-on (www.marriageencounter.org). He suggested that I take two weeks off from work and dedicate them to my family including attending the marriage encounter weekend. I arranged with my wife to attend that weekend and by the end of the weekend experience, I had resolved to rekindle the love with my wife and to participate in the raising of our two children. I recommend marriage encounter to married spouses because the experience enlightened me on how to save my marriage.

Alfredo

Alfredo is 42-year-old man. He has been married for 15 years and the couple has two sons, ages 13 and 9. Alfredo mentioned:

My second son is a special needs child and the relationship between me and my wife has been so strained since this second son was born. Before the son was diagnosed with autism, my wife and I blamed each other for what I called 'bad lack and a punishment from God to give us a child with such difficulties.' I developed a special affiliation for my first son and told my wife that she was the one to care for the second son. Years later, she revealed to me that my 'abandoning' our second son to her, hurt her so much. Her family members lived far from us, she had to quit her job to stay home to take care of our son and she had no one with whom to share her pain. She became depressed in the process and I suffered her constant rejections in regard to our intimate life, despite my frequent advances.

I became more sarcastic and critical of her for no apparent reason. One day, I guess, she was so frustrated and tired of my negative comments, she broke into tears and as she regained her voice, she told me to go and sleep in the basement.

It was there in the basement, on that sleepless night, where I had my "conversion experience". I sobbed and cried, whipping the tears with my hands. I realized how I had contributed to the problems in the marriage and family as well as hurting my wife and children. I put my pride aside and decided to ask for forgiveness from my wife and I also sought counsel from the priest who officiated at our wedding.

The priest helped me to put many things into perspective and suggested to take the child for a psychological assessment as well as seek marriage therapy as a couple. I shared the suggestions with my wife and we agreed with the priest's suggestions. Our son was diagnosed with autism and then started getting the respective treatments. I stopped blaming God, reconnected with my wife, happily married again, and mutually supporting one another in the raising of our children.

Robert

Robert is a 55-year-old man, who immigrated to the United States from Ireland when he was 35. Since his arrival, he has been working in the construction business. Two years after his arrival while in a bar he befriended a woman whom he later married. When asked about one of the challenges he has experienced in his marriage he attributed it to his over-dependence on alcohol. He elaborated:

> My wife and I are very serious drinkers, no wonder we met in a bar. The problem is alcohol has taken a great toll on our marriage. Every income we get is taxed by our use of alcohol and sometimes we are not able to pay our bills, not because we don't earn enough money, but because we spend it on alcohol. My wife sometimes has her friends over and instead of tea or coffee, they are served alcohol. Once I got into an accident and

I was driving under the influence of alcohol. The fines were so high and I am so lucky to be alive.

Alcohol has not only affected us financially and emotionally, but romantically we do not have a child together. My wife has a child from a previous marriage but she does not want to interact with us, she calls our house a bar. This kind of separation between my wife and her daughter has also affected me with my step-daughter because she blames me for encouraging my wife to drink excessively. I justify myself by saying I met you mother in a bar; I am not the one who told her to drink. However, such justifications just added fuel to the fire. On the flip side of the coin, my wife blames me for being the only alcoholic in the house.

Elaborating on his wife's statements, Robert quoted her to express the way she had addressed him:

'You [Robert] drink a lot and your prolonged use of alcohol has put us into tremendous debt and it is destroying our marriage. It is so hard and I am so heavy-hearted to say that I consider our marriage is dead because it is a sexless marriage and you are very depressed. I attribute all this to your excessive drinking. Why don't you stop, look for a sponsor and join AA?' (By AA, she meant Alcoholics Anonymous)

Robert added:

Although I did not want to listen to my wife's constant criticisms and blaming me as if she was not also a heavy drinker, I listened to her this time and looked for help with my drinking. I found an AA group through the help of my boss, whom now I consider to be my hero. After three years of joining AA, I have improved a lot, my wife has also joined another AA group and our financial situation has improved. Above all, we have become more intimate than never before.

Ivan

Ivan is a 70-year-old man. He was born and raised in Haiti, came to the United States to further his studies and received his doctorate in chemistry. He is currently retired and has been married for 46 years to his wife who is also from Haiti. Ivan mentioned:

> I dated many women as a young man. Most of them, it was just for fun until one of my uncles talked to me in a caring and yet challenging way. Among the things we discussed, I vividly recall: 'What qualities are you looking for in a woman you want to spend the rest of your life with?' Before responding, my uncle added: 'What kind of husband and father do you want to be?' Then my uncle raised his voice a bit and said: 'Man-up. Stop sleeping around and stick with one woman.'

Addressing the author, Ivan elaborated:

> Joseph, I am a man of faith and I believe in God. Now, I can say with certainty that God spoke to me through my uncle to help me decide about whom I wanted to marry and to focus on the need to be committed to her for life. I started thinking seriously about the meaning and responsibilities of marriage. I went back to my uncle and asked him for some advice about women and married life. Among all the things my uncle told me, I took to heart the following:
>
> i.   The most precious and most dangerous resources in this world are women, money and power. Men can kill one another for a woman. Once you find someone to marry, treat her well and with respect. Money is a good resource in marriage and every couple should maintain honest communications about money throughout their married life. Power can be used for good or bad. For instance, power may be based in one's knowledge, wisdom or leadership position and that may be used to liberate, help, console, guide, influence others or on the contrary to control, dominate and sometimes to kill others. Between married spouses, with all

cultural differences considered, power needs to be rooted in mutual respect and love. No one knows all the answers or has the final say on every smallest or greatest detail of marriage and family life. Each spouse should be willing to listen, share, give advice and take direction from one another.

ii. Dating is not like a job interview. It requires honest and ongoing communication. It is not time for bad mouthing about ex-girlfriends, but an opportunity to know one another, identify your needs, motivations for marriage, career choices, discuss religious beliefs, how to negotiate differences and resolving conflicts as they arise, discussing difficult topics and those which can be taken for granted, like having children and dual careers as well as talking about dislikes. Don't talk to impress in order to conquer and control but dialogue to build trust which will allow both of you to reach a mutual decision of whether to amicably end the romance or move on to the commitment of marriage for life.

iii. While still dating, ask the woman with a paying job: What do you think about putting our money together? After asking the question, keep quiet and wait for the response. If she responds: 'No, we need separate accounts.' Then, share with her your rationale for a joint account. If she still insists on separate accounts, inform her that it is time to end the romance and go your separate ways. My uncle elaborated upon the joint account: It is a reflection of the trust spouses have for one another. Of course, each spouse will have some cash money to keep and spend for some small expenses without explanation or need to inform the other.

Jimmie

Jimmie is 64 years old, currently a widower. Jimmie mentioned:

> I only received an elementary school education. I dated many
> women, and I did all this, looking for love. None of them
> responded to my needs compared to my late wife. At age 28,
> after dating many women, I met this special woman in a bar and
> we both bonded instantaneously; it was love at first sight. I
> guess we became quick friends because both of us needed each
> other's company. She had her unfinished business and I had
> mine as well. We both grew up in very difficult situations at
> home and unclean neighborhoods. My parents divorced when I
> was two years old. My maternal grandmother is the one who
> practically raised me, because my mother and father were both
> alcohol and drug users. I was exposed to a lot of things as child
> and teenager, which kept me fearful of people and nobody to
> trust.
>
> My wife also faced many hardships as a child and a teenager.
> She never saw her father and grew up only with her mom who
> was addicted to drugs. When I met her that night in the bar, I
> felt a relief in me, which I cannot put in my words. She was so
> outgoing, listened to me and I felt consoled by her caressing
> hands. We talked a lot that night until 1 am and she drove me
> back to my apartment. Within a month or so, I moved into her
> apartment, we lived together for five years, still drinking and
> using drugs as much as we could afford buying them.
>
> One day, I do not recall when, on our way back to our apartment
> from a bar, both of us were drunk and driving fast. I lost control
> of the car, ran off the road, hit a big tree and we both were rushed
> to the hospital with deep bleeding wounds and the car was
> totaled. News reached my maternal grandmother whom I had
> not seen in years. She came looking for me in the hospital. She
> cried on seeing my disfigured face, wounds all over my legs,
> arms and chest. She sobbed so hard that I became concerned
> that she might die in the hospital in front of the patient she had

come to see. She was sobbing and trying to console me. I told her: 'I promise you Grandma that after I recover from this accident, I will never drink and use drugs again.' She replied: 'That is what many addicts say when they are in trouble. They make promises they never keep.' She then looked me in the eye and said:

'Grandson, you are lucky to be alive. God has given you another opportunity to live, use it well. Join Alcoholics Anonymous (AA), you are the only remaining apple of my eye. Your mother used to tell me the same promises until she overdosed and we buried her four months ago. Sorry to tell you this sad news now, but I am tired of burying younger people than me. Be good, stop worshiping alcohol and drugs, and start worshipping God."

Jimmie mentioned that his grandmother's words, sorrow, and courage made him make an inner conversion and a definitive decision to stop using alcohol and drugs. Two months after his recovery from the accident, both he and his girlfriend went to AA, got supportive sponsors and two years later got married within a religious ceremony with his grandmother present. They spent twenty years together, happily married. They stopped drinking and using drugs ever since they were discharged from the hospital after that car accident. Over the course of their marriage, both Jimmie and his wife became regular church attendees, volunteered in many church groups and were active in their community. At age 40, Jimmie went back to school, learned about catering, opened his own restaurant and became a prosperous manager of his own business.

During the face-to-face interview, Jimmie mentioned:

I am grateful to God, to my grandma, my wife, sponsor, pastor and restaurant staff, as well as all the people who have helped me in one way or another. In 2015, my wife was diagnosed with terminal breast cancer, and later died. I miss her dearly and I am also glad that we met, survived that car accident, became clean together, supported each other and got married. I owe her a lot for all I am today. Though physically absent, she is still with me in many ways. My faith in the resurrection of Jesus also consoles me and reassures me that her soul is in the hands of the merciful God. Looking back as a widower, my faith in Jesus has helped me to realize that I will be with my wife in heaven.

I have hope that God was merciful to her and welcomed her to heaven. I am a firm believer in the power of God and His mercy and in the life to come. So, the journey I started with her in a bar will definitely end when we both meet in heaven. There we shall live happily ever in God's presence. I encourage other people as well to accept Jesus and the hope of his glorious resurrection. That hope has also helped me to cope positively with the grief of my loved ones, especially my wife and grandmother.

Mateo

Mateo is a Filipino man, born in the Philippines. At the age of 20 he immigrated to the United States with his wife, just after their second wedding anniversary. Mateo and his wife are both 49 years old. They are Roman Catholics and attend religious services once or twice a week. He works in electronics and his wife stays home to raise the children. He has a bachelor's degree and his wife has a high school diploma. He married at age 18;, they have four children, ages: 24, 21, 15 and 5. The family lives in a suburban neighborhood.

When asked about one of the challenges he has experienced in his marriage and how it was resolved Mateo explained:

> My wife is so involved in housework and caring for the children, which I understand and am grateful. On the other hand, I am a bit hesitant and ashamed to say that sometimes I get upset with my wife especially when I want to have sex with her. I feel like she has put me on a kind of diet, and almost wants to limit me to Saturday night. I was not like that when we were first married, she used to care for me and she seemed to enjoy it as well. It used to be frequent and sometimes she was the initiator. Now I

feel like I have to beg all the time and I feel rejected. She thinks I am inconsiderate and that I spend a lot of time on the computer instead of helping her with the household chores.

Whenever I reach home from work my wife wants to tell me almost everything that happened when I was away, and I have little patience now. She wants to communicate with me about many details regarding our children, her relatives and the neighbor. The situation has been stressful for both of us because she feels as much as she cares for the children, I should also listen to her as an adult. In my case as an engineer, I say what I want to say in a few words, but my wife says one thing with a hundred words. I think I would listen more to her if she also gives me the opportunity to talk. What happens is she asks me a question and while I am still thinking of the right words to use, she fills in the gap immediately and then blames me for not answering her questions.

My cultural background does not put a lot of emphasis on therapy but it reached a point when I asked my priest what I should do to improve the situation with my wife and he recommended therapy. We complied and it has helped us a lot. Now my wife knows to give me the opportunity to formulate my responses without filling in the gap. I have also learned that if I want her to collaborate with my requests in the bedroom, I have to help her with the household chores and the children's homework. This seems to help her reserve some energy for the two of us and it makes me more involved in the children's lives. I have also learned that being a husband and a father is not only being a provider of money but spending quality time with the family. I look forward to spending the rest of my life with my wife.

Eric

Eric is a 72-year-old retired military officer. He is a Roman Catholic and spoke with joy about having served his country well in the military and well as husband to his wife. They are currently in their forty-fifth year of marriage. The couple has two grown-up children and six grandchildren. Eric mentioned:

> I am glad to have married my sweetheart. She is a sister of one of my best companions in the military. Upon our first return from the first deployment, I went to visit my friend and his family. Upon arriving, my friend greeted me, introduced me to his father who gave a memorable handshake, his mother then greeted me and then his sister. Difficult as it may sound to say, I have to admit that as soon as I met his sister, I said to myself: 'She is so beautiful and I am to marry her one day.'
>
> After lunch with my friend's family, he asked if I would like to go with him to see his grandmother who was about five miles away. He invited his sister to accompany us. As soon as we entered his grandma's house, the grandma looked into his eyes with prolonged silence and then with a big smile told him:
>
>> *'Welcome home. I have missed you. I have been praying to God to keep you safe. Thank you for bringing your friend to see me. I am certain he is going to marry your sister. They seem to me like a perfect match!'*
>
> As soon as she said that, everybody in the room burst into laughter. I started giggling with a lot of joy and when his sister looked at me, we both smiled and laughed again. I winked at her and she smiled again. I am so grateful to God for my friend and his grandma. Her cited words served like an ice-breaker to my innermost fear. I was feeling so attracted to my friend's sister but I was so scared to say anything to her.
>
> Six months later, I married my best friend's sister. The wedding was wonderful. I asked my friend to be my best man and the bride chose the same grandma, to be her maid of honor. After

the wedding, we had a week honeymoon, went to our rental apartment and three weeks later, I was deployed oversees to another military responsibility. Again, difficult as it may sound to say, I loved serving my country in uniform and at the same time, I felt like I had abandoned the person with whom I had just married a few weeks before. Whenever I got a chance, I would call her and after talking with her, I felt a lot of joy and wonder about the power of being so connected with her in marriage.

My wife was so understanding and respectful of my duty to serve in the military and protect others. However, being physically away from one another made me so lonely and she certainly missed me. Eight months after my deployment, our first son was born. I missed being near both of them. I asked my young sister to visit them as much as possible. I am glad she was able to help my wife in many ways and the two of them have become great friends over the years. After my retirement, my wife and I had to undergo another phase of adjustment because we had to learn how to live with one another.

Eric added:

Since I am now retired, I have the privilege of doing the things which I enjoy. Among them, I spend some time reading the Bible and look for ways of relating it to my life experiences. The following three passages in the Bible are my favorite passages because I find them respectively applicable to the mentioned friend, to his sister (my wife) and to myself. The first two readings are from the Book of Sirach. The first is:

'A faithful friend is a sturdy shelter; he who finds one finds a treasure. A faithful friend is beyond a price; no sum can balance his worth. A faithful friend is a life-saving remedy; such as he who fears God find; for he who fears God behaves accordingly, and his friend will be like himself' (Sirach 6: 14 -17).

The second is:

'Happy the husband of a good wife; twice-lengthened are his days. A worthy wife brings joy to his husband, peaceful and full is his life. A good wife is a generous gift bestowed upon him who fears the Lord; Be he rich or poor, his heart is content and a smile is ever on his face' (Sirach 26: 1 – 3).

The third one is the following verse from the Book of Prophet Micah. I have adopted it and paraphrased it as my commitment for the remaining time of my life in this world:

'This is what the Lord asks of you [me], to act justly, to love tenderly, and to walk humbly with your [my] God' (Micah 6:8).

Dave

Dave is a 45-year-old Caucasian man married to an African American woman. Dave is a lawyer by profession and grew up in a white neighborhood. He attended a graduate university, which was far away from his home. There he was alone and started making friends with students from different racial, cultural, religious, social and economic backgrounds. He enjoyed sports and debating with some of his classmates. Among them was an African American young woman whom Dave felt greatly attracted to and described as: "very intelligent, beautiful, great sense of humor and exceptionally open-minded in her interactions with people of her own ethnic background as well as others of different cultural backgrounds."

Dave elaborated:

> It may sound ironic, after some conversations and interactions with this young woman, there came a time whereby I just kept daydreaming about her and yet worried to ask her out for fear that if the relationship became serious, I did not know how to tell my mother that I might marry a black woman. As a prospective lawyer, I laid down my arguments to present to my family members, but I could not let this opportunity go.
>
> On one Sunday afternoon, after attending church services, I asked her out and she agreed. We talked about many things

70

about our own families of origin, our dreams, the civil rights, which Martin Luther King Jr. worked for and died defending as well as his 'I have a dream speech.' After that wonderful Sunday evening, we both agreed that it was time to break the racial barriers for ourselves, 'focus on the content of our characters – while paraphrasing King Jr. and we started dating.

At the end of the semester, I went to visit her family and I was well received. The problem was with my mom. As soon as I mentioned to my mom that my girlfriend will come to visit, mom said: 'Bring a Caucasian only.' I replied by borrowing the words of Dr. King: 'Mom, I am hearing you and I respect you, yet at this point in my life, what matters is the 'content' of one's 'character' and unconditional love for one another which Jesus came to teach us. If one's color of the skin is what is necessary for the marriage to be successful, then people of the same skin color would not be divorcing.'

Mom kept silent for a moment and then replied: 'I am proud of you my son, not only are becoming a lawyer, but also a real follower of Jesus.' I replied: 'Mom, thank you; I am studying to become a lawyer; and my exposure at the university to people from different walks of life has helped me to become more convinced that it is time for us as a family and a society to go beyond some of our traditional prejudices.'

Dave added:

After convincing my mom, I did not care much about other people's opinions. Given the open-mindedness of my girlfriend, she was a delight to all the family members when she came to visit. Surprisingly, even Aunt Sue, who tends to say mean things about non-Caucasian people, she told me: 'You have to marry this woman, nobody else.' The rest is history. We celebrated our wedding at our local church. The religious minister who conducted our Pre-Cana workshops (trainings in preparation for marriage) included two profound sessions on the dynamics, challenges and strengths of interracial marriages. We found them very informative and we recommend them to others contemplating interracial marriages.

Rowland

Rowland is a 71-year-old husband with a Doctorate in Education. He was born and raised in a Roman Catholic family and continues to be an active participant in the Catholic faith together with his wife who was also born and raised in a Roman Catholic family. He attends church services one or more times a week with his wife. His father has an Irish background, his mother a German/Polish background and he prefers to identify himself as an Irish American.

Rowland and his wife have been married for 46 years and at the time they married he was 25 years old. They had six years of courtship and two months of cohabitation. The couple has three sons, ages: 43, 40 and 39, all living with their spouses and children in different states within the United States. Rowland and his wife are currently retired from their professional jobs and receive an estimated annual income of $170,000. The couple spent their first 29 years of marriage and child-rearing in an urban neighborhood, then ten years (empty nest) in a suburban area and currently eight years in a rural area during their retirement.

When Rowland was asked about one of the most difficult moments he has experienced in his marriage and how the challenge was resolved, he responded:

> During a sabbatical year in Arizona, one of our boys got into some trouble. We were far from our normal support system. He was acting out against a move he didn't want to make, and against our (in his opinion) strict parenting. We talked a lot about it, and I deferred to my wife's expertise as an educator. He refused counseling, so we went for counseling. It was not directly marriage counseling—more parenting counseling. We resolved the situation with his paying his fines, and by greatly relaxing his set of rules to two – harm no one and let us know where you will be.

Rowland added another challenge:

Both of our professional goals required more grad study, and this period coincided with our starting our family. Who would go to school? Who would pay the bills? Who would be responsible for the children (i.e. who stays home if one is sick?)? Where would we live? How would we pay the education costs? It was an ongoing conversation for nearly 10 years. We talked a lot, and always trusted that the other was being as fair as possible and trying to do what would be best for the family, including themselves.

Andrew

Andrew is a 35-year-old man and has been married for 15 years to a woman he met at work. The couple does not have any children and the woman blames herself for not being able to conceive. Andrew mentioned that he has tried to console her and assure her of his love for her, but she seems inconsolable. I would live with not having a child with the woman I love, but I can't stand her obsessiveness with cleaning and order in the house. He elaborated:

> It is hard to live with a person whose primary source of self-identity is just keeping busy. She wants to be productive keeps herself on the go all the time and she has difficulty expressing her feelings with me. She jumps from one activity to another and wants everything to be perfect. I'm not a psychologist, but I think my wife has Obsessive-compulsive personality disorder.

> I have read many books in order to learn how to live with her and it is very hard. She avoids sexual intimacy with me and I feel rejected. She is so conscientious about herself and seems to perceive sex as a dirty experience. Everything in the house has to be perfect or in order and flawless. She checks my work too. She comes to the garage to organize my tools then I look for them and I don't know where she put them. Preoccupation with details, order and organization seem to control her and I feel like a stranger in my own house.

On the other hand, my wife is a very nice person. She is caring and from time to time watches videos with me, though most of the time she is standing. She believes there is only one way to do things, her way. What has helped me to live with her is not to pay too much attention to what she says and does. I want to live in the house as if it is lived in and she also is learning the hard way that there is more to life than just keeping things in order.

Lorenzo

Lorenzo is a 43-year-old man, born in and raised in Ecuador, who migrated to the United States at age 19, leaving all his family members in Ecuador. He spent the first ten months staying with friends to reduce rent expenses. He described himself as a "very devout Catholic" giving a lot of credit to his maternal grandparents who used to take him to church every Sunday and learned to pray while living them since he was seven after the divorce of his parents. Two years after his arrival in the United States, he started dating a woman (fictitiously referred to here as Rosa) who also had immigrated to the United States from Ecuador. Lorenzo is fluent both in Spanish and English.

During the interview, when asked to identify one of the main challenges Lorenzo had encountered in his marriage and how it was resolved, he took a deep breath and said:

> I have experienced many challenges but I will focus on one which was so difficulty for me, but when I turned to God for guidance and grace, I was able to forgive my wife for having a child with another man while still married to me.

Lorenzo elaborated:

> I have been a truck driver for twenty years. I would be away from home for a week or two, come back home for three or four days and then back on the road. One day, I returned home and my eldest son, who was ten years by then seemed very strange

to me. This time, he was so silent, spent most of the time in his room and his mood was different than ever before. He seemed so upset and I did not know what to do. I decided to take him for a ride in our family car. As I drove, I made some jokes to make him laugh, but all seemed to fall on deaf ears. After about two miles, he asked me with a tone of curiosity and in a raised voice:

'Who is that man who comes when you are not here and he spends one night or two with mom in your bedroom?'

Lorenzo added:

I did not know what to respond to my son and decided to stop the car off the road at the nearest safe place I found so that we could talk without so much concentration on driving. We talked for about forty minutes, and that helped me to realize what was going on with my son. He was so torn inside between the loyalty to me and to his mother. ... Long story short, I believed my son and I thanked him for telling me. I was so heart-broken, I was angry and thought of confronting my wife, but refrained from saying anything to my wife who was due to give birth in three days. It was not easy to control of my emotions, I ran to the church and informed the priest about what was going within, and the fact that my wife was going to give birth in a few days.

The priest listened to me as much as he could, I cried in front of him, screamed but he cautioned me not do anything that could hurt my wife, the baby, myself or anyone else. Before getting out of his office, he gave me the statue of St. Joseph and prayed with me for wisdom and for the grace of forgiveness. I did not want to listen to what he was saying to me but as reflected upon his words, and I was found some inner peace and courage to move forward.

Within three days, Rosa gave birth to a baby girl who would have been the couple's fourth child, but after the DNA test, "that man" proved the biological father. All this took place after Lorenzo confronted Rosa four weeks after the birth of the child. Lorenzo elaborated:

> Even if I managed to control myself before the baby was born, my doubts intensified after I realized that the child seemed to resemble the man who used to work with "Rosa" at a restaurant. When I expressed to her doubts about my being the father to that child, she started crying and asked me for pardon. 'How can I pardon you?' I insisted. Then addressing me she said:

> 'This is not an excuse for what I did and I am not blaming you for my infidelity. However, your work as a truck driver takes you away from home for too long. You support us financially, but I'm so lonely after you go. I am the only one involved in the children's daily lives and homework.'

Lorenzo added:

> As she (Rosa) was talking, I was feeling so angry and in anger I told her: 'I am not going to raise another man's child... Leave me with my three children and go with your lover who heals your loneliness.' In that instant, she (Rosa) started to plead with me to forgive her. Instead, I asked her to take the child to her father, ask him to take a DNA test with the child; then sent her off to go and stay with her lover. She went with the baby to him. Upon discovering that he was the biological father, he rebuked her for refusing to abort the baby. He drove her to her friend's home, left her there with the baby, promising to come back later, but instead abandoned her with the baby and he went back to his country of origin.

> A week after staying with her friend, she (Rosa) realized that staying with 'that man,' it was not Paradise. He was humiliating her, calling her names and very mean to her. She called me crying on the phone, asking me to forgive her and allow her to come back to the house with her child. I was still upset with her. However, while pleading for pardon and expressing her remorse, I unintentionally gazed at the statue of St. Joseph the

priest had given me. I recalled how the priest had prayed with me for wisdom and for the grace of forgiveness. I cannot explain what happened to me, but let me say by God's grace, my anger subsided and I drove to meet her with the baby. As soon as I saw them, I looked that baby in the eye, and I heard my inner voice telling me: 'this child is innocent, take care of her and reconcile with your wife.'

Since that moment, I resolved to care for that 'innocent' child and started the process of forgiving my wife. It is not time for comparing apples to oranges. Reading the Bible has helped me to identify myself with St. Joseph as a dedicated foster father to Jesus. It is written in the Bible that when Joseph was betrothed to Mary (cf. Luke 1:26-56; Matthew 1:18-24), he ended up caring for Mary and Jesus. Maybe that is why the priest gave me the statue of St. Joseph! It has not been easy to let go of all this pain and betrayal, but I see a lot of positive changes in my wife and I have also given up being a truck driver. Now, I commute daily to work from home and it has been a great relief for my wife as well. Above all, my oldest son seems happy and doing well. He is no longer caught up into loyalty to me and his mother.

I'm glad there is peace now in my home. Thanks to God my wife did not abort that baby. I am a firm believer that life is scared and it should be preserved from conception to natural death. She is now four years old. I doubt I am the only man to go through this nor the last one. I have told you my story in great details so that others may do whatever it takes to forgive and reconcile with a repentant spouse, and more so, to care for 'the innocent' child.

Paul

Paul is a 77-year-old man born and raised in Uganda. He had a traditional wedding at the age of 24 with his wife Victoria (fictitious name), aged 20 by then. The couple has six children and they have been married for 53 years. When asked about one of the most difficult challenges Paul has experienced in his marriage and how it was resolved, he paused and then mentioned:

Today, it is what is termed domestic violence, but where I grew up, it was not a big deal to beat up one's wife. I regret it immensely.

The author asked Paul: "Would you elaborate on what you mean."

Paul elaborated:

I am not sure, but it seems that most of the incidents of domestic abuse are narrated by the victims and/or their advocates, but story is different because I was the abuser. In order to understand me better, let me inform you about the household in which I grew up. We were four: my father, mother, elder sister and I. Whenever my father was drunk, he would have a lot of arguments with mom and he used to beat her for no apparent reason. My sister and I would hide under our beds and we would here mom cry, yet felt helpless to rescue her. On his sober days, he was not a saint either. He was verbally abusive to my mother and would humiliate her in front of us, criticize her cooking skills, yet I thought my mom was the best cook in the world. During meals, mom would leave crying and go out of the house. Dad would follow her and push her back into the house.

The delicious meal mom had prepared lost its taste because of the way dad was mistreating mom. He would accuse mom for things she had not done and the next thing was to slap her and kick her. On one occasion, mom lost consciousness and that is when dad stopped beating her yet continued to be verbally abusive to her. I do not know why mom did not run away, I mean divorce my dad, but it was heartbreaking to see her suffer at the hands of my father. Sometimes, they would see dad and mom laughing together but in a couple of days, I would see bruises over her face.

Paul added:

I am so sorry for what I'm going to say because the abuse my mother endured from my father, I did it in so many ways to my wife after our honeymoon. My wife is so beautiful by my standards. So, I became so controlling of her and very jealous. Money was not a problem for me. I used it to build a fence around our house and I told her not to interact with the neighbors. I did most of the shopping so that she could stay inside the enclosed house.

Back in the day, there were no cell phones. We had a landline in the house and I told her to use it only for emergencies to call me at work. I cut her off to visiting so often to see her relatives and friends. I asked her to inform her relatives and friends not to come to visit without my permission. One day, she broke one of the rules. She came out the house and I found her out the house talking to the neighbors. As soon as she saw me, she rushed to the house but she knew that I had also seen her. Inside the enclosed house, just the two of us, I interrogated her why she had left the house without my permission? Beyond responding, I lost control of my anger and I beat her severely. She cried and apologized, but I was so furious that I enclosed her into one of the rooms for three hours.

After letting her out of that room, I reminded her of the rules I had set for her and the consequences for breaking them. I was 27 by then, she was 23 and we had no children yet. The next day she woke up very early to prepare breakfast for me as usual, but I did not eat it, as another way to punish her.

I left for work, went to a restaurant for breakfast and then to the office. At around 11.30 am, my sister showed up to my office without any prior appointment to inform me about the promotion she had received at her work. I congratulated her and took her out for lunch. During lunch, we talked about many things, reminisced about our parents and the lessons learned a lot that way. At one point, my sister asked me a question which influenced me to change my life as a husband to my wife and all the positive changes that resulted thereafter. She asked me:

'Looking back at how our father mistreated our mother, what kind of husband and father are you becoming?'

Before responding, she interrupted me by saying:

'I am not asking you to answer me, but to think about all the pain our mother experienced at the hands of our dad and how we both grew up in fear of dad. Good luck in your marriage.'

Paul mentioned that after that lunch dialogue with his sister, he went to his house, closed himself in the room he had closed his wife in the previous day and cried while recalling what his dad had done to his mother. He realized how he had started to harass his wife and to repeat what his father had done to his mother. He did not go to work for three days. He emphasized:

I was so ashamed of myself, depressed and had no appetite. I hated the man I had become to my wife, the rules I had set for her and for beating her based on my insecurities, jealousy and hurting an innocent person in the same way my father used to hurt my mother. On the following Sunday, I went to church with my wife. Coincidentally, one the readings on that Sunday was about St. Paul's journey to Damascus to persecute the Christians there and about his conversation to later become one of the greatest missionaries of Christianity (cf. Acts of the Apostles 26: 12 - 18).

Paul added:

After the church service, we (Paul and his wife) went home and there I asked my wife to forgive me for all the harm I had caused her. I thanked for the patience she had expressed with me and I told her about how that reading in church about St. Paul's conversion had impacted me so much. My wife remained silent and a few days later accepted my apology based on the changes she had started to see in me.

Paul also mentioned his wife revealed to him that had he not changed his mistreatment of her and the house rules, she had started to plan a way to escape from him. He cited his wife's words: 'I could no longer live in a house which had become a prison with a warden who did to me whatever pleased him.'

Paul praised his sister for initiating the process which saved his marriage, as well as his patient wife and the reading in church which empowered him to ask his heartfelt apology from his wife. By the time of the interview, Paul revealed that he was a "happily married man" with his "beloved wife" and the couple had six children, 13 grandchildren and four great-grandchildren and had celebrated their 53rd wedding anniversary. Paul was spending a significant amount of his retirement time as a volunteer in one of the local prisons coaching men, using his personal stories to help them on how to reintegrate into society and their families after being arrested for domestic violence.

Peter

Peter is a 72-year-old widower, an African American man and was married for 50 years. He married at the age of 20 to an 18-year-old woman whom he had grown up with in the same neighborhood. Peter mentioned:

> We had three beautiful girls and two boys. Unfortunately, we lost our youngest son to drugs and one of our daughters to HIV/AIDS. As parents, we suffered these losses and we took them to heart. We held each other's hands and cried together. It was only our faith in God and the support of the family and the church community that helped us to handle this terrible grief of parents burying their own children. My other two daughters and son are very successful in their marriages and professions. They all put their energies into study: my son is a medical doctor; one daughter is a registered nurse and the other is in the military. All have given us grandchildren and we cherished them together before my wife died.

81

We are all Catholics. My children used to sing in the church choir and they also sang Gospel music with other children in the neighborhood. Painfully for me, they are not going to church a lot these days and it hurts my soul. I go alone after the death of my wife. Her death has made me so helpless and I feel lost. I live alone, I eat alone, and I sleep alone.

I have thought of remarrying in order to have someone to live with, to do things together, to go to church together, to share a meal and to give one another company. I want to enjoy my retirement with someone and to travel where I am able to do so. To my disappointment when I shared my desire to remarry with my children, one of my daughters and a son became so furious with me, and my son said "no, no, no. "The other daughter left the decision to me. I can't think of any reason for their denial other than imagining that they are still grieving the loss of their mother. Whatever the case, I am resolved to remarry for the reasons I stated before.

Stephen

Stephen is a 62-year-old man, born and raised in the Philippines. He got married at 28 years old to his high school sweetheart, who was 26 years old at the time.

When asked about one of the challenges they faced in their marriage, he expressed with deep sorrow the chronic sickness of his wife. Elaborating on it he said:

> After the birth of our first son my wife became very sick and her sickness was incurable. We tried different treatments, moving from one doctor to another while my parents were taking care of our son. I cared for my wife as much as I could with the help of my mother and sister. Practically, we were married only four years in which we enjoyed life together. The next 30 years were all covered by going from one doctor to another.

It was so stressful for me as a care taker and for those 30 years it was difficult for us to be intimate as a couple. In desperation after 15 years of faithfulness I am ashamed to say I broke my vows with a woman who was a widow. Our relationship went on for five years and when I confronted myself, I felt so much guilt because I was not living up to what I had vowed at the Altar of the Lord. I knew in my heart that in health and in sickness I had to be faithful to my wife, but what I called the human condition took over my soul.

The turning point in my life came about after I asked myself would my wife go out with another man if I was the one who had been sick, the response was most, most, probably not. She was a very caring, humble woman and she finally died in my arms. My grief for her is only known to God because there is no single day that passes without thinking about her. She was the first woman I had sex with in my life; she also confided in me that I was the only man she ever had sex with.

My wife thanked me for caring for her while holding my hand so tightly with all her energy and asked me to pray with her the prayer of the "Hail Mary". We prayed it together, slowly, holding our hands together. About five minutes after the prayer, she opened her eyes one more time and we looked each other in the eye, and then she died peacefully. [Stephen took a moment of a brief silence, a profound breath and silent tears flowed from his eyes; and then he added]:

I miss my wife so much. She was my love, my sweetheart and will remain so. I look forward to meeting her again. My life will never be the same. I know what it means to be loved by a wife and to put into practice the vows we professed at the Altar of the Lord. My hope is in the Resurrection. She is with Jesus now, and when my time comes to go, I will see her in Heaven.

Meet each female participant

Anna

Anna is a 61-year-old woman, married for 38 years and has spent most of her married life as a stay-at-home mom. After the children left home, she decided to become more dedicated to serve in her church as a volunteer on a number of committees. She is a Roman Catholic, attends church services almost on a daily basis, especially daily morning Mass and her husband joins her at the Sunday Mass. She identifies herself as a German American. She received an associate's degree during her formal education and her husband has a master's degree. The couple got married in 1980 and they have four children, ages: 33, 31, 29 and 26.

When asked to identify at least one of the greatest challenges experienced in her marriage and how it was resolved, she mentioned:

> My husband lost his job when we had four children ages 10-17. Our finances were extremely tight with our oldest attending college in the fall. We gave up on a lot of the extras; I supported him emotionally and also went out to get some part-time work to help with the finances. Six months later he found work, but still, that time of not knowing in between was hard. By supporting one another we got through it, and by working together it made our marriage stronger. My parents had been in a similar situation, and they handled it in a similar way. I learned from them.

Anna added:

> Our son was expelled from school for an unfair circumstance, involving another boy in his 6th grade class. We discussed it together, and went into the school together to the principal to explain the circumstances. He received only one day of expulsion, versus 3-4 days that were originally determined.

Again, working together and communication were key issues and that helped get things resolved.

Ellen

Ellen is a 67-year-old Catholic woman, attends church services once or several services per week. Her parents are of Irish descent and she identifies herself as Irish American. She is a registered nurse. She left her parents' house under very difficult circumstances and spent nine months in the house of her prospective mother-in-law as well as her future husband. Eventually, they moved into their apartment, got married when she was 21 years old and they have been married for forty-six years. He husband is also Irish American, 72 years old, and both earn a combined annual income of $100,000 plus, before paying taxes.

When asked about one of the greatest challenges that she has experienced in her marriage and yet found a way to live with it in a more productive way, she responded:

> We did eight years of fertility treatment without success. It was stressful. Then after many prayers, God brought us a baby girl through adoption. When she was a teenager, her behavior was troublesome. My husband felt it was Ok and she would outgrow it. We started to argue about her on daily basis. We went for marriage counseling which reminded us to work together and how much we loved each other.

When asked for any suggestion she had for other spouses struggling with infertility in their marriage, Ellen emphasized:

> Infertility can cause stress in a marriage. Spouses should have open discussions with each other but don't put blame on either person. If you love and respect each other, you can overcome any obstacle in your marriage.

Ellen added:

My husband and I finally decided to adopt a child. She was almost two years old when we adopted her and she is currently 39.

When Ellen was asked to describe briefly one event in her married life, she said she has found her faith in God to be a great resource in saving their marriage she stated:

> My faith in God is very strong. So is my husband's. This helped our marriage to be strong also. When we had our infertility problems we prayed together and did novenas. We put our trust in God that if he wanted us to have a child, he would bring us one. My patron saint is the Blessed Mother. In May 1980, we did a Novena to her. In August, I was in church and felt that I received a message we would have a child soon. I even told my sisters-in-law because they also know how strong my faith is in the Blessed Mother. I was working as a nurse and befriended a social worker who was being bullied. In October, I received a call that there was a baby for adoption from her. We were able to take our four-day-old daughter home from the nursery. Our daughter was born with a birthmark identical to mine. I told my husband that is a sign from God and the Blessed Mother that she was meant for us to keep. May, August and October are the three months we celebrate the Blessed Mother.

Joyce

Joyce is a 55-year-old medical doctor and has only been married once. She was born in Uganda and completed most her of studies in Uganda. Her parents made connections with the parents of her husband and arranged their marriage. When asked about the arrangement and involvement of her parents, she said:

> In retrospect, I have come to appreciate the time my parents took to choose a well-behaved man for me. Unlike some of my friends who met their future spouses at the university, during school, most of my efforts were dedicated to my studies. I was

kind of taken back in my thoughts when my mother told me that she and my dad were in serious communications with the parents of a young man in the neighboring village. The four parents talked among themselves, and then a meeting was held at my parents' house with the young man who came with them to meet me. I was 22 years old when I first met my prospective husband and we progressively fell in love as time progressed and we discovered the qualities and talents both his parents and mine had 'implanted and nurtured' in us while raising us.

I was still a virgin when I met him and he is the first man and only man with whom I have ever been intimately involved. My parents walked us through all the traditional and cultural details related to getting married. We also received pre-marriage counseling from a Catholic priest who officiated at our wedding.

Beyond a reasonable doubt, that priest helped us so much. There are issues that our parents couldn't talk to us about in clear and definite terms, but that priest left no stone unturned!!! By the time we got to say "I do" we had received an excellent preparation and resolved to do whatever it takes to make our marriage succeed. Many men in my home area are still so dominating of their wives and the priest helped my husband to consider me as an equal partner. I am happy to witness that he is a different man compared to what my friends tell me about their "macho" husbands. He treats me as an equal partner, he asks for my opinion and listens, we negotiate our differences and I also respond in kind to his goodness and areas of improvement.

Two years after our wedding, we came to the United States. He already had a job and I wanted to finish my Doctorate of Medicine. He supported me financially and I dedicated myself to study. Based on the recommendation of that priest, my husband opened a joint account for both us even if I was not contributing to it. I had access to the money and we have maintained our communications about money, especially before making any major purchases. Ever since I got my first pay check, I also deposit my income on the same joint account. It has worked for us.

Sarah

Sarah is a 47-year-old woman, Roman Catholic and attends church services one or more times a week. Her parents are both of Polish descent and she identifies herself as Polish American. Her highest level of education is a bachelor's degree. She got married at age 26 to a police officer and the couple has two children. Elaborating on one of the greatest challenges she faces is having a son with a mental disorder while her daughter, who is generally healthy, has become so distressed due to her ongoing preoccupations and inability to successfully help her younger brother.

Sarah also reported experiencing self-blame, emotional fatigue, guilt, jealousy of other people's children, yet she is committed to cherish and care for her son. One of her main concerns is: "What will happen to my son when one of us dies or both die?" After a moment of silence, she responded to her question: "God will provide for him someone."

Chen

Chen is a 53-year-old woman, who came to the United States from China at the age of 13. She is a Buddhist by religion and is very active in her faith. She has been married for 28 years to a man of Chinese background, who came to the United States at the age of 10. The couple has two children ages 19 and 23, they live in an urban neighborhood, both of them work together in a highly demanding job. They enjoy working together. When asked about one of the challenges they have experienced as a couple she mentioned:

> My husband did not know how to cook and would not do anything to help me unless he was asked. He imagined that it was very easy to cook as 2+2=4. He would not even help me, even when I was sick, not even to feed the children and that

bothered me a lot. One day, while a bit upset, I asked him to cook because I was sick. He wanted to order food out and I asked him not to, and instructed him how to fix something simple. Progressively, I have invited him to cook with me and he has learned a lot. He now helps with the cooking and has been active in the raising of our children ever since. It may seem that this was not a major conflict to an outsider, but it really bothered me and I am glad he now helps me.

Another source of conflict has been the influence of my mother-in-law on our marriage. At the beginning of our marriage, she tried to control me, telling me what to do, give me orders and was so intrusive in our marriage. As time passed by, I spoke to my husband to ask his mother to give us some space in our marriage and we moved a bit farther away from her. It seems she now respects me more because she has seen how successful I am in my business with my husband and in the raising of our children.

Being a dual-career couple has been productive for us and my husband respects me and always encouraged me to work. The money we bring into the family we put it in the same joint account and that has empowered our relationship and communications. At the beginning one of us had more spending than the other and we resolved this by the other spouse taking charge of the account for six months. Ever since we started communication more about how much we want to spend and we are very frugal.

Our marriage stability and satisfaction is based on true love and trust. As Chinese people, we use the word love primarily in romantic relationships and between spouses. It seems the word love is very common in the American culture, and that is not the case with us as Chinese. There are different types of love and we have proper terminologies for each type of love in contrast to the way the word is used in the United States. For instance, we speak of filial piety instead of love between a parent and a child. Regarding true love this love is sacrificial, implies a profound commitment toward the other and maintains loyalty without easy access to divorce. We do our best to resolve problems instead of walking away from a relationship.

Cynthia

Cynthia is a 45-year-old woman, daughter of parents of Irish descent. When the author asked her to share her insights about the factors which contribute to stability and satisfaction in marriage, she took a deep breath and then said in raised tone of voice: "NO ALCOHOL." The author asked her to elaborate on what she meant and she mentioned:

> Alcohol was the main reason for my running from my parent's home to my maternal grandparents at age 13. My father was drinking too much and used to fight with my mother over very small things. He would start off an argument over something insignificant as: 'Where is my blue shirt?' Mom's telling him: "I washed it and it is not yet ironed' would make him shout at her: 'What have you been doing all day. It is the one I am going to wear tomorrow.' Then he would either continue arguing with mom or come to shout at me and my young brother for not doing our homework from school even if we had already finished it.

Cynthia added:

> My dad would wake up the next day as if nothing had happened the previous night and he was so nice with us, smiling and talking nicely to mom, my brother and I. This made me think that alcohol is one of the worst enemies that can destroy a home and its family members. It reached the point that almost every day, my father came home drunk and my mom would tell us to go to our bedrooms and pretend that we were already sleeping. I know the adage: 'A bad worker blames his tool,' but in my case, I hate alcohol. It turned my father into an alcoholic. Bankrupt, dishonest, he was terminated from his job for overdrinking and it eventually contributed to his death at age 42. My mother became a widow at age 40 my brother and I became

91

orphans at ages 17 and 19. My grandparents had to attend the funeral of their only son and my children will never enjoy the company of a grandfather. I hate alcohol. Alcohol kills. My father's alcoholism made my mom homeless and I am glad that my husband does not drink at all.

Lea

Lea is a 26-year-old Caucasian woman. She was born and raised in a Roman Catholic family in New Jersey. She has been married for two years to a Christian man after seven years of courtship. When asked about when she knew her husband she mentioned:

> We met in high school; we went to high school together, dated and broke up, then came back together in college and have been together since. During the seven years of courtship, I came to know his family better and he also knew my family well. Today I describe my in-laws as 'awesome'. My husband and I feel a sense of stability and satisfaction now in our marriage. It is more of this sense of security and love we have for each other, and the time we spent together during courtship that helps us to hope for the best for our marriage.

When Lea was asked about how she knew her husband was the right man to marry she said 'when you know you know'. Both of us value some independence from each other have room for mutual friends and separate friends, we both contribute financially to our marriage and we maintain quality communication. When asked about some of the fears she had but never communicated before marriage, she mentioned:

> Who will stay at home once we have children? If we go from two incomes to one, that can be stressful. At which point do we stop splitting family houses for holidays and do it all together?

When asked to clarify what she meant by "at what point do we stop splitting houses for the holidays…?" She explained: "I mean, at what point do we become an independent family unit, rather than spending all our holidays at our parents' homes."

When asked about one of the challenges she had experienced in her marriage she referred to her health, and she elaborated:

> If you are not healthy it adds another level of stress. When I am experiencing fibromyalgia pain, It is hard for me to get around and be productive. It then adds stress to him to make sure I feel ok, but also to get done everything I didn't do and what he also has to do. (She added) that raises concern about maintaining our income to provide for the needs we have and the bills we accumulate.

Teresa

Teresa is a 56-year-old woman from Ghana and has been living in the United States for the last 12 years. Teresa and her husband are both Roman Catholics, and they attend church services at least once a week. Teresa received a diploma in education and her 57-year-old husband has a master's degree. Teresa was 27 when she got married and her husband was 28. The couple has one child. When asked about one of the difficulties the couple has experienced and how it was resolved Teresa responded:

> Our individual career progression demands forced my husband and I to live in different countries for close to 10 years. The relatively 'independent' lifestyles in a way established different 'kingdoms' which initially made it difficult to settle down when we eventually lived together. We clashed often on decisions affecting the running of our home and parenting our daughter. With time, both of us adjusted to each other, improved our and communication, and we got over most of our differences through a mixture of compromise and understanding.

Emphasizing what has helped her to resolve the problem she experienced due to distance was her faith in God's grace that one day they would be reunited and live together as a family. Teresa added:

> I also chose to trust my husband and not second guess his actions and whereabouts. I believe that he wants what is best for me and our family ultimately.

Jessica

Jessica is a 33-year-old woman, Caucasian and has been married for 10 years. During college, she dated many boys and became pregnant on a number of occasions due to unprotected sex. During the first three months of her first pregnancy, she was very afraid about the pregnancy; her boyfriend abandoned her because she was pregnant. She turned to her mother for guidance, her mother told her to have an abortion, rather than risk her education and career. Seven months after the abortion, she was pregnant again and this time she decided to have another abortion with the help of her boyfriend. This boyfriend later abandoned her and she became pregnant again after one year, this time she did not consult anyone, but proceeded with an abortion on her own. By the end of the school year she had started to feel so depressed about the abortions after seeing that one of her classmates had given birth to a beautiful baby girl.

One year after school she started working at a local store and started dating one of her co-workers. After three years they decided to get married and Jessica became enthusiastic about becoming a mother. Two years went by after the wedding without conception. In the next two years, she experienced three spontaneous abortions. Jessica began to blame herself and question if after so many abortions, now experiencing spontaneous abortions, was God punishing her. Her husband was so supportive or her and he was Catholic. He suggested that Jessica join the Rachel Program. Jessica joined the program and came across many other women in the program who were also having very similar experiences and questioning as to whether God was punishing them for their previous styles of life. Jessica mentioned:

If it had not been for the coordinator of the Rachel Program, I would most probably have continued to think that God was punishing me and the other women in the group. The coordinator, shared with the group that she had also thought God was punishing her but she had realized after speaking with a priest that God is merciful and calls people to conversion and forgiveness. I believed the coordinator and I also went to speak with a priest. The priest was very understanding and compassionate. He listened to me and suggested that whenever I am ready, I should go for Confession and resolve to amend my life. After my Confession and receiving Gods absolution, I still struggled with forgiving myself, but my husband supported me and reassured me of God's unconditional love.

Two years later, I became pregnant again and gave birth to a beautiful baby boy. My spirituality has improved and I am a firm believer now in Gods mercy and in the courage to forgive oneself because holding onto the guilt is to question God's mercy. Who am I to question God? Thanks to my husband, to the Rachel Program, to the priests and the fellow women who have supported me throughout my experience I encourage other women to do whatever it takes to keep their babies and bring them to full term without any excuse or fear.

Karen

Karen is a 66-year-old woman, Roman Catholic, who has been married for 47 years and the couple has two children. They cohabited for five years after she completed high school. When asked about one of the problems they experienced as a couple, and how it was resolved, she responded:

A difficult time in our marriage was having my husband work steady nights and raising two small children ages 2 and 4 years old. I felt a heavy burden when he left for work having no help with simple household chores, raising the children. Even though he was home during the day, working nights, he would need his rest and sleep until late morning or early afternoon. Eventually, I adjusted. I had to. He was the breadwinner. When he had free time, he showed what a good husband, father, and provider he was. He showed he loved me and his family by the time he spent with us when he could.

Suzanna

Suzanna is a 45-year-old woman, who was born in South Africa and immigrated to the United States with her parents at the age of 5. During college, she fell in love with a young man, who she apparently considered to be lonely. She went on to become a social worker and three years after her studies she married the man. They have been married for 20 years and they have one daughter. Asked about one of the challenges she has encountered in her marriage she started sobbing and then made a funny laugh to which she said:

> I am laughing at myself because of the predicament I put myself into and the guilt I feel for not reading the warning signs and red flags of my prospective husband when we were dating. As a social worker, I should have known better, I regret my desire to help him and it is too late to divorce him and for the sake of our daughter I will stay. Briefly put my husband has been diagnosed with narcissistic personality disorder. Our marriage is conditioned by him and I feel trapped. He has a way of seeking attention all the time, has no consideration for my feelings, sexual intimacy is superficial and it is only on his own terms. He argues a lot, he sets many unrealistic expectations about me and our daughter and dominates all the conversations.

> It is only my professional training and personal therapy which have helped me to live with a husband who is narcissistic and he is father of my daughter. His sense of entitlement drives me crazy. He is so self-centered, very dogmatic in his beliefs, manipulative and wants to take credit for everything I do. Therefore, I recommend that during dating partners should be attentive to their own mental health and that of the person they

are dating. Some of these mental health disorders don't change with marriage.

Linda

Linda is a 38-year-old woman, who immigrated to the United States from Chile. She came after her husband had been in the United States for four years. When asked about one of the challenges in her marriage and how it was resolved, Linda started sobbing and after taking a deep breath she said that these four years of separation were very hard for both of them financially, relationally, and as young parents. Linda mentioned:

> My husband and I discussed at length about the advantages and disadvantages of leaving our country and moving to the United States. It was not an easy decision, but with everything considered my husband came without documentation in order to improve our lives and to escape from the dangerous neighborhood that we lived in. He left me when I was four months pregnant and I had to depend on my parents for almost everything. A year later he started sending us some money and the situation became a bit better, but the loneliness we were both feeling was intense. I don't know why I started doubting his fidelity, but the idea passed my mind several times. In the third year since he left, I asked him to send us money so that I could come to the United States with our child. He helped us as much as he could and we were finally reunited. Surprisingly even after coming here I still felt lonely because my husband was busy working and I was now far from my family.
>
> It is very hard to maintain a conversation as an adult with a 3-year-old son. Fortunately, I started going to church and I found people there with whom I started to interact and made friends. A year later my young sister asked me if we could help her to come to the United States. My husband agreed and we sent her the money. After three years, she managed to join us. She lived with us because it was cheaper and there was no way she could

get an apartment without working. In the meantime, I had started a nice job and I spent a lot of time at work and my work shift was different from my husband's work shift. My sister was very helpful with my child and I felt a great sense of relief because she was taking good care of them. Now I don't know whether to blame myself or not for taking a night-shift job, but I think that leaving my husband alone with my sister opened the door for them to become romantic.

On the other hand, given all the help I had given to my sister and the confidence I had in her I don't think she should have paid me by sleeping with my husband. I blame my husband also for betraying me with my sister. An affair would have been heartbreaking enough, but it was so much worse because it was my sister. It is very hard for me to overcome this. However, I also realize that holding on to blaming them or myself hurts me more. Consequently, I have prayed to God to give me the grace to forgive him and my sister as well as myself. Progressively, I have managed to forgive him for my well-being and he seems to have stopped his extramarital affair. He goes to church with me, receives the sacraments and Communion at Mass.

Based on what I have gone through and my ongoing doubts as to whether my husband can ever be trusted, I recommend that people should respect their in-laws, establish good relationships with them and also maintain clear boundaries with each of them.

Christine

Christine is a 28-year-old woman, was raised in a Roman Catholic family in India and has spent only two years in the United States with her husband. They have been married for five years. She describes herself as a very devout Catholic, honest and wants to spend time with her husband. When asked about one of the great challenges she has experienced in her marriage she described it as follows:

I am open to children and my husband also wants children, but he is not open to having them in the near future. He works so hard and sometimes even brings work home and that affects our time together. Being away from home and already married five years without a child and still in limbo of when it will ever happen sometimes, I end up so lonely, depressed and angry at my husband.

I don't want to use artificial family planning methods, especially those which involve putting chemicals in my body. This decision also complicates my sexual life with my husband for he is not ready for children but wants my company on a regular basis. This challenge is not yet resolved but we have started to speak about it and I am becoming more understanding of the reasons my husband wants to delay beginning a family. We are both legal immigrants and we don't have permanent status yet, our finances are still tight, our families in India are dependent on our small income and we are still paying our student loans.

Marie

Marie is an African woman from Ghana. She is a 39-year-old, a postgraduate, a Presbyterian, and currently attends religious services one or more times a week. Her husband is also 39 years old. He is a Methodist, attends religious services once a month and is also from Ghana. They got married at the age of 25, have been married for 13 years and have one son who is 11 years old. The family lives in an urban neighborhood. Based on their cultural background they did not live together before marriage.

When asked about one of her challenges in marriage, she mentioned the stress she feels in sending money back to her relatives and friends in Ghana. She elaborated:

I am the only person in my family who has received higher education and who is out of the country. I don't make a lot of money but I am expected to support the people back home. Unfortunately, some of them even live in better houses and have better jobs than me but they still demand a lot from me. Being in the United States even complicated the situation for me because those who have not been in the United States think that dollars are everywhere and can be picked as leaves of coffee.

This demand has brought some tension with my husband because he thinks that I should not be sending them the money every time they request it. His relatives are better off financially than mine and I tend to think that by telling me not to send to those who really need it, he is being mean and inconsiderate. Most of all I am hurt because sometimes I have to send my parents some money without his knowledge. They are elderly and my brother, who is with them, does not have enough to care for them. They are the ones who sacrificed for my education and for many good things I have obtained in life. I feel torn between loyalty to my husband and to helping my relatives. There is no definitive solution to this tension in our marriage except to say that since I am working and getting paid it is ok to send them money from my salary.

Doris

Doris is a 69-year-old woman, received her doctorate in education and has been married for 46 years. She was born and raised in a Roman Catholic family, attends church services one or more times a week and is a volunteer for a number of community activities in the church. Doris's father is of Irish cultural background and her mother's parents were of Irish and Italian descent. She identifies herself as Italian and Irish American. Doris got married at age 23, in 1972 and together with her husband, who is also Roman Catholic and a doctor, have three sons, ages: 43, 40 and 38. Doris is currently retired, and the couple receives an estimated annual retirement income of $170,000. Doris has the experience of having lived in an urban neighborhood for almost 30 years, ten years in a suburban area and currently eight years in what she describes as a "rural" community.

Doris and her husband mutually agreed before marriage to support one another to advance academically, to support one another in raising their children and to be dual-career couple. When asked about how has being a dual-career couple positively impacted her marriage stability and satisfaction, she mentioned:

> The impact has been enormous in making us better people and partners: co-equals in all financial and major family decisions, and able to enjoy both our professional and family time. We have had to cooperate, communicate, and follow through on commitments to balance everything off, but always saw the negotiations as a WIN-WIN arrangement. We EACH got to pursue high level careers AND remain closely connected to the lives and activities of our three sons. Our sons got the benefit of two engaged parents with different skills and interests to enrich their experience and education.

> Both of us were willing to sacrifice a lot of short-term gratification for future payoffs of healthy, happy children set on positive future trajectories, and careers that advanced nicely for each of us. The whole experience is one I would describe as 90% really hard work and 10% joy, with the joy making the work completely worthwhile. We fastened our seat belts, took the ride, held on, laughed and sang, and found deep satisfaction in our marriage and in our lives. Now, as retirees, the balance has shifted – much less work and more joy as we embrace grandchildren and selectively choose our volunteer projects and community work.

Furthermore, this mutual support between Doris and her husband is reflected in the following situation in which Doris was asked to identify and describe a very difficult moment she has experienced in her marriage and how it was resolved. She responded:

I have experienced a devastating professional setback, but it did not impact my marriage. In fact, this is the situation where my husband and I quickly assessed the situation, determined that no one we loved was harmed or in danger, and trusted that God would help us get through the difficulty of it. Being in this marriage helped me weather that situation and stay balanced.

Joana

Joana is a 33-year-old woman from Mexico. She came to United States at the age of 17 with her aunt. She was born in a Catholic family and raised Catholic. After four years in the United States, she decided to become a Pentecostal and met her boyfriend in the same Pentecostal Church. Joana told her Catholic aunt with whom she was living that she was going to move to her boyfriend's apartment. Joana elaborated:

> Both my boyfriend and I are Pentecostal and I don't have enough money to rent an apartment alone. He has a good paying job, he is a citizen in the United States and if our relationship works out, I have dreams of going back to Mexico with him to be married there with my parents present. We will start out by living together to get to know one another. If both of us feel comfortable enough to get married, we will be more convinced of making a life commitment to one another.

Joana added:

After informing my Catholic aunt about my plans to go and live with my boyfriend, she asked me:

> 'Will you live as brother and sisters then until you make up your mind?' I replied: 'Aunt, I respect your old school practices of 'waiting until marriage to have sex, but I think that for some of us who have lost that patience and made experiments in that area, we still need to be supported.' Aunt replied: 'I understand what you are saying and my main message is that irrespective of whom you decide to experiment with, just in case you become pregnant, never abort the baby.'

A year after Joana moved into her boyfriend's apartment, she gave birth to a baby girl and named her after her aunt, who had encouraged her to keep the baby.

Raquel

Raquel is a 35-year-old African American woman. She has a 10-year-old son from a previous relationship, as well as a 5 -year-old son and a 3-year-old daughter with her husband. During an interview with the author, she mentioned:

> It may sound that I want to do the things backward. In other words, I gave birth to a child and now seeking to get married instead of getting married first and then become pregnant and giving birth to a child. The thing is that I cannot change my past but in my teenager years, I really longed and still hold on to the dream of getting married. I am not blaming my parents for having lived together for four years and then separated, but because of that, I never had a model of marriage to emulate. My mom did her best to raise me and my young brother, she worked two jobs to support us, finances were tight and we missed going to school at least two days in a week.

> I cannot explain how I managed through high school, but after that I could not continue. We were so poor and I befriended a man who had promised to help me get a job so that I could help my mother with rent and other bills. I did not even have money for transportation and that man offered to come for me and take me to work and then bring me back. I did not know how to return the favor, so when he asked me out, I said yes and then I found myself with greater challenges than the ones I had before. I became pregnant at age 19 and then he left me on my own. I felt so lonely and on two or three occasions, I experienced some difficult thoughts and peer pressures to abort the baby.

> I give thanks to God and to my mom for her unconditional support in midst of poverty, my faith in God became stronger

and I resolved to keep my baby and I gave birth to a baby boy. I am a firm believer that life starts at conception and the baby in the womb has the right to be protected from all harm. Looking back, I thank God for all the support I have received. I recalled my grandma's words as soon as she heard that I was pregnant: 'Keep the baby and you will be happy for not having innocent blood on your hands. That is why you are alive today because I decided to keep the pregnancy of your mother and she in turn kept you alive.'

Raquel added:

I am glad my grandma did her best as a single mother to raise a child, and I am grateful to my mom for raising me as a single parent. Now, I am grateful to God for all the graces received as well as all the people who have helped me as a single parent to raise my son. However, nothing has taken away my dream of getting married. I want to break this cycle of single parenthood for my next child or at least to provide my son with the opportunity of having a stepfather.

I also recalled the adage that my grandma used to quote to me: 'Some men do not buy the cow if they can get the milk for free.' Inspired by the wisdom within this saying, I resolved not to return any favor to a man with my body without making a commitment to go together before the Alter of the Lord. I later realized that the more I respected myself and became more focused on seeking for a committed marriage partner, the more men respected me. Those who were coming only for my body and not for me as a person, sooner or later realized that I was not so desperate nor all that generous. They left on their own and I maintained my dignity.

By God's grace, Jack came into my life and we got married in church. He was mature and had a career of his own. He is an African American and a Catholic man and a chemical engineer. Jack and I have two biological children, ages 5 and 3, as well as my 10-year-old son, who has Jack not only as a stepfather but a man who really cares about him and a father-figure in life.

Jean

Jean is a 73-year-old woman who immigrated to the United States from Uganda. She came in an emergency situation to attend to her husband who had been involved in an accident. The incident left the husband permanently paralyzed from the waist down and in a wheelchair. They have been married for 50 years and she gives a lot of credit to God for the survival of her husband and for being able to conceive a son with the help of professional doctors.

When asked about one of the challenges she has experienced in her marriage she expresses with deep sorrow the pain of her husband becoming paralyzed and the difficulties she has experienced of becoming primarily a caregiver instead of just a wife. Jean credits her faith and love for her husband because if it was not for true love she doesn't know how she would have handled all she has gone through and she continues to experience. Jean's marriage story and suggestions will be elaborated on later in this book.

Lucy

Lucy is a 65-year-old woman, who was born in South Korea. She and her husband, who is also South Korean, came to the United State as a married couple. Her husband opened a coin laundry business in Manhattan and they worked together. The business was very successful and they managed to raise money to educate their two sons without any school loans. Lucy's husband is retired and she is semi-retired, she works part-time in a nursing home. She emphasized that the money she earns is for her personal account, because she believes a woman should have some money to spend with no questions to ask.

When asked about a difficult time the couple experienced, she mentioned the aftermath of September 11, 2001, as follows:

> Our successful business, which we had worked so hard to establish and maintain, was lost. My husband and I became so depressed, and it was a very, very hard time as we ended up being so overstressed we started arguing, verbally attacking one another even on very insignificant matters. As a couple we became so distant, we lost interest in one another and we lost many friends and acquaintances, whose status we could not measure up to. I became so concerned about the future of our marriage and I found myself looking for the door to go back to the Catholic Church.

> I am happy to say that prayer has helped me to go beyond material things and refocus on our marriage, my husband and my children. I pray, even though the financial situation has progressively improved, I keep up with my prayer and trust in God. I attend daily Mass, participate in Bible Study and in a prayer group.

Lucy said as bad as the experience was it brought her back to God and for that she is glad. She mentioned that her stability and satisfaction in marriage has been enriched by the work ethic she found in her husband. She attributed this work ethic in the arranged marriage, because those that arranged it focused on the virtues and values within him as opposed to over-focusing on material successes and outward appearances. Her children have also been sources of grounding for her marriage; they were both open to having children and worked together to live together as a happy family.

Elaborating on housework she made accommodations when her husband was still working and she did most of the house chores. However, after his retirement she was upset that her husband was not collaborating at all. Eventually she addressed this question with him and he has started to help with the dishes, cleaning and shopping together. She commented that her husband does not attend church, but they now travel as a couple, nationally and internationally, as tourists and they go on religious pilgrimages together. Given these improvements in the home, she has started to enjoy her retirement.

Lucy's current concern is about her sons, ages 38 and 34, for not being in any committed relationship. One is an accomplished medical doctor and the other is in business. She would prefer that they marry South Korean women. However, if that is not possible, she is open to women from other cultural backgrounds.

Sonia

Sonia is a 33-year-old married woman in an interracial and multicultural marriage. She was born and raised in the United States by immigrant parents from El Salvador in the midst of many extended family members. She is the second youngest of five siblings. She is fluent in Spanish and English. She was raised in a Roman Catholic family, regularly attending Sunday Mass and is speaks so happily about being Catholic. During the interview, she spoke with big smiles reflecting her joy for being the first person to receive a Bachelor of Arts degree in her nuclear family. Two months after she started working, she met a man at work with whom she fell in love and who later became her husband (fictitiously named in this book as Dr. Adrian).

When asked by the author to identify and elaborate on one of the most difficult challenges Sonia has experienced in her marriage and how it was resolved, she mentioned: "I have suffered with how to fit into my husband's family by proving myself to his mother and sister."

Sonia elaborated:

> While dating, I had no problem with my future mother-in-law and sister-in-law; maybe because I had fewer contacts with them and they did imagine that the dating might lead us to marriage. However, on my wedding day, I overhead my mother-in-law bad-mouthing me to my sister-in-law saying: 'I can't imagine that my son has married this girl who is not a doctor. That is not good. I am so upset with my son for marrying a

woman who is not Hindu and Indian.' The sister-in-law responded to her mother: 'You are right mom; we are a family of doctors and she is not a doctor... I told my brother not to marry her. She is now a member of our family. Unbelievable!'

Sonia added:

Listening to them bad-mouthing me on my wedding day, about my not being a doctor and all the other stuff, I felt so hurt and humiliated. Even if I was the first to get a BA in my family, it did not count in that instant. I felt like I had never gone to school at all. Thank God, I managed to keep calm on the outside, faking smiles, but in my heart, only God knew what was going on. Within the first three months after the wedding, I tried to prove myself to my mother-in-law and sister-in-law that I am intelligent and capable of doing many good things. I later realized that all efforts to prove myself were not working and I became so depressed after failing to please those two women.

I did not want to put my husband in a situation of conflicting loyalty between me and his mother and sister by telling him what the impact of what I heard them say about me on our wedding day and my failed efforts to please them. Consequently, I decided to seek professional help from a therapist. I was scared, depressed, spending so many sleepless nights, experienced very low self-esteem, upset, humiliated. The therapist helped me to gain my voice, stopped trying to prove myself fruitlessly, I regained my self-esteem and sleep. Writing down the positive self-affirmations as recommended by the therapist was and continues to be very helpful. I realized that I am not the problem and I should not let their insecurities, unrealistic expectations and prejudices dictate how I live my life. I have overcome the feeling of not being good enough. I told myself that once they to get to know me, their perceptions of me might change. During the therapy sessions, I also realized that what makes marriage successful is not primarily whether the two spouses are doctors or not. Surprisingly, my sister-in-law is who used to speak so proudly about being married with

108

another doctor is currently divorced. She now lives with her parents and she has started to thank me for being a good wife to her brother.

I am so grateful to God that my husband is very understanding and supportive of me. We discussed many things before we got married, especially how to raise our children, we agreed that they will be baptized in the Catholic Church and continue to receive other Sacraments in due time. My husband respects my Catholic faith and religion, accompanies me and our children to Sunday Mass on a regular basis and I also respect his Hindu religion. My mother-in-law and sister-in-law have gotten to know me better as a person. I am hardworking, good at cleaning my house and progressively getting better at cooking. I no longer compare myself to women at my own detriment and being patient has helped me not to give up. All these inner changes are helping me to progressively build cultural bridges and to enjoy my marriage with less stress.

Esperanza

Esperanza is a 34-year-old woman, born in Colombia and immigrated to the United States with her parents when she was 13 years old. Esperanza and her husband (fictitiously named Pablo) met in high school, became friends and dated for a while, separated during college, each dated other people, until they finally reunited. At the time of the interview with Esperanza, they have been married for seven years. Pablo was born two years after his parents immigrated to the United States from Cuba. Both Esperanza and her husband are fluent in Spanish and English.

When asked to identify one of the major challenges Esperanza and her husband have experienced in their marriage, and how it was resolved, she mentioned:

> I do not know whether I can call it one problem because it is composed of many other parts. The problem started immediately after the wedding. Pablo's family started

pressuring us to have children as soon as possible. Pablo and I tried to resist their insistence for the first year, and then we decided to move to another State to reduce the tensions with them. Even after moving to another state his parents continued to call us and demand that we should start a family. Pablo started to pressure me to start a family. I didn't want to and we started having arguments between us. Long story short, we decided to seek professional help from a marriage and family therapist. The therapist was very understanding and helped each one of us to do a set of inventories and identify our priorities. I will not speak for my husband but I recall that this is what I got from the therapy sessions: I realized that the crucial problem was not starting a family or not. The real issue was that I was focused on my career, paying off student loans and to work as many women of my generation, and advance myself professionally.

Esperanza elaborated:

Reflecting on the therapist's question: What is your description of successes in life? I realized that my description was focused on having as many material things as possible, work to get as much money as possible, have fun, focus on my self-advancement as a woman, enjoy as much sexual intimacy as possible, and to have a style of life which would allow me to enjoy my life to the max before having children.

As I reflected deeper and deeper on what other people call pondering, I became aware in the therapy sessions that in order to start a family, I had to restructure my priorities, redefine success and make tough choices which most probably are in contrast to the contemporary perceptions of success. The therapist insisted that people who make changes in therapy or after therapy, have the tendency to give up on these changes. Consequently, I had to turn to the wisdom mentioned by Martin Luther King, Jr. to become a social misfit in order to maintain the changes I had suggested for myself.

110

The interviewer asked Esperanza" What do you mean?

Esperanza replied;

> Martin Luther King, Jr. said 'the future belongs to those whom society considers to be social misfits.' In other words, there was no way I was going to start a family if I remained focused on today's description of success. This includes, but is not limited to, having a big house, highest education, making a lot of money, be well travelled and as sexually active as you wish and with whom you want.
>
> I confronted myself and I revisited traditional values which my parents had taught me at home. For instance, to value the people entrusted to my care, work for the wellbeing of children, the poor, the elderly, and to go back to the church. Above all I recall my grandma's words which she used to recite to me from the Bible. "The Lord has told us what is right and what he requires of you: to act justly, to love faithfulness, and to walk humbly with your God" (cf: Micah 6:8).
>
> I am so grateful that we went to therapy. Just before our therapy sessions ended, I resolved to restructure my priorities and asked God for the grace to persevere in the decision I had made, learned how to resist peer pressure from the people of my generation and we started a family.
>
> I am happy to report that we have a 3-year-old boy, who has brought us together as a couple and as a family more than most of the material successes which we were chasing without finding lasting joy in them.

Maggie

Maggie is a 48-year-old African American woman, married to a 52-year-old African American man. Her husband is fictitiously referred to here as Joshua. Both Maggie and Joshua are professionals, make a lot of money, and are very active in their Baptist Church.

When asked about one of the challenges the couple has experienced in their marriage, Maggie paused, started sobbing, and then started talking at length:

> One day my husband approached me to tell me about what our 20-year-old son had told him. He (Joshua) asked me to go to our bedroom because he wanted to tell me 'Something important and difficult to talk about.'

> I wondered what it could be and my mind wondered from telling me about a serious illness to a death in the family. On reaching our bedroom he was panicking even though we were just the two of us in the house. Then he started saying:

> 'I don't know where to start (silence). Our son told me three weeks ago that he wanted to tell me 'Something very important. I feared for the worst, yet I did not want to scare him for fear that he could change the topic if I appeared very scared. He asked me to go to his room, while you (Maggie) were at work.'

Maggie informed the author that she told Joshua: "Stop beating about the bush. Tell in clear what words what our son told you."

She elaborated by citing Joshua's words:

> 'Our son told me that he is gay and has been active in that style of life for two years. He expressed the emotional turmoil he has gone through and the risk he took to tell me with the hope that I can tell you and understand him.'

Maggie, while sobbing, went on to inform the author:

> I looked my husband in the eye and we both started shedding tears. We both held each other in silence. Afterward I told him that maybe it is my fault that our son has become gay. My husband instead told me that maybe he was the one to blame. We both expressed our frustration to one another and in the coming weeks we both became more depressed, ashamed,

blamed God, and blamed ourselves. We finally decided to look for help from our Pastor.

Maggie added:

I told the Pastor that I don't approve of homosexuality and my husband added: neither do I. The Pastor seemed different on that day when we were sitting with him in his office than when he speaks in the church. He seemed more compassionate, more understanding, and he listened to us as we expressed our pain. By the end of the meeting with him, I felt that I shouldn't continue to blame myself and I felt less shame and more loved by God who gave us this son to care for. When we reached home I cried a lot and continued to wonder why my son, why me and my husband had to face this reality. I questioned myself whether we should tell our family members or not and I did not know how each would react to the news. I had more questions than answers. I continued to share my concerns with my husband, who looked me in the eye and said words which have helped me to feel more peace.

Maggie cited what her husband mentioned:

'You and me, we don't approve of homosexuality, but first and foremost this is our son. We are not going to throw him out of the house, we are not going to abandon him, otherwise, to whom will he turn to if he can't turn to his parents! He (Joshua) insisted in a louder voice: 'Our pain and struggles seem like those of grieving for a loved one who has died. We are grieving the loss of the dreams we had for our son.'

Maggie added:

After that painful conversation in which my husband made an analogy to grief, I went to our family library. Surprisingly, I found there a book which I had not read. It was titled: *On Death and Dying,* by Kubler-Ross (1969). Although I was not literally mourning a death of a loved one, as I was reading that book, I started identifying myself with a lot of insights in that book

113

while struggling to come to terms with my son's sexual orientation. I was experiencing recycling feelings of denial, anger, bargaining with God and depression. It took me time and faith in a merciful God to reach acceptance. Above all, when I recalled that what my mother used to say: 'Once a parent, you are always a parent,' together with what my husband had told me: 'first and foremost, he is our son,' I found some relief, and I will keep holding on to those insights.

Olivia

Olivia is a 70-year-old Caucasian woman, earned her doctorate in developmental psychology and spent a lot of years teaching in different colleges and universities. She is currently a widow. She was married to her husband for 52 years until he died in 2013. The couple had two children, ages 45 and 41. Olivia received her doctorate at the time when her prospective husband was completing his master's degree. The two of them decided that Olivia would start working and her husband would go for his doctorate.

Olivia elaborated:

> I was the sole breadwinner and all expenses were on my income. My husband and I both valued education and he worked so hard to finish his Doctorate of Philosophy. After his graduation, we opened a joint account together and it has been like that to this day. We communicated about our money, how to spend it, when to start a family and how to integrated our inheritances into our joint account. After the birth of our first child, we were so happy and we were ready for the second, and many more. However, our second child died three days after birth and it was a great loss and it brought a pain that we have never recovered from completely.
>
> I was raised Lutheran and my husband was a Roman Catholic and very devoted to his faith. As a matter of fact, he contemplated the priesthood and joined the seminary for a few

years. By the time I met him, he had left the seminary on his own account, but he was so enthusiastic in his faith that I wound up converting to Catholicism. I embraced Catholicism with great love and we both attended Mass every Sunday. We both had a spiritual hunger and we searched for churches with excellent preachers and those focused on social justice issues. No wonder instead of a diamond engagement ring I put on a sapphire, which is a blue stone ring, this was our way of boycotting the exploitation by the diamond brokers.

When asked about what contributed to their marriage stability Olivia highlighted that they were both interested in one another because they valued academic achievement, spirituality, mutual respect, raising of children and the excellent example of married life from their parents. Olivia spoke with high regard about her being the first woman in her family to become a doctor. She credited her husband's intellectual curiosity to her mother-in-law, who was also a Doctor of Medicine.

Elaborating on one of the most difficult times in their marriage Olivia spoke with tears in her eyes about the death of their second child. She mentioned that her late husband during the time of his death had not come to terms with the baby's death and was still struggling with that grief. Talking about this grief together and consoling one another and pouring their hearts into their two live children is what she referred to as "sources of relief to that unresolved loss."

Olivia's grief intensified after the prolonged sickness of her husband and the eventual death. However, she credited her faith in the Resurrection, prayer, memorial Masses, and the hope of meeting her loved ones in heaven. In a special way, she mentioned, that even if she were to remarry, she would still hold on to the sweet memories of her husband who had died. She added: "Some days are heavier than others, but I speak to him and I know he is still with me every day."

Josephine

Josephine is a 75-year-old woman, a practicing Roman Catholic, and she has been widowed for seven years. She married at age 33 to a Polish man and they never had children. Elaborating on her marriage stability and satisfaction, she mentioned that:

> My husband and I were mature when we got married. He was 32 and I was 33, both of us being mature meant we respected each other's view and we married because we loved one another. We worked together in his business but before that I had worked on my own and had saved a lot of money. That is the advantage of staying with your parents until you get married, so you do not have to spend money on rent. We built the business together; my husband was a mechanic and I worked in the office.

When asked about the most difficult challenge she faced since she got married, Josephine elaborated:

> Losing my husband is a great pain that will never get out of my heart. I miss him every day. People speak of being each other's half in a marriage and I know now what it really means. I speak to him every day and I allow myself to listen to him going back in the ways he used to speak back to me. He was a man of few words, liked to listen and then would say something profound. That is why I speak more to him now because he is a great listener. Those who think I am crazy to say I speak to a dead person it is their problem.

> Both of us because we were mature when we got married, mature meaning older, we were open to children but nature did not bring them. Surprisingly we never talked about it between the two of us. As a woman, it still hurts me that I was not able to bring a child into the world. Because we did not speak about it, to this day I do not know who had the difficulty between the two of us or both of us. This is another challenge which I feel also hurts me and now it will never be.

> I don't want to blame men for dying early, but the truth is there are very many widows left living for a long time and remarriage is not easy for women. Therefore, I recommend men take care

116

of their health, keep up with their medical appointments and also not overstress themselves with financial concerns, which seem to contribute to their anxieties, stress, heart attacks and premature death. Finally, based on my faith in the Resurrection I hope and pray that one day I will be together with my husband again in heaven.

Part 3

Influencing factors of stability and satisfaction in marriage

This chapter is a reflection of the responses which the participants shared with the author of this book. The author has made a few modifications to some of the responses, but most of the information is presented here using the direct words of each participant. The goal is to maintain the integrity of the participants' feedback based on their life experiences so that the readers get access to the participants' original narratives and suggestions for establishing and maintaining stability and satisfaction in marriage.

Additionally, it is important to point out that all the participants described in Chapter 1 were in their first marriages. In the following chapters, the author has integrated some of the observations that were mentioned by remarried participants, who contributed to his book *"Stability and Satisfaction in Remarriage"* (2023). Based on their firsthand experiences and words of wisdom, the goal is to learn how to make marriage as stable and satisfactory as possible.

Although the identified factors for stability and satisfaction in marriage are individually described in the following pages, it is important to clarify that they are all interconnected and interrelated. The author developed the following 35 factors from the feedback he received from the participants. Even if these factors could be further analyzed and reduced to a lower number, the author decided to maintain them as 35 to reduce the risk of compromising the meaning and significance of each factor.

Based on the feedback from the participants, some factors were identified by all the participants and others by a varying number of participants. In this book, instead of presenting these factors by focusing on how many participants identified any given factor, the author decided to present the factors by establishing a kind of step-by-step progression of some of the different milestones or phases in marriage "from between discerning the vocation to marriage to being together in heaven." Whenever necessary, specific numbers of participants' and/or their respective genders will be mentioned in the book. However, even if an insight or experience was mentioned by only one participant or fewer, it is included in this book because of its significance and possible contribution to lives of other people, who may be inspired or benefit from it.

Based on above-mentioned observations, the author has integrated some of the findings of his doctoral research on marriage, as written in his book on stability and satisfaction in remarriage, into this book in order to help the reader become more knowledgeable about marriage and remarriage. The following tables (Tables 3 and 4) illustrate some of the data about the study participants, who contributed on the author's book: "Embracing Stability and Satisfaction in Remarriage". The fictitious names of the participants are maintained in this book whenever referenced.

Code	0001M	0002M	0003M	0004M	0005M	0006M	0007M	0008M	Saturation
Alphabetical pseudonyms in order of conducted interviews to saturation point	Abraham	Bernanrdo	Charles	Daniel	Elias	Fred	Godfrey	Henry	xxxx
Age	70	62	70	47	50	54	51	53	
Cultural-ethnic background	Jewish American	Italian American	German American	Puerto Rican (Hispanic) raised in U.S.	Denied any: "Neither" (German & Swiss Parents)	African American	Scottish English	Irish American	
Highest level of formal education	Ph. D in Psycho-logy	One year of college	Grade 12, 7 years navy training	College Graduate	Some college	Ph. D. student (clinical psychology)	Two years in college	Law school (Ph. D.)	
Religion	None	Roman Catholic	Roman Catholic	Roman Catholic	No religious affiliate	Roman Catholic	Episcopalian	Roman Catholic	
Age at firts marriage; and duration of first marriage	20,40	20,20	22,25	21,15	23,7	24,15	21,7	32,11	
Children from firts marriage and from second marriage	1,0	2,0	4,0	3,0	3,2	1,1	1,2	2,1	
Time in years between 1st. and 2nd. marriages; and time in remarriage to present	28	2,19	2.5,21	2,8	3.5,16	2,10	4,21	11,8	
Number of step-children	1	1	0	2	0	1	0	0	
Current residential neighborhood	Suburban	Suburban	Suburban	Urban	Suburban	Inner city	Urban	Suburban	
Annual family income in remarriage (U.S. dollars in thousands)	Over 130	90-130	75-90	45-55	55-65	75-90	75-90	Over 130	

Table 3. Demographic summary for the remarried male participants.

Code	0001F	0002F	0003F	0004F	0005F	0006F	0007F	0008F	Saturation
Alphabetical pseudonyms in order of conducted interviews to saturation point	Alicia	Beatrice	Catherine	Dora	Elizabeth	Felicia	Grace	Hilda	xxxx
Age	58	64	53	52	60	53	65	58	
Cultural-ethnic background	Italian	Puerto Rican (Hispanic)	Italian & Polish	Peruvian (Hispanic)	English, German & Italian American	Puerto Rican (Hispanic) raised in U.S.	African American	German & Welsh	
Highest level of formal education	Some college classes	Third year of college	College Graduate	Complete college to be a nurse	One year and 6 months of college	Second year of college	Half (1/2) year of college	Post-masters (licensed terapist)	
Religion	Pentecostal	Roman Catholic	Roman Catholic	Roman Catholic	Roman Catholic	Roman Catholic	Baptist convert to Roman Catholic	Quaker	
Age at firts marriage; and duration of first marriage	21,17	20,10	22,8	20,5	18,5	18, less than 1 year	20,25	19,12	
Children from firts marriage and from second marriage	1,0	5,0	2,0	2,0	1,1	1,1	5,0	1,2	
Time in years between 1st. and 2nd. marriages; and time in remarriage to present	1,8	8,27	4,20	9,18	2,31	1,33	2,16	3,25	
Number of step-children	1	0	0	0	0	0	0	0	
Current residential neighborhood	Suburban	Urban	Urban	Urban	Urban	Inner city	Inner city	Suburban	
Annual family income in remarriage (U.S. dollars in thousands)	Over 130	45-55	75-90	75-90	35-45	90-130	75-90	45-55	

Table 4. Demographic summary of the remarried female participants.

121

Part 4

Influencing factors of stability and satisfaction in marriage

In 1999, I went with two friends to a Chinese buffet. Just before finishing the meal, each one of us randomly picked up a fortune cookie out of the three that had been provided to us. After opening mine, I read the phrase written on a small paper inside the cookie. I am so glad that I picked that particular cookie because the phrase made a lasting impression and a transformation in my life. The phrase was: *"If you think education is expensive, try ignorance."* This phrase was a great source of encouragement while struggling to study and pay for my graduate studies in marriage and family therapy, doctoral program in family psychology. Based on some of the acquired knowledge from those studies, lessons about my family of origin and various cases in my pastoral and clinical work, I have been able to confront and reduce my ignorance about marriage and family life.

Study Session 1

Education about the beauty, current realities and
complexities of marriage

All the participants mentioned that anyone interested in marriage needs to learn about the realities and the complexities of marriage and family life. Rushing into marriage without any knowledge of what you are getting into, as well as holding on to misconceptions about marriage and/or embracing unrealistic expectations, were considered grave dangers to the success in marriage. Lee elaborated:

> People interested in marriage should learn about marriage in the context of its historical, social, cultural, economic, spiritual, and religious perspectives as well as the current political influences on such a beautiful institution. However, some of those influences are more destructive than constructive. Throughout the centuries, marriage has brought families together and blood relationships are formed through marriage. As any institution, the foundational, conceptual framework and the practice of the Institution of marriage must remain the same. Otherwise, it is no longer an Institution it was designed by God to be. Some of the family roles may be shared and negotiated but we have to admit and collaborate with God who created us as men and women. We as humans need to admit that we cannot fool Mother Nature. Our efforts to change men into women or women into men are going to be very dangerous in the long run. A lot of precious resources and time will be wasted and lost. The more we try to change what is already within our biological setup, the more frustrated and confused we will become.

It is important to discern whether one has a vocation and lifetime commitment to heterosexual married life or not. Married life, as described by the all participants in the research, is a "vocation" or "calling from within oneself," between a man and woman, by entering into a covenant of love and mutual self-giving. All the participants mentioned that marriage is not a profession or a career. Marie elaborated:

> My vocation to marriage may have started from a mere attraction to my high school sweetheart but as time went by, I realized that the attraction I was having for him was different from my desire to become a laboratory technician. I was raised Catholic and I had learned from my parents that marriage is for life. Consequently, I started questioning my motivations for getting married to John when we reunited after completing our college degrees.

Elaborating on the past and current contexts of marriage, Miguel mentioned:

> In the past, when divorce and having children outside of marriage were almost taboos, both many men and women entered into marriage together for the first time. People in the past used to grow up and marry and live in the same neighborhood. Compared to the past centuries, our contemporary society is experiencing a very high level of cohabitating partners, incidences of divorce, single parents, long-distance lovers, technological advancement, and many women in professional paid jobs, many remarriages, changing household roles, dual-career couples, and a lot of mobility within States, outside of States and internationally.

> Consequently, anyone preparing for marriage or whoever is involved in preparing couples for marriage needs to know about the influences of each one of the variables and others in regard to stability and satisfaction in marriage. Additionally, in our contemporary societies and religions, it is most likely that a person interested in entering marriage for the first time may end up getting married with another person who has had one or more romantic relationships and in some cases with a person who has young or adult children from previous relationship(s).

124

Therefore, each person entering marriage needs to become knowledgeable about what makes marriage successful for first time couples as well as in remarriage. Knowledge is power.

George emphasized:

> Marriage is beautiful. I would say that some responsibilities in marriage actually give life, rather than take it away. Caring for another faithfully steadfastly is one of those. Additionally, there are peaks and valleys in every relationship. Going through them together reveals depths that aren't possible to plumb when one leaves to find someone else every time there's a valley.
>
> Living for another is thrust upon you. It's like a graduate school in maturity. There's also a new purpose to your marriage in caring for children, as well as the joy they bring. Living for another in thrust upon you, and sometimes you don't feel like obliging so much, constantly. Fatigue makes cowards of us all.

Independence and Interdependence

Doris:
> Over our 46 years, the partnership has become stronger and tighter. We work to be on the same page with respect to major family decisions and interactions – child-rearing, jobs, home bases/communities, churches, extended family, friendships, and politics.

Marie:
> We lived apart for a long time so whenever we got together, we did as much as we could to make up for lost time. There's always intellectual discourse because of our different professions and interests. We have individual and joint goals we are working toward (further education, investments, vacations. etc.) so we plan together,

encourage each other and keep each other informed. Our daughter and matters concerning her keep us entertained.

Jean identified some of the following difficulties she had at the beginning of her marriage and how they have helped her to cope with them by learning to be independent and interdependent:

> One year after our marriage, my husband went for further studies out of town for two years. He returned on school breaks (three times a year). The 5th year of our marriage my husband left the country for further studies (it was hard). One year after he was gone, he had an accident that left him paralyzed (that was hard). I did my best to survive, support myself, be there for my husband and I also appreciate my family members and friends for visiting me frequently, as well as his family members and friends for checking on me.

Ivan mentioned:

> Marriage is between two people who are first of all independent, each with a sense of self-identity, knowing what he or she wants and does not want. Some people do not know what they actually want in life and in a marriage. Once one attains a sense of independence, knows what he or she wants or does not want, as were as what can be negotiated or not, then, that person can wholeheartedly enter into a relationship of interdependence without losing his or her identity and yet open to share life with another person in a lasting and mutually satisfying commitment of love.

Andy's criteria of whom to marry:

> Analysis of our similar backgrounds at that time, I felt we came from very simple backgrounds; and physically she was who I wanted.

When asked, what helps you to avoid the risk of your marriage relationship become a boring routine, Andy responded: "It will get boring when what bonds you together changes "and when the spouses are "people-dependent" instead of interdependent.

According to Lea, in marriage, there is a need for:

> Independence apart from each other. Having your own friends and your own interests apart makes for healthy separation. Then you have more to discuss with each other and you can pull the other person into that section of your life during times.
> Sometimes we go out with our friends separately and sometimes together.

Lea added the need to clarify:

- Who will stay home once we have children? If we go from 2 incomes to 1 that can be stressful.
- At which point do we stop splitting family houses for holidays and do it all together.

- Communication is important in marriage. My spouse and I have mastered the art to be able to effectively communicate and make sure we are on the same page about what we want and need in life.

- Steady income is also necessary to provide for the needs we have and the bills we accumulate.

Differences between the wedding and marriage and their interconnectedness

All the participants, including those who cohabited before marriage, mentioned that the day of their wedding was so significant in their lives. The wedding day is one day and marriage is meant to be until death, yet that one day continues to stand out in the memories of all of the participants.

Matthew made the following observations about his wedding day:

> Once Rosa and I decided to get married, we agreed that we were to get married in the Church. We did not have a lot of money to spend on the wedding, yet we prepared it within our means and it was so special. It turned out to be one of the most important days of my life and it is constant point of reference for me and my wife. Some of our preferred rituals of celebrating every wedding anniversary include making every effort possible to attend Holy Mass together and having a date night.

Cynthia elaborated on the importance of her wedding day as follows:

> I have sweet memories of my wedding day, some of which are difficult to put in words. I will not forget that day as long as my memory serves me. That day marked a significant milestone in my life. As applies to many married couples, my husband and I count the number of years we have been married from the day of our wedding. On our wedding day, I experienced an internal transformation within me and hopefully my loved ones were also touched in one way or another. I became a "wife" on that day and it is a dream I have held in my heart since I was fifteen. Alex became a "husband" – a state of being which he informed later that he also longed for since he was seventeen.
>
> My close relatives as well became another big family of relatives primarily because of my exchanging wedding vows with Alex. For instance, his mother and mine became mothers-in-law, our fathers became fathers-in-law, Alex also became not only a son but a son-in-law as well and I also became a daughter-in-law to his parents and a sister-in-law to his siblings. What a day that transformed our lives! No wonder Alex and I have decided to celebrate every wedding anniversary, not only the silver jubilee and the golden jubilee.

128

Keys to the knowledge of the complexity of marriage

As keys are important to open doors, consider the following keys regarding the knowledge of the complexity of marriage.

- Handling the complexity of marriage

- Awareness and acceptance of one's contribution to marriage

- In-depth communication that is reinforced by trust

- Taking courage to trust again

- Caring for mentally and emotionally challenged children

- Friendly relationship with children (and stepchildren)

- Ability to ask for help from trusted loved ones and/or professionals

- Accepting support from trusted relative and friends

- Humor and optimism, especially in hard times

- Doing things together with spouse

- Complementarity, equality and equity in marriage

- Acknowledging whatever each partner brings and takes from the relationship

- Consistent and mutual respect

- Kindness, generosity, shared view that the relationship is built on mutual collaboration and effort

- Ability to share with others and overcoming a deeply rooted selfish attitude that makes constant focus on: "Me," "My," and "I"

- Better spending habits by both spouses

- Integral maturity that encompasses the whole life of the individuals

- Ability to forgive as a manifestation of maturity and personal growth

- Overcoming transference issues in marriage based on unresolved issues from one's family of origin experiences and/or past romantic experiences (e.g., infidelity)

- Making use of accumulated knowledge through experience

- Appropriate response to the unkind and continuous aggressive behaviors of the ex-spouse

- Maturity based on ability to slow down to think things through, accept one's personal limitations, seek professional help, and if necessary to resolve them, and start to implement prevention strategies

- Overcoming frustration, anger, and/or guilt from past relationships

- Kindness to self and consideration for others

- Knowledge of what you are getting into

Study Session 2

Motivations for Marriage

The participants mentioned various reasons for entering into marriage. Some of those reasons were right and were risky. Therefore, it is important to do a self-evaluation to assess the appropriateness of one's reasons for marrying and also to listen to other people's approvals, concerns, constructive criticisms and/or disagreements regarding the upcoming marriage. More often than not, people who marry for the wrong reasons then end up disappointed, frustrated, hurting themselves and/or their partner, or ultimately experiencing divorce. Some feel they have "fallen in love" even before they heal from the wounds and baggage from their family of origin and/or prior romantic relationship(s). Others are not sure of what they really want, whereas others have hidden agendas and/or unrealistic expectations about the partner and marriage. Those who marry for financial support from the partner but without committed love may experience financial security, but sooner or later may realize they are lonely and miserable.

On the other hand, even though Maggie's motives for marriage were not based on love, she mentioned that it is important to explore one's motives before marriage. Maggie clarified that one of the motivations for marriage was that entered marriage to escape from home and a dangerous neighborhood. She elaborated:

> I feel envious of my friends who marry because of love. My case was different. I had a painful and prolonged difficult experience during my adolescence. My parents were constantly fighting, separated and then got together a number of times until they finally divorced when I was fifteen. My dad was an alcoholic and my mother had to work long hours while I took care of my

younger siblings. We spent some nights without food. We were very, very poor and lived in crime-ridden neighborhood. There were also drugs users and dealers in the neighborhood. After some classes of college, I decided to move and get married to a man who was older than me because he lived in a safer neighborhood and he seemed financially stable. Honestly, I am the one who asked him to marry in order to escape the poverty at home and the environment with a lot crime. I am glad he turned out to be a very good man and we are happily married.

My experience

Based on what you have read in this session, reflect on your own personal experience. Answer as honestly as possible the following questions regarding marriage.

1. What is motivating me to marry?

   _____

2. What motivated me to get married the first time?

   _____

3. How am I planning for marriage?

   _____

4. What do I have to do to avoid my past mistakes?

   _____

5. What areas of my life do I have to improve in order to succeed in my marriage?

   _____

6. How am I preparing the other significant people in my life in regard to my plans for marriage?

_____

7. What are my expectations in marriage? Which ones are realistic and which are not?

_____

8. What factors do I think influence stability and satisfaction in marriage?

_____

9. What kind of a spouse do I need, in order to establish a stable and satisfactory marriage?

───

────────◆◆◆◆◆◆◆────────

Keys to exploring the motivations for marriage

As keys are important to open doors, consider the following keys to exploring the motivations for marriage.

–   Explore and identify your needs in specific and concrete words

–   More often than not, human behavior is needs driven

–   Be interested in marriage without being desperate and impatient to marry. Desperate people tend to make desperate decisions and take desperate actions

Study Session 3

Awareness of one's genesis of marriage journey and
significance of courtship

Many people today struggle to find a spouse, and some are desperately searching without a lot of success. The following examples are some of the ways the participants found their respective spouses:

Lea when asked to describe briefly how she came to meet and know her current spouse, she said:

> We met in preschool. We went to high school together, dated and broke up, then came back together in college and have been together since.

Additionally, when Lea was asked to describe briefly the factors which helped her to become convinced that this is the person she should marry to, she emphatically responded: "When you know you know."

Miguel mentioned that he met his wife at church "through worship ministry." In regard to the factors which helped him to become convinced that this the person he should marry, he mentioned: "Same vision regarding faith, life, family, and career."

Ted:

> I met my wife when she was 13 years old and I was 18. My best friend (who was dating her) introduced us because he wanted my opinion. I thought she was the most beautiful thing imaginable. He stayed with her until she was seventeen. He joined the Air-Force. They broke up and I wanted to approach her but I was torn because of my friendship with her ex. When

he broke up with her, he told her to invite him to the wedding. He knew we wanted each other. She eventually chased me; I didn't run too fast.

Joyce mentioned:

The time for courtship (dating) is a precious time that should be well invested. During courtship, the partners should clarify their motives for marriage and honestly communicate them with each other to make sure that they are on the same page. Otherwise, better to stop the marriage plans before it is too late.

The courtship stories shared by the participants indicated that some courtships were short in duration and others longer. There was also an arranged marriage which the participant described with a positive evaluation, yet cautioned that it may not be the best choice for everybody. That participant's moral and cultural backgrounds influenced her to find pertinent reasons of appreciation of an arranged marriage and its limitations.

Additionally, regarding the best use of the duration of courtship, Rowland emphasized:

Don't remove a fence before you know why it was put there. Our ancestors had a lot of wisdom in establishing that time not only for the partners, but also their family members, to learn more about one another and make many decisions which are pertinent in establishing a foundation for a stable and successful marriage.

Olivia, based on her professional experience of working with individuals, couples and families as a psychologist, clarified that some partners need to seeking professional help if needed before marriage.

Accordingly, Carter and McGoldrick (1998) noted: "Courtship is probably the least likely time of all phases of the lifecycle to seek therapy. This is not because coupling is easy, but because of the tendency to idealize each other and avoid looking at the enormous long-range difficulties of establishing an intimate relationship. While the first years of marriage are the time of the greatest overall marital satisfaction for many, they are also a time of likely divorce. The degree of mutual disappointment will usually match the degree of idealization of the relationship during courtship…" (p. 238).

Therefore, partners contemplating marriage are encouraged to seek professional help before and during courtship. Kelley and Burg (2000, p. 139) recommended, "Settle as many issues as you can before you get married. It is easier to separate an egg before you scramble it."

Olivia also observed:

> I have come across many individuals who take a lot of time looking for 'Mr. Right' or 'Ms. Right.' Some seem to move aimless and/or endlessly move from one relationship to another looking for the 'Right One.' Others become stuck and never take any step for fear of not getting the 'Right One', waiting for the 'Right One' to appear. Some also seem like they do not know what they really want, yet determined to keep searching for what they do not know. I think there is no Mr. Right or Ms. Perfect. Every person has character flaws and areas of improvement to work on, and others are difficult to changes, even with professional intervention. Therefore, it is important to identify some of the key areas to look into within oneself, the other and in the relationship in order to identify what can be negotiated and the un-negotiable.

Ted, who eventually knew what he wanted, stated:

> I am convinced that you can look deeply into someone's eyes and look right into their soul. Her soul was as beautiful and pure as anyone's could possibly be. I had dated a lot of girls in my youth. Each one, at the start, looked like the perfect person. Eventually, after we had gotten to know each other, I would find little flaws. I would break up with them because they weren't perfect. My wife was different. I found the same small flaws, but I would tell myself, "I could live with that." After a while, I realized that it wasn't the flaws that were most important. It was her soul that I wanted or needed.

Ellen:

> We first met when I was 13 years old and he was 18. I was dating another boy so we were just friends. I broke up from the other boy and I was then single and so was my husband. We still were very close friends. We would go to church every Sunday with each other. He helped me with my English class in college which made us be together more. Our first date was wonderful. After two years, we got married and we have been together ever since for 46 years.

When Ellen was asked to identify the factors to become convinced that this is the person she should get married to, she responded:

> My feelings were different from other boyfriends. The chemistry between us was very special and we could feel it. I hated being away from him. He always treated me with respect and love. We both had strong faith in God.

Albert:

> Learn who the person is that you might be marrying show them your true self if you know what that is. If they accept you then you have a good base.

Rowland:

> Friendship – we knew each other for years and had many shared positive experiences, including two years where we could only write to each other. We knew each other well when we finally lived in the same area and became more romantically committed.

> We were both in our respective college choruses for a joint concert and met at the social afterwards. We were 19 and 17 in 1966. We exchanged addresses and occasionally wrote letters since there were several more concerts planned over the next two years. There were a few casual visits to show off Boston and Philadelphia, and a group trip to Mardi Gras in 1969. Then I went to Africa in Peace Corps for two years, returning to

Boston for grad school in 1971. Finally, we were in the same place, in our own apartments. A year later we got married. It was a lengthy process that allowed us to know each other well, but not completely.

When asked to describe briefly the factors which helped him to become convinced that this the person he should get married to, Rowland replied:

> She was smart. She liked children. She worked hard. She had a sense of joy about life. She sang. She was up for adventure. She was OK with uncertainty. She shared the same faith. We laughed together. She was willing to get married.

Doris:

> My husband and I, we dated 5 years before our engagement which led to learning more about each other: our likes, dislikes, moods, meeting family, enjoying holidays, traditions. However, I feel that each of us had parents who had long marriages, until the spouse's death. My parents were married 30 years, but only because of my father's untimely death at 56 years old. My husband's parents were married almost 60 years. I saw the example through them, what a true marriage should be.
>
> We used the 5 years of dating to grow in knowing each other in good times and in bad times. Our parents' long marriages exemplified what the unity of love, and it is what defines marriage. Till death do us part.

Olivia mentioned that people also need to overcome the fear of embracing marriage for life. It is important to be cautious but also too much fear can be dangerous.

Additionally, Doris, when asked about personal experience and her advice to people interested in marriage who are still fearful of the long-lasting commitment, she wrote elaboratively as follows:

In 1964, when I was a child of about 15, I told my Catholic parents that I thought marriage was problematic, because it gave people license to get careless with each other. I proposed a system of 5-year contracts as the alternative, so people would be motivated to be more careful and caring toward their partner, such that they would want to renew the contract when the time came. My parents were horrified, and my mother offered all kinds of societal arguments about why this was wrong-headed thinking. I was unconvinced. Finally, she said: "Well, if you want to have children, it's a lot easier on the children." I thought this was a good reason for marriage.

Having chosen marriage, and experienced a very fine marriage for 46+ years, I think my mother's final argument falls short. Having children is NOT enough reason, because the marriage lasts a lot longer than the parents' care of children. So, here's what I would say to an interested but fearful couple:

If your like, respect, and attraction and admiration for your partner are mutual, and you believe you can help each other continue to grow and develop to be your best self, consider these questions:

Doris continued with her advice to contemplating marriage as follows:

These relational qualities are non-negotiable. If you strike out with this opening statement, don't go further, and do NOT get married!

- ***Are we friends who can share honest feedback?*** *[emphasis in bold made by Doris]*

- *Do we share the same values? Religious/spiritual beliefs?*

- *Can we count on each other to be trustworthy?*

- *Do we have the same work ethic?*

- *When we work together on something, do we complement each other in a way that is satisfactory and productive?*

- *Can we solve problems and resolve differences together?*

- *Do we have compatible views about money – spending and saving?*

- *Do we laugh at the same jokes?*

- *Do we have similar expectations about having and raising children?*

- *What will that look like?*

- *Do we have the capacity to respect and support each other's professional pursuits?*

- *What will that look like?*

- *Can we see us with each other's extended families over time?*

Doris continued:

> If your responses to the above are mainly 'Yes,' then you are looking at a relationship that is moving forward with a lot of strength and momentum. Marriage is right for such a relationship. It gives you a special ticket to plan an exciting, long-term future, to dream together with a lifetime friend and companion, and together, work on making that dream a reality.

> Years ago, when I was still a teenager, there was a coffee table-type book called *The Family of Man*. It was a photo essay of people around the world. My favorite section showed couples. The caption read: 'We two are a multitude.' This is the image I want to suggest as some of the potential that a great marriage represents. Through marriage, you touch and shape the future, and continue to move the "Family of Man" forward. Even without children, a married couple in great friendship and partnership can be a force for good in a community. Being married demonstrates your ability to make and keep a commitment.

Marie:

> I met my husband through mutual friends when we were in high school. We spoke on the telephone for a while (no mobile phones at that time). I fell in love with him the first time I saw him. At that time, I was just looking for someone who had nice, clean and 'manly-looking' shoes.

Marie elaborated about how she became convinced that this the person she should marry:

> At the time, my husband was more convinced that I was the one for him and his enthusiasm carried me along. We courted for a long time and were compatible with each other. He was easy to be with, easy to be in love with. He always behaved better around me. (I've always known my husband to be a hot-headed young man growing up. Even to date, hearing about some of his past exploits surprise me!) He saw me differently and always treated me special. He protected me. On my part, no one else could be him and that feeling is still there. He became my standard for everything in a man and he still is.

Marie emphasized the importance of communication as follows:

> Communication and teamwork are soft skills that are essential to any successfully run organization. Poor communication or lack of communication can create barriers in a relationship that make it difficult to rationalize what you are (still) doing together. Neither my husband or I are mind readers; therefore, we choose to communicate as per previous responses. Bottled up feelings can fester, making mountains out of a molehill. Awareness of a partner's communication style is important – for instance, there are individuals who would rather not talk in the heat of the moment and would rather sleep on the problem first to avoid saying something they may later regret. Making your partner aware of this up front will make them understand that you are upset but your style is to sleep on it – which also helps one calm down enough to address the issue more rationally/logically.

Jean mentioned that she met the man who later became her husband at work. "We were working together." Elaborating on the factors which helped her to become convinced that this was the person she should get married to, she said:

> We were working at a boarding school that required some teachers to supervise student night studies. He was one of the teachers to do rounds from 7:00pm to 9:00pm and he always did his turns. Every morning the school had student and teacher assembly that he always attended. School had staff meeting twice in a term that he attended. During staff meeting discussions, he had good ideas that the school adopted. He got along with staff members. Had a sense of budgeting. He was clean.

Additionally, Jean identified the following factors which have contributed to her marriage stability and satisfaction:

> I knew my spouse's family and the discipline the father had on the children.
>
> We dated according to our faith – No actions before marriage.
>
> I loved him and trusted him.
> He was employed and well-liked by co-
> workers.
> He was willing to let me have my little sister live with us.
> He could control socializing with friends.
> He would trust me enjoying my friends' company.

Doris described how she came to meet and know her spouse as follows:

> We met at our Catholic colleges (me in Boston, him outside Philadelphia) when our choral groups got together for a concert. He was a sophomore, and I was a freshman. We corresponded by letters (back in the day) for more than a year and began a friendship that grew when I spent the summer after my sophomore year waitressing in Atlantic City (his family lived on the mainland, and I got together with him, and all the children

142

in my beach "Family" on weekends). We continued to correspond, and he invited me to a chorus weekend in Philadelphia in the fall of his senior year.

Still becoming friends, I called him during the winter to see if he was around on a weekend I was going to be in Philadelphia, and he told me he and two buddies were driving to New Orleans for Mardi Gras (and would I like to come along)? I said okay and found two friends. We drove down and experienced the city and the festival, and at the end of the week I decided I should seriously consider marrying this man, after watching how he dealt with logistics and intense people issues during this trip. The sands shifted for both of us at that point, but he left for Sierra Leone and Peace Corps immediately after graduation, so we now corresponded via aerogramme as I finished my final year of college and got my master's degree. Finally, he came to Boston for grad school and I began to teach. We spent a year seeing each other regularly (in the same city at last), going to Mass together, and getting to know each other up close before agreeing to get married. Actually, I had to make the case for marriage. He had to agree, or take a hike.

Teresa emphasized that it is important for partners to learn about anger management and self-conflict. As much as partners may love one another, some people have a quick temper, say things which they later regret and/or keep intra- and interpersonal hurts to themselves, and it reaches a point when they explode with anger, and end up doing a lot of harm. Domestic violence tends to spread from anger.

Some of the participants mentioned that they had difficulties with controlling their anger in general and in a special way toward their spouses. Some clarified that they did not have difficulties with anger as such, but had observed its negative consequences in the marriages and families of their relatives and friends in work environments and more so expressed during road-rage incidents. Consequently, based on some of the participants' input, other resources and author's experience, the following strategies are included here in this book as a resource for whoever may be interested.

Study Session 4

Understanding the implications of deciding to
marry or to cohabitate first

All the participants mentioned that making the decision to marry is one of the most important decisions they have ever made in their lives. The word "become" married is used here instead of "get" married to highlight the change which takes place within oneself and between the two partners, as well as the couple's relatives and other significant loved ones. What you "get," you can lose or give away. Becoming a husband or a wife transforms each of the individuals at almost all levels of the human experience (for instance: marital status, moral, ethical, social, cultural, spiritual, religious, economical and professional). The relatives' statuses also change due to the marriage relationship which has been established by the two partners. A mother remains a mother and yet also becomes a mother-in-law; the same for the father, who at the marriage of his daughter or son also becomes a father-in-law. A brother or sister also becomes a brother-in-law or sister-in-law as a result of the exchange of the nuptial vows between the spouses. Consequently, individuals should be prepared to assume this significant change.

Based on personal experience, participants were asked: "'" What advice do you give to people interested in marriage but who are still fearful of the long-lasting commitment?"

Mateo responded:

> If you love the person, go for him/her (get married). Cohabitation is another name for insecurity and lack of committed love. Love is the key to marriage life. Period. If the other person does not love you in return, end the relationship. Marriage is built on the foundation of committed mutual love.

144

Committed love does not need experimenting with one another. You either love the other person as he/she is or not. If you are still comparing one to another, make up your mind about whom to get married to, with the awareness that each person has virtues and limitations, including those whom seemingly influence you to feel so excited whenever you meet them. Once you start living with them, you come to know them in their true colors and without making the decision to love each person as he/she is, you may spend your entire life without getting married.

Andy responded:

They should know themselves first; then they should realize it's a journey. There will be many turns, but it is not to be feared. It is one day at a time. No guarantees, but they can enjoy good times.

According to Ted:

Yes, you have plenty to fear…but… the rewards of a life together with the one you love cannot keep you from becoming the person God had in mind for you. Remember your early years. You feared 'first day of school,' 'taking your driver's road test,' 'first job interview' I can go on and on. Get over it…Fear never goes away; you just fear different things.

Doris gave the following advice for people interested in marriage, but who are still fearful of the long-lasting commitment:

Avoid marriage until they overcome this fear. Marriage is a lifetime commitment. Loving one another is just a part of marriage. It comes with ups and downs and they have to be mindful of that.

———————◆•◆•◆•◆———————

Description of cohabitation

Some of the participants had cohabited before they got married and they shared some of the advantages and risks of cohabitation based on their lived experiences. Additionally, some of those who got married without cohabiting also shared some insights about cohabitation by focusing on the observations they had made from the lived experiences of their cohabitating loved ones.

Joana mentioned:

> Like many people today who cohabit before marriage, I decided to live with my boyfriend primarily for financial reasons. My parents were so concerned that my boyfriend and I decided to rent an apartment together, but I still had a lot of student loans and living alone is too expensive. We chose to rent a new apartment together instead of moving into his own rented apartment to set a tone that both of us were starting afresh and on equal footing. Moving into his apartment, even if it is rental, had a negative connotation for me. He used to constantly refer to the apartment as 'my apartment' and I did not feel comfortable moving into his apartment, so we could start talking of 'our apartment.' I had to remind him to speak of our apartment, as both of us were paying rent from our individual salaries.
>
> Living together before marriage also helped us to test our compatibility before saying 'I do' (pronouncing our marriage vows to one another). We also looked for an apartment near our places of work and that helped us to overcome our long-distance relationship. Living together therefore benefited us by saving money (due to split rent, utilities, food, etc.) We spent more time together, revealing and knowing our true colors and learning to be together.
>
> It may sound contradictory but it is the truth, looking back, I am glad that we had some heated arguments and conflicts over some of the daily chores and the challenges of living with another person. We avoided wishful thinking that those

problems will just disappear by themselves. Instead, we decided to sit down and focus on resolving the problems without attacking one another, neither projecting blame, humiliating the other nor quitting. My mother had inculcated (drilled into me) the wisdom of addressing the problems to find solutions without attacking one another.

Consequently, when my boyfriend and I experienced some disagreements during our cohabitation, he started the blaming game and wanted to quit. I told him what my mother had taught me, he listened and we started to search for solutions to our problems. Progressively, we grew closer together, learned to listen to one another, mutually respected each other as persons and we became more equipped in discerning the wise words to use in moments of heightened emotions and when to let go.

After such trials and advancing together in conflict resolution skills, we decided to move to the next level. Most of my student loans had been paid off and I had learned the lesson of not letting any minor incident be exaggerated nor misinterpreted beyond its boundaries.

On the other hand, Doris cautioned:

Cohabiting has its risks. Not getting married ... can put you in a state of ambivalence or drift, where you can't move forward with confidence on important life decisions – like having a child, going after a particular job, relocating to a different place, buying a home. Okay, you can buy a pet, but that's about it. My experience is that relationships either move forward or stagnate. If the partner you are with does not give you forward momentum, find a new partner – fast. Don't waste time on a relationship that is stuck.

Nelson mentioned:

I understand that every couple is unique and I respect that. However, I am old-schooled and a great believer in using courtship as opportunity for learning about one another as much

147

as possible. My grandmother used to caution me of the risks of cohabitation or in her own words: 'Be careful of the dangers of practicing on the stage.' She groomed me to become a respectable man to women and the need of identifying at least three non-negotiables about a woman I was going to marry. She advised me as follows: "Although the opposite poles of a magnet attract each other, marriage is not for complete opposites when it comes to age, beliefs, values, culture, religion, education, work ethic and geographical locations."

He continued

> Before I completed college, whenever I went with my sister (in her twenties) to visit Grandma, whenever we were bidding her farewell, she would tell me: 'Look for a woman with whom you want to be committed to, not a booty-call (that is, a meeting for casual sex).'

> My first girlfriend was so caught up in her head into the romantic story and whenever I brought some important things to talk about during our courtship, she could not listen. She wanted to move in with me and with the cited words of my grandma ringing in my ears, I told her 'No. I do not condone hook-up culture which approves having casual sexual encounters with no relationship.' 'We are not going to practice on the stage.' I later realized that she was using me as an escape from the home of her abusive and alcoholic father. We broke up and I was relieved. Faithful to my grandmother's words of wisdom, I found the love of my life, and we have been married for seventeen years.

This is the "One" I am going to marry

Eric was one of the participants who mentioned that as soon as he saw Maggie in a supermarket, he instantaneously said to himself: "This is the woman I'm going to marry." Janet, likewise felt the same conviction as soon as she met William at the university. She elaborated: "Beyond

148

reasonable doubt, as soon as I saw, Willy (William), I knew in my own heart that he was the 'One' for me." Both Eric and Janet expressed and informed the author that their love at first sight was accompanied by experiences of inner peace, trust, conviction and hope for the best. Each immediately did his /her best to get the telephone number of the person who had attracted his/her attention. By the time the author asked Eric and Janet to participate in responding to his questionnaire for this book, Eric and Maggie were in their forty-fifth year of marriage while Janet and Willy had just celebrated their thirty-fourth wedding anniversary.

 On the other hand, participants like Doris, took a lot of time to discern the qualities of their respective future spouses. For example, when asked to describe the factors which helped Doris to become convinced that "Jack" was the person with whom she should get married to, she gave a detailed list of what contributed to her final conviction and resultant decision to get married with Jack. Doris mentioned:

> From my observations, and our many discussions, I knew, he (Jack):
>
> - Respected women. He was always very polite and a gentleman. I remember thinking that I would like his mother when we first met. She had taught him well
>
> - Expected me to have and pursue my own work
>
> - Was smart, curious, fun to be with, interesting, and able to make me laugh in unexpected ways
>
> - Was not afraid to work hard and expected to succeed
>
> - Was calm, balanced, fair, and a good problem-solver in a difficult situation
>
> - Spent his money carefully, and took care of his things
>
> - Liked children (lots of beach time with my little neighborhood friends in Atlantic City) and could talk and play creatively with them. They liked him too

- Wanted a family

- Was able to call me out (nicely) on silly comments or behaviors – when he did this the first time, I decided this was almost enough reason to marry the man. It really impressed me that he cared enough to tell me I could do better, and that he did it in such a kind way

- Was largely uncomplicated. He said what he meant, and kept his word and commitments.

- Could hold his own in any intellectual conversation without being offensive

- Liked to sing, go camping, and spend time outdoors

- Had good friends whom I also liked

- Could fix things that were broken, and build things

- Was relaxed with my parents, siblings, and extended family. He was easy socially, and liked people

- Came from a nice family and extended family that welcomed me immediately and graciously, as soon as they saw we were getting serious

- Was interested in growing as a Catholic in a post Vatican 2 world

- Liked Boston culture, music, museums, sports teams, and would be happy to stay there.

- Liked travel. Peace Corps exposed him to the world, and all kinds of food. He was respectful and appreciative of people from different races and cultures. He was a humble, rather than ugly American

- Was a considerate lover who had not had multiple partners (back to respecting women)

- Would never make me worry about how he presented himself, what he said or did, such that I would always be able to be proud of him. When I articulated this to myself, and recognized its importance.

The author asked Mike to describe what helped him to become convinced that the woman he was dating was the woman he should get married to, Mike mentioned:

She was smart. She liked children. She worked hard. She had a sense of joy about life. She sang. She was up for adventure. She was OK with uncertainty. She shared the same faith and religion with me. We laughed together. She was willing to get married.

On the other hand, when Lea was asked about how she knew who to marry, she briefly responded: "When you know you know."

Advantages of Participating in Marriage Preparation Programs (e.g., pre-Cana or engaged encounter)

Ivan mentioned:

The pre-marriage helped me to put things into perceptive. I knew in my heart that I was ready to marry my sweetheart but I was still self-centered. I recall during our pre-Cana program two couples left the program. I knew both of them and I contacted them afterwards. Each of them admitted that the program helped them to realize that they were going to get married for the wrong reasons. Each realized that he/she was not ready for the responsibilities within marriage.

Anna added:

Pre-Cana helped me to integrate God and to develop a deeper marital spirituality before marriage. After our engagement, we met with the pastor in our parish and we had very informative meetings together. He explained many things to us about our faith, the preparation of the wedding ceremony, we chose the readings for our wedding and we experienced a deep connection with the priest who accompanied us in our understanding and living the Sacrament of Matrimony.

Study Session 5

Considerations for marriage to someone formerly married/separated

Description of dating and marriage preparation

Traditionally, courtship or dating refers to the time partners spend getting to know one another and discussing a number of topics that are geared at helping each of the partners make up his/her mind whether to proceed with the relationship or to part in peace before they become engaged. The duration of courtship varies from couple to couple. Some people just spend weeks or months dating another, while others spend years.

In regard to dating after divorce, custodial parents have a number of considerations to take into account in comparison to those dating without children from a prior marriage/relationship. Once a person becomes a parent, the children become a top priority. Consequently, custodial parents ought to date with extra caution in order to reduce the risk of exposing children to one's dating partner. Because dating partners have the potential for separating, this not only hurts the partners but also the children if the children have formed a relationship with the partner. Therefore, time for dating or courtship has its values and limitations. Getting to know one another is important, but some people do not express their real motives for marriage, whereas others have a significant set of unrealistic expectations.

Marital history refers to the experiences I have from my previous marriage. It involves the "who," the "how," the "where," the "why," the "how long" I was with him/her, as well as a multiplicity of feelings, thoughts, actions, and behaviors I experienced during my former marriage. It also includes the experiences I had as I observed the marriage of my parents and how I was influenced by the marriages of other significant people in my life. It is a history that I cannot change but one I can learn from by exploring the impact it has on me right now and as I move toward the future

Experience of others

Many participants mentioned that they strongly attributed their remarriage stability and satisfaction to the lessons they had learned from their families of origin and their past experiences of marriage. At the time of the interview, those seven participants reported that their parents were divorced at least once. However, for the sake of illustrating the impact of marital history on remarriage, two detailed stories have been selected: one of a male participant, Bernardo, and another of a female participant, Elizabeth.

Bernardo stated:

> I do not blame my parents for having divorced when I was nine years old. They had their reasons for doing so. However, since I grew up without seeing my father and mother living together, expressing love for one another and love for us [their children, my sister and I], all that had a negative impact on my life. Even when they got married with other people, their remarriages also ended in divorce. As a result, when my first marriage ended in divorce, I felt guilty because I saw myself repeating what my parents had done. Surprisingly, my daughter also had children in her first marriage, then divorced, and is now remarried. Therefore, for the success of my second marriage, I am putting into practice what I have learned from my past mistakes and those of my parents and my daughter. Now I believe that history tends to repeat itself unless lessons are learned from it and put into practice.

Elizabeth mentioned that her remarriage stability and satisfaction were in one way or another influenced by the experiences she had gone through while growing up. While elaborating on her family of origin, Elizabeth stated that the divorce of her parents, when she was four years old, affected her very much because she ended up living with her mother, a woman whom she resented for many reasons. Some of these reasons included the way Elizabeth emphatically described her mother as an alcoholic, who spent most of the time away from home dating other men. Elizabeth stated:

My mother was never satisfied with one person. My mother needed recognition from a lot of people. I think that was her sickness. I didn't recognize that, of course, until I was older. But she did have a sickness. She drank a lot. She wasn't a fall-down drunk but her first priority was herself, not her children…I resented my mother very much; I resented her lifestyle. I resented the way she lived. We had nothing; I resented that and took my anger out on her because we had nothing.

[Elizabeth added:] We had no family life; she didn't keep in touch with her family. We didn't have cousins. We didn't have uncles; we didn't have aunts, so to speak. Once in a great while we would have family. You see other people, you go to school with bad clothes, people make fun of you, and you have no real friends, because nobody wants to be bothered with you because you are trash! That is what we were. We were trash. I mean, I look back now and say my mother tried. She was single, she went to work every day but my mother thought about herself. I needed a pair of shoes. I can remember this. I needed a pair of shoes really bad. I had holes in my shoes, and she wouldn't buy them because she had to go out to the bar that night. She had to have money for that bar, and that was more important to her. I did resent that.

Based on this resentment, when her mother remarried Jim, Elizabeth felt a strong attachment to Jim because she found in him a lot of compassion and understanding. Elizabeth elaborated on her relationship with her stepfather as follows:

> Very good from what I remember. I remember specifically one time he [Jim, my stepfather] came home for lunch. He had a cake in his lunch box or something and my mother gave all the cake to my younger half- brother [Jose]. Then my stepfather took the cake and cut it in half and we got half and half. That I remember. I remember good things with him. He was a good man. Unfortunately, he passed away just after four years of living together.

Many participants reported that the lessons they had learned from their first marriages and/or from the experiences of their second spouses helped them to avoid many mistakes in their second marriages. A typical example was one that Daniel narrated in detail, illustrating the precautions he was taking to reduce the risk of transference issues that had started to affect his second marriage.

Among all the participants, Daniel provided a detailed description of marital history which is worthy citing because of his profound insights. It is important to note that Daniel used the colloquial phrase, "you know," several times simply as a connective between his ideas. When queried about his marital history, Daniel responded:

> We [my second wife and I] have spoken about our past marital experiences. Actually, she has spoken a lot more than I have about my divorce because I have always spoken about things that happened in my [first] marriage to her and she has told me everything basically that has happened to her in her [first] marriage. This helps us to understand what each one of us expects, OK. ... Her situation was a lot different because her ex-spouse traveled a lot, and ... he was with other women. She found out that, afterward, he had children, you know, while they were still married, so that was a different situation than mine. I

156

didn't have that problem … but it did affect me somewhat because she went through so much with that situation. And her divorce, I think that, it kind of like it carried over to me because she was very, um, not pressure, she was very, not jealous either but she was very watchful of different things I did. You know, she was being careful that I wasn't doing anything. You know, because she already was so hurt so much before that, and she didn't want the same thing to happen to her. And I knew that; I know that.

Daniel added:

Sometimes we had situations where I would turn to her and say, you know what, you have been really hurt too bad with him that you are really starting to take it out on me. I told her a couple of times. Maybe I shouldn't have, but I wanted to tell her that, because I realized she was bringing up her past and bringing it on to me when really, she shouldn't have. But that's part of learning, you know, that's part of the learning. If you don't say something to her, then how is she going to know? So, I think one of the things to help us bond is to let each other know what we didn't like about the previous marriage. So, you know, and, by me telling her what I went through with my wife, with my first wife, she will be careful not to do those things. And the same thing for her, you know, I'm careful. You know, I don't try to, you know, give her any idea that something is going on.

Given such experiences of marital history, when Daniel was asked about what was contributing to his remarriage stability and satisfaction, he replied:

Yes, yes, because [now] I know what hurts her. I know what doesn't hurt her. … and I try to keep it there. I keep it in that frame of mind, you know. I think that is important; you know you might make the same mistake.

Hilda shared a narrative of how she overcame her transference issues with her second husband, a situation that almost contributed to the ruining of her second marriage. The following dialogue gives a clear sense of how previous marital experiences can negatively reinforce transference in a remarriage. Hilda emphasized:

My first husband was physically and verbally abusive to me. I developed a lot of fear toward him. It even reached a point where the mere sight of him made me to become very anxious and lose track of whatever I was doing.

Unfortunately, when my second husband and I got married, whenever he made a comment about something that I had done wrong or had forgotten to do, then I would withdraw from him, be silent for a day or two. This was because I imagined that, if I would respond to him, he would become more verbally and physically abusive to me and shout at my son as my first husband used to do.

I recall a particular instance when I kept silence for almost three days without saying a word to him. That happened after he told me about his discomfort on the pretext that I had consulted my son, instead of him, about which restaurant we would go to for dinner. I was so terrified that was going to become a big issue and probably lead us to separation.

When asked how have the two of them resolved that, Hilda replied:

On that same day, I decided to ask pardon from my husband and explained to him how my ex-husband used to beat me and shout at my son whenever we had an argument. So, my second husband, with a smile on his face, and with a great sense of humor said "I am not your ex. He then gave me a big kiss, and we started talking again.

When asked whether she had other arguments after that and how she reacted to him afterward, Hilda responded:

> Of course, yes. I am sure it is not uncommon to disagree once in a while for people who love and care about one another. Ever since, whenever my husband sees me withdrawing from him, he says "I am not going to do you harm. I am not ____ [mentioned her ex-spouses' name]. Then, the two of us start laughing and hug one another.

In addition to overcoming the risks of transference in remarriage, by the time of the interviews, all the participants had learned significant lessons from their past marital mistakes in both the first and second marriages. For instance, the participants who entered their first marriages thinking that they were in love acknowledged during the interviews that they were not motivated by love per se when they entered their first marriages. They had motives other than the love that bonds the spouses together. Catherine said that she no longer believed in the adage that "love is blind" because marrying for the wrong reasons is what makes people perceive love as blind.

Based on the lessons learned from past marital mistakes, Catherine and several other participants suggested that divorced parents should avoid the risk of marrying for the wrong reasons. Some examples included: sole interest of sexual expressiveness, begetting children and/or alimony, pregnancy of the female partner, impatience, that is, claiming that it is too long a time to wait or it is too late to get married, extreme dependence on others, feeling uncomfortable living alone, wanting to get out of one's parent's house or escape a bad marriage, or as Fred (an African American participant) said: "I married a Caucasian woman because I wanted to experiment with a person of another race."

Some participants suggested that divorced parents contemplating remarriage make the best use of the time between the end of the first marriage and the beginning of the second marriage. Based on their retrospective experiences, those participants said that although they had not adequately utilized that duration constructively before they remarried, they considered it a golden opportunity for healing from the wounds of divorce, further education, introspection, spiritual growth, purifying one's motivations for remarriage, dating with a lot of prudence, and comprehensive preparation for remarriage with the help of competent professionals in providing remarriage services.

My experience

Based on what you have read in this session, reflect on your own personal experience.

1. What motivated me and/or contributed to my getting married to my former spouse?

   _____

2. What did I learn about myself based on my first marriage?

   _____

3. What did I learn about my former spouse during my marriage and/or after divorce?

   _____

4. What do I still miss from my first marriage?

   _____

5. What factors contributed to my first divorce and what must I work through before entering a second marriage?

   _____

6. What are the resources I already have (e.g., relatives, friends, spiritual and material) that I can rely on as I enter (re)marriage with all its benefits and challenges?

_____

_____

_____

_____

_____

Keys to dating and (re)marriage preparation

As keys are important to open doors, consider the following keys to dating and marriage preparation.

- Slow down before you start seriously dating and behaving romantically with a new partner

- Date appropriately and make a profound preparation for marriage with your partner

- Inform the children involved when the right time comes

- Give yourself time to heal from your emotional, spiritual and/or wounds

- Dating ought to start by developing friendship first, mutual respect between companions

- Hold in-depth talks about children, expectations, money, sex, personal history, family of origin, parenting skills and disciplining of children

161

- Anticipate that your teenage child might react with a negative attitude toward your prospective spouse, especially if the teenager still has hopes that you and his or her other biological parent will reconcile and remarry

- Be aware of your marital history, interpersonal dynamics in your family of origin, in your first marriage

- Be clear about your motivations for (re)marriage, develop right and realistic expectations, know the consequences of your actions and be flexible in order to adjust well to changes in marriage

- Prenuptial agreements are extremely necessary especially between very rich partners

- Let each partner sell his or her residential house or apartment so that the two partners (and custodial children) can move into a new house. If one of the two partners has to move into the other's house or apartment, that move must be on a temporary basis

- Focus on exploring and addressing the likely problems in marriage rather than paying more attention to the color of the wedding gown and/or where to spend the honeymoon

- Acknowledge that marriage is hard, complex, especially if it involves children from the previous marriage. Marriage involves a lot of work because you marry a family, not just a person, and that is outside of your control. Therefore, include the in-laws in the remarriage arrangements because they are constantly present in your marriage

- Take advanced studies because that might also help you to get a better paying job

- Be extra prudent in regard to dating, know the challenges involved, and keep up with your parenting roles while dating

- Establish and maintain consistent house rules and roles

- Know that conflict is inevitable in all human relationships

- Be aware of the potential areas of conflict in marriage

- Learn the skills of conflict resolution and practice them

- Understand that cohabitation has its advantages and disadvantages, and it is still not encouraged in all religions, societies, and/or individuals close to you may not approve of it

- Look primarily at what your part will be in the marriage, what you might not be doing now, and how your faults might affect the marriage

- Maintain chastity during courtship and be careful with other people's money

Let me explain this key with the words of my Grandmother. She was a great teacher. I recall the way she coached one of my sisters to be very careful while dating and to watch the dating habits of other people. Above all, I remember almost every word I overheard while Grandmother as follows while cautioning my sister who had started dating a rich man:

> Be careful with him. Know what you need out of the new relationship. Don't rush into marriage. It is true he has a lot of money but you should marry the person not his money. I understand money is very important in marriage but he may or may not give you the money. Secondly, maintain your chastity throughout the courtship. Don't fall into the trap of thinking that you need to sleep with him before marriage in order to assure him that you love him. If he threatens to leave you because you are not generous with him in that sense, let him go. That is a clear sign that he cares less about you than that he wants to instantly gratify himself. Care about him too.
>
> Training yourself to wait from being intimate with him. You will bring mutual benefits and you will maintain your dignify if

things don't work out with him. Don't change the rules of the game [Grandma added with a raised voice]. Remember: all behavior is needs driven. You may call me old-fashioned and now that I am over 80 years old, I care less about what people think of me. I am saying this to help you and your partner to spend the quality time you have to talk through the important details regarding remarriage. Instead of day dreaming that premarital sex will automatically make him love you,stick to the rules of the old lady. I see further while I am sitting down than you while you are standing up. I say this because I care and love you. Teach him to respect you and respect him too. Finally, both of you should do an AIDS blood test before being intimate. I repeat: do not change the rules of the game. Good luck!

Reinforce marital stability and prevent divorce

In an effort to help couples attain and maintain the marital stability and satisfaction that prevent divorce, contemporary couple therapists encourage couples to invest themselves together in the foundation of their marriage, assess whether or not their expectations are realistic, develop emotional intelligence, learn to express emotions appropriately, prevent distress (especially because it affects communication motivation and sexual intimacy), promote marital adjustment, reinforce couple strengths, and validate interactive process in contrast to avoidant and volatile communication (Burleson & Denton, 1997; Gottman, 1994b; Johnson & Greenberg, 1994).

Professional therapists have suggested that marital partners should learn and practice problem-solving or conflict resolution skills, have open and mutual negotiation dialogues about finances, sexuality, parenting skills, setting clear boundaries with in-laws, attain a level of acceptance that some aspects cannot be changed, stop attempting to change one another, maintain a significant level of shared spirituality and prayer time, learn to forgive oneself and the other, constantly maintain the purpose(s) of their marriage, learn to negotiate differences of opinion, and whenever necessary join a support group and seek professional help before the problems escalate (Ahrons, 2004; Ganong & Coleman, 1989; Kerr & Bowen, 1988; O'Leary, Heyman & Jongsman, 1998).

Study Session 6

Description of clear boundaries in remarriage

Clear boundaries are described here as the invisible barriers or limits that are designed within a given society, culture, family or system. These boundaries regulate the level of communication and the acceptable type of contact or separation between individuals involved within a given subsystem (e.g., stepfamily) so that they can interact with each other in healthy ways, respecting each other's space, time and rights. This allows the individual to become independent, to be dependent on others, as well as interdependent with them without becoming fused or caught up in rigid interactions with others.

Experience of others

Six participants mentioned that it was difficult for them to separate themselves completely from their former spouses, especially because four participants had joint custody of their biological children. Alicia said:

> Immediately after my divorce, I did not want to have any contact with my ex-spouse. I was so angry, frustrated, and fed up with him. Unfortunately, I had to live with the bitter truth that, because of the child we had together, I had to maintain constant contact. I realized that as I kept being angry and distanced from him, the more I suffered because I could not sit down with him to plan what would be in the best interest of our child.

Alicia added:

I changed my attitude toward him, and my understanding of how his mother had badly treated him while growing up helped me to forgive him. So, when I changed the perspective and way of relating to him, he also changed. Then we started to communicate well. Ever since, we both respect each other, and planned together the wedding of our son, together with the help of my second husband and his second wife. Therefore, I have learned that, though divorce ends a marriage, it does not end the family. My ex-spouse and I are now close, and we can relate as friends.

On the other hand, Geoffrey mentioned:

My divorce with my ex-spouse was generally amicable. I have never had any fight or major argument since I married my first wife and even after our divorce. Even now that makes me understand better why many relatives were shocked by our divorce. On the other hand, I have to clarify that, ever since I remarried, I have taken serious measures to make sure that my on-going amicable relationship with my ex-spouse does not become too intimate, and hence put my second marriage in jeopardy. We are very close as parents and friends, but distant enough to avoid the risk of falling back into romance. My second wife is also very respectful of my on-going friendship with my ex-spouse, and the two do some shop- ping together once in a while. All these healthy interpersonal relation- ships have also contributed to my remarriage stability and happiness.

My experience

Based on what you have read in this session, reflect on your own personal experience.

1. What are the benefits I have received by establishing and maintaining clear boundaries with my ex-spouse?

   _____

2. What is hindering me from establishing and maintaining clear boundaries with my children?

   _____

3. What are the dangers of involving my custodial child(ren) in all aspects of my personal life to the point that I tell the child(ren) everything about my life?

   _____

4. What have I learned from the participants' experiences that I would like to integrate into my life in regard to clear boundaries?

   _____

———————◆•◆•◆•◆———————

Keys to establishing and maintaining clear boundaries in remarriage

As keys are important to open doors, consider the following keys to clear boundaries.

- Know your own and others' boundaries and respect them

- Do not get romantically involved with any adult child or relative of your spouse. [This is focused only on adults because sex with a minor is a crime and never to be tolerated!]

- Respect and treat your stepchildren well

Study Session 7

Interracial marriage experiences and recommendations

————————◆◆◆◆◆◆◆————————

Miguel:

>Initially as interracial couple, our cultural traditions and habits contributed to misunderstandings. AS we improved our communication, we were able to identify elements of our diverse cultures.

Marie

>Although initially challenging because my husband and I were not co-located, being a dual career couple in somewhat related operations, gives us insights into the different operational aspects of our respective fields, which provides a good consultative forum/soundboard.

————————◆◆◆◆◆◆◆————————

Study Session 8

Committed to Love

————————◆◆◆◆◆————————

> 11 Now may God himself, our Father, and our Lord Jesus direct our way to you, 12 and may the Lord make you increase and abound in love for one another and for all, just as we have for you, 13 so as to strengthen your hearts, to be blameless in holiness before our God and Father at the coming of our Lord Jesus with all his holy ones. [Amen.] (1 Thessalonians 3: 11 – 13)

The word "love" has become one of the most frequently used and misused words and we attach many different meanings to it. I hear people say phrases like: I love my car, I love my job, I love my swimming, I love my dog, I love my football, I love my boss, I love my church, I love gardening, and so many other statements.

In this book as well as my book on remarriage, the focus is on committed love and it is described as a permanent decision each partner makes to offer one's self to the other and to accept the other partner unconditionally. This type of love is an act of the will, a choice not an obligation, mutually given and received. It reflects God's unconditional love for human beings beyond our imperfections. It involves self-sacrifice, sharing ordinary life together, as well as loving the partner beyond his or her physical appearance. Committed love is grounded in kindness, loyalty, fidelity, sacred trust, forgiveness and reconciliation, and caring for the partner's loved ones (e.g., children, elderly parents and others in need). Committed love is manifested in specific actions, including nonromantic ones (e.g., putting out the garbage and doing chores). It involves seeking mutual satisfaction and growing in holiness.

It is also important to clarify what committed love is not. It is not a mere feeling. It is not selfish, temporary, stagnant, exclusively romantic, boring, nor rooted in lust, jealousy, unrealistic expectations, possessiveness, fantasies, wishes, and lack of knowledge about self and/or the partner. It is not a love one falls in or out of, but a love which each partner breathes in and out till death do they part.

Contributions of the participants

The participants expressed their convictions in similar words and related phrases: that committed love is the most important influencing factor of stability and satisfaction in marriage. Even if the participants described love in many different ways, all of their descriptions fell within the following categories: love of self, love of the partner, mutual love between the partners, love of children and attentiveness to their needs and love toward the multiple extended family members. For the purposes of facilitating the conceptualization of these multiple categories of committed love, each category will be described separately.

Love of self

All the participants mentioned that they had come to the realization that committed love starts with love of self. For instance, Grace expressed:

> I have realized that the more I love myself, the more love I am able to give and share with others. Otherwise, without loving myself, I feel like my love for others is insincere. I am pretending to give to others what I do not have. Whenever I do not love myself, I start to desperately demand my husband for

attention and if he ignores me, I feel angry at him because [I start to think that] he is mean.

According to Elías:

> I learned to love myself by paying attention to my own wounds and brokenness as a result of my divorce. It was hard for me to confront myself, and to admit that I was in pain. I knew that I needed healing before I could proceed with my plans for the next marriage. However, I told myself that "I had to learn to love myself by focusing on how to address and resolve my painful past."

Based on a biblical passage, Fred stated that it is not bad to love oneself. Otherwise, why would Jesus have commanded his followers to love God and others as they love themselves! Fred emphasized:

> Jesus said: 'Love others as you love yourself.' Therefore, I have also learned to love myself. Love of self after divorce and before remarriage does not mean becoming narcissistic. It is about establishing a good foundation for feeling good about who you are as a person, developing your personal identity, exploring the unique person you are, your talents, limitations, dreams, needs, likes, dislikes, priorities, fears, and accepting your uniqueness.

Henry emphasized:

> Love of self goes hand in hand with the knowledge of self because the more you know about yourself and love yourself, the more you are able to learn to love and know about other

people. This makes it possible to establish harmonious relationships with others without dominating them. Likewise, you don't allow yourself to be dominated by others. It is a win-win situation for people who individually have a conscious, mature, honest, positive, realistic and unconditional love of themselves.

Elaborating on love of self, Alicia stated:

> I felt a real need for a man in my life. I could not imagine myself remaining unmarried for the rest of my entire life. I remained a single mother until the age of thirty-eight years. However, I was convinced that I would not get married with any man from the street. So, I started setting some of the things I would look for in a man before getting married with him. I had a chance this time to choose a man and I used it.

> After my first divorce, I realized that there is no perfect man and no perfect woman in the world. So, I started to look for a man whom I would at least tell myself that his personality was matching the basics of what I wanted in a man to get remarried with. Fortunately, I got him and he is the one with whom I currently share a very happy marriage. I give myself credit for doing whatever it took me to love myself. I set up the qualities I wanted to look for in a man and I abided with them until I got the right one for me.

Love for the partner

Most participants highlighted that it is important to develop a love for the person you want to marry. Dora stated:

> After two months of dating my current husband, I realized that he had some of the qualities that I wanted in my spouse-to-be. However, I also realized that he was not a perfect man. He was a good man but I could not stand his smell of cigarettes. It was not easy for me to accommodate all his limitations. I realized that I was not perfect either. In the final analysis, after some negotiations about our differences of opinion and dislikes, I made a decision to love him and we have been married for 18 years.

Some participants also mentioned that love for the other involves, among other things, knowing the other's cultural background, religious affiliation, likes and dislikes, hobbies, favorite food, and fears.

In regard to the other's religious affiliation and likes, Geoffrey stated:

> Even if my second wife agreed to have our marriage celebrated in my Episcopalian Church, I have realized that she is still attached to the Catholic Church, and I encourage her to continue praying at home the Catholic prayers she likes a lot, especially the Rosary. I love her and respect the teachings of her religion even if I do not agree with all of them. Because of the love I have toward her, I let her go to socialize with her friends. Sometimes I accompany her to visit her friends just to make her feel supported because she likes to socialize and network with other people to help the people in need. She also likes to go shopping with her friends and my daughter from the previous marriage. They love one another and that makes me have a greater love for her. My second wife also likes to cook and invite her friends at home. I entertain her friends and help her with the

washing of the dishes. I do all this because of the love I have for her.

Mutual love

Based on the descriptions of mutual love by all the participants, it can be deduced that mutual love is a complex concept with different connotations. However, all of them agreed on describing it as a bond of trust and caring for one another. Abraham clarified:

> Immediately after my first divorce, but before I married my second wife, I dated a number of women. The lesson I learned during those series of dates was that marital love is a two-way street. Later on, I realized that some of those women I had sex with did not actually love me. They were only interested in having a nice time, yet I had felt that I had fallen in love with them.
>
> Well, after some time, I started to realize that some of them seemed to have fallen in love with me, but I cannot certainly say that I really loved any of them. I was primarily seeking them out for sex and to hide away for some time from my loneliness.

Most participants considered mutual love not to be an overnight product. It is a process that involves a journey of growth, self-giving to the other and a give-and-take experience. It involves mutual fidelity, loyalty, unconditional commitment to one another and the ability to be there for one another in joyful and painful moments of life.

In a special way, when asked to describe how mutual love between partners in second marriages differs from that of the partners in first marriages, all the participants pointed out that the uniqueness is based on each partner's conscious decision not only to love his or her spouse, but also the partner's children from the previous marriage. Many

176

participants mentioned that love involves the ability to grow together beyond conflict, the ability to love the person, without focusing too much on the person's possessions, but who he or she is as a person.

Many participants stated that mutual love involves peace, companionship, feeling secure, trust, tranquility, and above all the ability to enter into a nonjudgmental and constructive dialogue with one's spouse. They also agreed that the ability to laugh and to eat together are also very important in reinforcing mutual love. Likewise, many participants expressed that mutual love is based on mutual respect for one another, honesty, and transparent communication.

Most participants considered sexual intimacy to be their greatest expression of mutual love. Grace expressed:

> Sex is wonderful, the best thing in the world, but with the right person, and only the right person, it can be the most out-of-this-world experience.

Elaborating on the notion of mutual love, Beatrice emphasized that men and women lack the knowledge and practice of how to treat one another. No wonder then, Beatrice stated:

> Every woman should learn about how to treat a man and vice versa. This requires preparation and self-challenge because people always run the risk of getting remarried primarily by instinct and/or physical needs.

Mutual love was described by all participants as a decision, based on commitment, to be there for the person "no matter what" [added Catherine], and the ability to enter marriage by prioritizing love before anything else.

Love of children and attentiveness to their needs

All the participants highlighted that whatever happens to the children affects the parents. Grace emphasized: "Once a parent, you remain a parent for life; even grown-up children turn to their parents for advice and support." These participants, by virtue of being parents when entering remarriage as custodial parents, expressed that the love for their children and their attentiveness to the needs of the children have highly contributed to the couple's remarriage stability and satisfaction.

All participants stated that, for at least the first three years of remarriage, none of them paid sufficient attention to the needs of his or her child(ren) for two main reasons: (1) the remarried parent's lack of knowledge regarding the unique needs and challenges faced by children of remarried parents and (2) the remarried parent's emotional investment in pleasing the partner. Such pleasing was prioritized because the custodial parents were struggling to make the second marriage work in order to reduce the risk of another divorce.

As all the participants later realized, the parents' lack of identifying and paying attention to their children needs not only affected the children but also affected the stability and satisfaction of their marriages in a negative way. This was particularly applicable to remarried parents with adolescent children from a first marriage. The following paragraphs highlight some of the children's needs and challenges which the participants identified. They suggested that remarrying and remarried parents should pay a lot of attention to them.

For instance, Fred suggested that parents should be attentive to children who blame themselves for their parents' divorce. Fred made this suggestion after realizing that his first son from the previous marriage had taken onto himself the responsibility of having failed to save the marriage of his parents.

Several other participants also mentioned a similar story about their children. However, they acknowledged that the failure of the first marriage was not their children's fault. Additionally, female and male participants reported that, after remarriage, their children struggled for more than a year while grieving over the lost fantasy that their biological parents would remarry. These participants also reported that their adolescent children rejected disciplinary rules from their respective stepparents.

Remarriage ceremonies also have an impact on the significant others of custodial parents. For instance, twelve participants reported that it took them more than a year to realize how their adolescent children experienced conflict of loyalties and guilty feelings for having attended the wedding ceremony of a biological parent with a non-biological parent. Some children, as reported by nine participants, struggled with feelings of resentment and anger with themselves for having failed to forgive the biological parent for remarrying.

Several participants mentioned that their children had difficulty in handling feelings due to the loss of privilege and of being the center of attention as a result of passing from being the only child to living with other stepsiblings and/or half-siblings. These feelings were also reported by two male participants as still a problem for their adult children, already in their thirties, because it involves sharing the inheritance from their parents with their stepsiblings.

Without referring to their children, some participants mentioned that they have witnessed the children of their friends in second marriages having profound concerns and fears that their parent's new marriage might also end in another divorce. Unfortunately, the participants reported that those concerns and fears have started to have negative effects on those children because some of them seemed very preoccupied about the risk of experiencing another divorce and another adaptation situation.

All the participants highlighted that parents contemplating remarriage should pay attention to the children's developmental needs and introduce their prospective spouses at the right time. This involves prudent dating, whereby the parent ought not to introduce his or her biological children to everybody he or she starts to date before making a commitment to live together. Otherwise, breaking up with a particular person might also affect one's children.

After acknowledging that it might not be easy to date a compatible partner the first time after divorce, most participants cautioned that parents contemplating remarriage should avoid the risk of playing out their romantic experiments with different partners in front of their children. According to Henry, "It is heartbreaking for the children to see their parents with a different stranger every now and then."

Loving attitude toward multiple extended-family members

Most participants mentioned that they had found it very helpful, within their remarriages, to extend their love to different members of their extended families. Catherine discussed this further in the following interchange:

> Ever since I knew that I could not change my fate, I resolved to change my attitude. I had to accept the bitter truth that, even if signing the divorce papers officially indicated the legal ending of my first marriage with my first spouse, those signatures did not terminate our family. My ex-spouse and I continued to be significant others to one another because we had children who needed to be in contact with both of us after the divorce. By the same token, for the sake of the children, I sought family therapy for myself and the children in order to learn how to handle the conflict of loyalties between me and their father. They needed him and they needed me and they still need both of us.

Daniel stated that he did whatever was possible to keep in contact with his former spouse for the sake of the children:

Every attempt was in vain. That woman has a lot of psychological issues and they are really affecting the children I had with her. Nevertheless, I managed to reconnect with my ex-in-laws and they are very understanding, friendly with me, have compassion for my children and me. This is because they know that my ex-spouse is a trouble-maker. Fortunately, keeping a healthy relationship with my ex-in-laws (especially my mother-in-law, father-in-law and brother-in-law) has relieved me of the stress and guilt I have been feeling for my children to grow up while disconnected from their maternal relatives. I have realized that, ever since I reconnected positively with my ex-in-laws, the relationship with my second wife has also improved. For instance, if I want to have a good time with my wife for a weekend or have another honeymoon experience, we can leave my children in the safe hands of their maternal grandparents.

Grace commented on her experiences as follows:

My love toward significant others included making a conscious decision to embrace a positive attitude of forgiving my ex-spouse. I did this after realizing that the more I held on to blaming my ex-spouse and keeping the grudges we had ten years ago, the more I suffered from the resultant anger of recalling the events that surrounded my divorce. I realized that my lack of forgiving him was negatively affecting my relationship with my current husband.

Given these observations, I felt challenged to decide between holding on to blaming him or forgiving him. Four years later after the divorce, with the help of a religious minister, I made the decision to forgive my ex-spouse for whatever he did to me. Ever since, I started to feel better. However, I admit that was difficult for me to let that anger go because I still think that I was faithful to him and he is the one to blame for cheating on me. Nevertheless, I had to let go of holding on to my sense of self-righteousness because the emotional price I was paying for it was draining all my emotional resources and integrity.

All in all, based on the results of this study and after a step-by-step and systematic analysis of the data (Strauss & Corbin, 1998), the selected central theme from this data is committed love. All the other selected themes seem to be coherently interrelated with this central theme. The criteria for choosing this theme to be the central theme is based on the unanimous consensus and experience of all the participants that love is the most influencing factor for both remarriage stability and satisfaction.

All the participants' contributions were a synthesis of their short-term and long-term experiences that go beyond what each knew, did not know, did and/or did not do at the time of entering their second marriages. Unless otherwise stated, whatever was reported in this study reflected the participants' views at the time the interviews were conducted and during follow-up sessions.

Appropriate Emotional Expression of love should be shown continuously

Jesus Christ is the model for love. Based on Sacred Scripture, Jesus loved by way of encountering the whole person (body and soul). Suggestions for men and women:

i. Read about Jesus's healing of the leper (Mk 1:40-45) and about Bartimaeus (10:46-52).

ii. Read about the woman at the well (Lk 4:4-30) and the woman with a hemorrhage (Mk 5:25-34).

Marie:

Self-love (NOT SELFISH LOVE) – The Bible (1 Corinthians 12:31 – 13: 8) refers to faith, hope and love; and stresses that the greatest of these is love. Love is complementary, and I believe that my self-love is a clear demonstration of my capacity to love another. Marriage merges two people to become one, and my love for that single unit reflects my self-love. We are both career-oriented, xx years into our marriage with one child. Navigating the delicate balance between our individual career progressions and family life has sometimes resulted in our being in different locations, particularly in my case. My husband has been really supportive and also does not hold me back from developing myself and my career interests, and we discuss the implications of any career moves on our lives and family before we make the final decision.

Agree to disagree – No-one is perfect, myself included, and everyone has something they would like to or wish they could change about themselves. This is an acknowledgment that we will sometimes disagree. We make every effort to solve our problems, big or small internally amongst ourselves. In this regard, we communicate freely and understand each other's point of view, bearing in mind that 6 looks like a 9 from the other side. We establish the causes of our disagreements to distinguish what is tolerable if it continues and what is not acceptable if it continues.

Love and desire – My husband may not be perfect, but I accepted his marriage proposal because I found him perfect for me, despite my own imperfections, and is the only man I want. My commitment is for life. Therefore, I cannot see myself setting up a home with another person. My advice will be to choose someone you can stand to be with for a long time, while fully acknowledging that he is imperfect. During courtship, it is common to note certain imperfections or displeasing habits, and many women are known to persevere while forward planning to change the man once they get married. It is best to determine whether you can accept the "full package" as-is before marriage.

Doris:

> Our marriage is grounded in a deep friendship and commitment to help the other become the best person he/she can be. We knew each other for six years before we married. In that time, we explored values, interests, work ethic, politics, religious beliefs, and good patterns of honest communication that we're able to celebrate and also to challenge the other person respectfully. We found a lot in common. Over time, we have become best friends.

Lea mentioned:

> Love is not something you fall in and out of. Love is a choice you make every single day. You choose to be with that person and to see them as essential to your life. So, make sure you always are finding the reason you are choosing to love.

Anne expressed:

> Marriage has its rewards, mostly it is great to be together, always have that one person to depend on and know they are always there for you, in good times and in bad. No one is perfect, we have to forgive one another and let some things go, but love remains. The little things don't matter. You don't have to worry they're going to walk out on you. A marriage commitment makes you work out your differences, you can't just walk away. You support one another. So much can go unsaid when you spend so much time together, growing and maturing together.

Ted:

Love, compromise, forgive, work hard to make your spouse have a motivation or reason to become happy. It's the little things sometimes. Just say thanks and I love you. It doesn't cost you anything.

Albert:

Trust in my spouse, the support of my spouse, equal responsibility and cooperation in decision making, family duties divided by ability and preference.

Ellen mentioned:

My husband and I have a true love in our hearts. We do everything in our day thinking about each other. We have full trust in each other, which allows freedom in our daily life. Respect is a very big problem if you don't have any in your marriage. If you don't respect each other when you have children, they won't respect you either. It is important to have compromise in your marriage. Decisions can't always be one-sided. This is why communication is so important. A couple should work together daily to make decisions that are needed.

Ellen added:

We truly love and respect each other. We communicate daily and enjoy each other's company. I live my life for him and he lives his life for me. We always think of each other.

Miguel:

To define commitment as a gain rather than a loss. With marriage, the individuals are not losing their "liberty" but they are gaining "companionship"

My experience

Based on what you have read in this session, reflect on your own personal experience.

1. What do I know about myself in terms of personality, talents, weaknesses, likes, dislikes, desires (interests) and goals that I want to achieve in my lifetime?

2. Which of the following were my primary motivations for the first marriage?

    O   I thought I was in love

    O   Companionship: needed somebody to be with

    O   Female spouse was pregnant

    O   Wanted to have children

    O   Wanted to get out of parent's house

    O   It was time to get married

    O   Wanted to have on-going sexual expressiveness with the same partner

    O   Curiosity and rebelliousness: wanted to experiment with a person of another race

    O   Other:

3. Which of the following summarizes the major attitude in my current marriage?

- ○ Love of self

- ○ Love for your partner

- ○ Mutual love

- ○ Love of children and attentiveness to their needs

- ○ Love toward multiple extended-family members

- ○ Other:

Keys to committed love

As keys are important to open doors, consider the following keys to committed love.

- Having the right motivations for marriage

- Focusing on realistic expectations about marriage and prospective spouse

- Compatibility, involving the picking of the right partner or "chemistry match"

- Love involves making a decision and a commitment to marriage

- Love of children and attentiveness to their needs

- Intelligent and emotional maturity

- Unconditional love

- Self-identity and personality qualities (e.g., reliable, responsible, sociable, easy going, kind, reasonable spending habits, perseverance, joyful, spiritual, independent and dependent)

- Mutual love between partners

- Love toward the multiple extended-family members

- Maturity based on one's experience

- Ability to handle and resolve conflicts to arrive at mutually acceptable decisions

- Children's mental status

- Wisdom that focuses on knowing your position and roles in the marriage

- Forgiveness is part and parcel of maturity

- Love of self and love of the partner

- Sense of order, structure, and flexibility with self and others

- Awareness that all marriages are difficult and the need to work hard for the relationship to succeed

- Perception of remarriage as an iceberg

- Compatibility: described as enjoying some of the same things and values

- Keeping up with the lessons learned by from one's past mistakes that contributed to the end of the first marriage (e.g., marital infidelity and overfocus on work at the expense of marriage and family life) in order to avoid the risk of making the same mistakes again

- Parent's realization of the pain and losses suffered by the children as a result of parental conflict and divorce and resolve to make the second marriage work so that the children do not face the same fate again

Study Session 9

Integrated maturity and personality compatibility

————————◆•◆•◆•◆————————

In an effort to establish a sense of priority among all the factors identified as influencing marriage stability and satisfaction, it was determined from the research results that all the participants described committed love as possible because of each partner's integral maturity. In metaphorical terms, as sunlight is important to chlorophyll during photosynthesis, so is integral maturity important to committed love for marriage stability and satisfaction.

It seems that the communication that reinforces marriage stability and satisfaction is not a matter of communicating or dialoguing about any topic, at any time, in any place, with any other person, but communication that is geared at building relationships, solving problems, and communicating maturely instead of a mere venting of one's emotions without due consideration for the recipient(s) of the communication.

The same rationale could be applied to the other primary and secondary factors that were identified. A typical example is in reference to maturity and finances in marriage. Based on the collected data, many participants stated that intelligent decisions have to be made before spending money, and other decisions that go along with money (e.g., deciding whether to have a joint account or separate accounts).

Whenever the participants applied maturity to marriage stability and satisfaction, most of them were describing it as a fruit of perseverance, earned through hard work and through overcoming hardships. Some participants spoke of maturity as the ability that had helped them to maintain self-control in emotionally charged moments in their marriages.

At the time of the interview, all the participants seemed to have what Kerr and Bowen (1988) referred to as a high "differentiation of self." They expressed themselves with clarity of feelings and thoughts, yet, while listening to their stories about their first marriages, they seemed to have been in these earlier marriages more driven by their emotions (e.g., love perceived as being "head over heels" or limited to romance) than a balance of thought and feelings. Based on what was learned from all the participants, remarriage stability and satisfaction appear to require individuals with an above-average level of differentiation of self.

In analyzing how the participants presented the details about their first marriages, most of them had a differentiation of self that was below average. It seems that each participant's acquired higher differentiation of self may have played a significant role in positively influencing his or her remarriage stability and satisfaction.

In elaborating on the importance of hardships and maturity, Fred highlighted: "Whatever does not kill you makes you to grow."

From the participants' descriptions that however tough their divorce process and its consequences were for most of them, all the participants reported having grown in one way or another through their divorces. Examples of related areas of growth included forgiveness, compassion, patience, and ability to take risks, as well as self-improvement through education, spiritual growth, and the courage to seek help. Maturity is a core domain in marriage stability and satisfaction because it helps the individual to be in control of his or her life, to make coherent decisions, and to assume responsibility for his or her actions.

Experience of others

Some of the participants highlighted that maturity is one of the most important influencing factors in marriage stability and satisfaction. However, based on how each participant described how he or she conceptualized maturity, it was not a mere notion of one's chronological age that determined his or her level of maturity. Accordingly, Catherine exclaimed: "My second husband is ten years younger than me, but mentally he is above me!"

Based on the participants' descriptions of maturity and how they applied it to marriage, maturity is a complex concept. For instance, several female and male participants described maturity as an individual's ability to independently make coherent decisions and that individual's ability to put into action the decisions made. On the other hand, Geoffrey mentioned:

> A mature divorced parent should be capable of assuming responsibility for his or her past, present, and future actions. One of the greatest lessons I learned, as I was struggling to come to terms with my divorce, was to stop blaming other people for all my actions and wrong choices in life. This included learning to confront myself by reflecting upon my personal contribution to the previous divorce.

Likewise, Bernardo stated:

> Now, when I look back at my divorce, however difficult it may be for me to admit, the truth is that I was responsible, in one way or another, for my previous divorce. It takes two to make the marriage work and it takes two to break it.

Elaborating on the importance of integral maturity and self-love, Hilda stated:

At the time of remarriage, I was more focused on finding a companion to overcome my loneliness. What I have learned along the way is that I lacked the appropriate degree of maturity to love myself better. Integral maturity is indispensable for every partner contemplating remarriage. This implies maturity at different levels (e.g., emotional, spiritual, moral, interpersonal, and ability to handle conflict with prudence). Maturity is also based on the ability to slow down, think things through, not rush into another marriage before resolving one's baggage.

Furthermore, many participants stated that seeking professional help after divorce is also an expression of maturity. This includes a willingness to make an effort to work through his or her frustration and guilt from the first marriage. This requires honesty and self-love. Charles said:

Maturity embraces the ability to hold on to realistic expectations in a second marriage. One should be able to decide when it is the right time for him or her to enter a second marriage.

Many participants mentioned that they felt seriously hurt by their former spouses because all the events that surrounded the divorce and ultimately the divorce itself marked an irreversible change in their lives. This was based on the intensity of the pain, suffering, humiliation, and shame related to their divorce experiences. Four participants mentioned that they experienced thoughts of retaliation toward their former spouses, but they did not carry out any imagined act of revenge. However, according to these participants, their pain and related losses from the divorce persisted until each discovered a real solution that they referred to as forgiveness based on maturity.

Grace clarified:

Real forgiveness is a manifestation of maturity, especially when people acknowledge their own contributions to actions that have brought pain, humiliation, or loss of any kind.

Bernardo stated:

> I did not experience comfort in my heart and the ability to move on with my life after divorce until I took a decision as a mature person to forgive my ex-spouse. I also had to make another tough decision of forgiving the family friend whom my ex-spouse went to bed with while we were still married. As I look back now, I guess becoming more mature and understanding my contribution to her marital infidelity helped me to forgive my ex-spouse and that family friend. I guess, if I had not forgiven them, I would still feel very hurt.

Some participants stated that recovering one's integral health is an act of maturity and it has a significant influence on remarriage stability and satisfaction. Henry remarked:

> Being healthy in terms of mind, body, spirit, and emotionally helped me to enter my second marriage with a sober mind and helped me to discuss tough issues with my current wife before remarriage. Good health also helps me to relate with my significant others without becoming extremely dependent on them, but rather relate with them maturely and interpersonally.

Along the same lines, Beatrice cautioned divorced parents who are still single:

> Do not stuff somebody into your life before feeling whole about yourself. You need to be independent in order to establish an intimate relationship, without feeling the exaggerated urge to have someone into your life or looking for others to fill into the hurt parts of yourself.

Additionally, Grace spoke of compassion and forgiveness as integral parts of maturity.

Even though my first husband had cheated on me, had a child with another woman while we were still married, and I was very angry with him when we divorced, I managed to forgive him before he died

After divorce, I converted to the Catholic Church, and during Lent, a priest at my new parish encouraged us during the homily to visit the sick, especially those who were lonely. Surprisingly, the priest gave us that homily during the very moment when my ex-husband was sick and lonely. I don't know how to say this. Anyway, I had vowed never to forgive my husband. However, that homily really turned my life upside down.

After Mass, I felt a strong urge to talk with my ex-husband but I did not know how my second husband would react about my going to care for my ex-husband. After some serious thought, I acted maturely by letting my husband know about my ex-husband's illness and I asked him to accompany me to go and visit him. He [second husband] welcomed the idea and … and was happy because I had included him in the visit. He even suggested that I could stay more days alone with my ex-husband in his final days. It was a very powerful experience. We talked a lot, he asked me for forgiveness, and I forgave him. After his death, I arranged for his funeral and I really feel happy that I had the opportunity of reconnecting with him before he died. I have realized that life is too short to go around not talking to your family and in-laws. I really believe in forgiveness with everybody, including the people who had seriously hurt me.

Elías also considered himself to have become more mature in his second marriage in comparison to his first marriage. When asked about what he thought had contributed to his great sense of maturity, Elías said:

> I perceive myself wiser in the second marriage because I no longer put all the blame for my divorce on my ex-spouse. I have learned to assume responsibility for my actions. I have learned to be realistic and not to expect everything to be wonderful in remarriage, because life is not that way and people are not that way either.

Elaborating on this acquired wisdom and maturity, Elías suggested that divorced male parents preparing for remarriage should primarily look at what is their part in the marriage, what they each might not be doing, how one's faults might have contributed to the first divorce.

Many participants mentioned that counseling and psychotherapy were part and parcel of maturity insofar as they contributed to those participants healing from the wounds of divorce. Those participants considered counseling and psychotherapy to be very helpful in setting the tone for establishing stability and satisfaction in second marriages.

Accordingly, in a post-interview note, Hilda wrote:

> I think the whole key to marriage and remarriage is counseling! I can't stress this enough. I think I should have gone through this process the first time I got married.

Several participants highlighted that maturity involves the way remarried people strategize working with their family members in order to avoid family tensions. In this regard, Elizabeth clarified how her second husband's business with his brothers has strained her marriage as follows:

> In the last few years, the relationships have strained a lot. I resent not having the closeness of family. Even though we are older, and thank God, my sons both grew up with their uncles and that was fine, but now everything is kind of strained. In the

business, the guys have different views. One has one view and another has another view. They clash.

Many participants mentioned that maturity included their ability to discern how to apply the knowledge gathered from daily life events or information to strengthen their second marriages. A typical example was that of Elizabeth, who prudently applied to her marriage a technique that she had overheard on a television channel. She overheard that technique at the moment when the stability and happiness in her marriage had started to be affected negatively by her husband's demanding and stressful work. The television message that Elizabeth recalled was: Giving a strong hug to a loved one reduces his or her stress. Consequently, Elizabeth started to give a strong hug to her husband as soon as he came home from work. Elaborating on the impact of that hug on her marriage Elizabeth said:

> Whenever my husband comes home from work, I give him a big greeting because that changes his mood. Always I have learned to stop whatever I'm doing, and come out and say: 'Hi, how are you? How was your day?' If I greet him like that, he becomes a better person. If I just say: 'Hi, how are you, hey, how you doing?' he comes in miserable. Now, I truly believe in that hug. I heard it on the TV one day, and I applied it to my husband, and it really works.

Emphasizing the notion of forgiving one's former spouse as an expression of love by the one who forgives, Alicia stated:

> Currently, I do not care whether my ex-spouse acknowledged his mistake or not. The most important thing for me is that forgiving him has made me feel better about myself and improved the love I have for my second spouse. This is because

I am no longer wasting my energy ruminating about the past abuses. Instead, I am more focused in the present and how to keep my second marriage successful. So, you see, forgiveness of the ex-spouse has had many benefits for me. Therefore, I recommend that those who find it harder to forgive should do it at least for personal reasons if they cannot for other motives. I have experienced that forgiveness heals the one who forgives, and it is based on love.

Mateo commented that integrated maturity calls for paying attention to everyone's contribution to the household. When asked, based on personal experience, how has being a dual-career couple negatively impacted your marriage stability and satisfaction, Mateo responded: "Not applicable as wife does not work." On further analysis, Mateo revealed that his wife does most of the household chores and most of the responsibilities of raising the children as well as taking them to school, doctor's appointment. Being a stay home parent does not mean you are not working. Work should not be limited to getting paid.

Lea identified the following challenges which she faced at the beginning of her marriage at the same time how they progressively contributed to her integrated maturity:

- learning to live in the same space
- adapting to each other's habits
- sharing time
- appropriate emotional expression and to express it continuously
- communicating about what bothers us and working through it

Lea identified the following factors that have contributed to her marriage stability and satisfaction: "communication, trust, independence, steady income and healthy amount of intimacy."

Lea elaborated:

- make sure you're on the same page

- make sure you can be comfortable with what the other person is doing and saying
- allowing each other to have their own identity outside of the couple
- allowing for stress-free living without hyper focusing on money
- connecting on a deep personal level

Ted:

> Emotional Compatibility: We are both calm people...able to resolve our conflicts amicably (most times). We are not prone to violent outbursts. This keeps our battles from becoming major friction points in our relationship. I received good advice from my mother. "Never go to bed angry"

> Physical Compatibility (love is blind): We each thought we were beautiful. It took us a while to realize that the beauty was on the inside.

Elaborating on integrated maturity, Ellen added comments about becoming parents or not.
Ellen noted:

> Our marriage is very strong. We truly love each other. *We discussed what our life would be like if we were unable to have children before we got married* (Italics added by author to highlight when conversation occurred). It didn't matter to us either way. Our faith helped us deal with our infertility. We left it up to God as to whether he wanted us to have a child.

Ellen emphasized:

> Infertility can cause stress in a marriage. Have open discussion with each other but don't put blame on one person. If you Love and respect each other, you can overcome any obstacle in your marriage.

Charles:

> The main challenges men and women face in marriage are focused on issues involving finances, health, and fidelity.

Doris:

> FREEDOM TO GROW. We expect to grow continuously – individually and as a couple. Early on, we realized that change is inevitable. We agreed to view our development as ongoing, and promised that we would keep each other "in the loop" as our personhood and ideas evolved. We did not want to wake up some morning to a stranger in the bed. Having this understanding gave us freedom, as individuals, to explore new things, people, and ideas that interested us. And because we are best friends, we are eager to share the direction of our thinking – even to try it out on the other person and get feedback that is honest, yet safe.

Doris added:

TRUSTING PARTNERSHIP. We are partners – in every sense of the word. At first, we were all about fairness and equality, and set our target for a 50/50 partnership. But that was not practical. We learned to be flexible, considerate of the other person's needs, and to give as the situation demanded. Sometimes it was 50/50, but often 20/80, or 60/40, or 100/0 – whatever was needed to make our family healthy, functioning, and stable. We also learned not to keep score – to trust that the partner is giving what he/she can, in that moment, and to value that contribution. We have each other's back, and are considerate about sometimes filling in the gaps or cleaning up unavoidable messes that the other person makes. We don't complain – today it's his mess – tomorrow it will be mine.

Jean mentioned that integrated maturity in regard to her marriage involved:

- Focusing on bringing up our child in a family where both parents are there for him was important

- Loving each other and caring for one another's feelings helped marriage going

- Remembering vows proclaimed and facing the church community kept the marriage going

Based on personal experience in her marriage, Jean suggested the following advice to people interested in marriage but are still fearful of the long-lasting commitment:

- Make sure you love each other

- Discuss how your finances will be handled

- Be able to communicate freely on issues that may bother you

- Keep God in your marriage – Prayers (Some days may seem like hell but prayers and focusing on good times you have shared with your spouse)

- Try to keep busy when necessary so your mind is occupied and give time to family also

Doris clarified that there are many pathways to growth, including learning how to resolve the difficulties people encounter in marriage. Based on personal experience, Doris elaborated:

> My husband and I needed to work on each other to shape a positive and productive exchange that would nourish our relationship, now that we were together every day. Here are some examples of what that looked like.
>
> I was unhappy in my first job (working with terrible administrators). I complained a lot, until finally my husband suggested I do something about it – go back to school and get credentialed to position myself for leadership so I could "be the

change I wanted to see." He did not let me wallow in misery, and pushed me to take charge and do it better. I listened, realized he was wise, and applied to school.

I had a tendency to complain about most things, and brought this into the marriage. Again, my husband gave me feedback that I was sounding like my mother, a "cup half empty" person. I was horrified, and worked very hard to adjust my attitude and change the way I was coming across. I was not showing my best self, and he cared enough to stop me in my tracks and challenge me to get to a better place, in friendship. This is one of the reasons I married him – for his willingness and ability to call attention to my unattractive behaviors and redirect me. Had he not done that, I think I would have continued down a path of self-inflicted misery, and made the marriage a difficult burden for both of us.

While I had too much to say, my husband did not at first. This required some creative work and adjustment on both our parts. Early on, his work was technical and mine was with people, so he came to the dinner table with little conversation. I pushed him with questions like: *Did anything interesting happen today? Who did you have lunch with? Did you have any fun conversations? Did anything unusual happen on the subway ride home?* Over time, he found there were aspects of his day that he could share. As work shifted and became more people-intensive, there was lots to talk about and mull over together – whether it was about work or colleagues or organizations or our church community or our children. First child was a super challenge.

Mateo:

Our marriage is based on Love, Trust, Respect for each other, Compromise and Communication on a daily basis. My wife and I have a true love in our hearts. We do everything in our day thinking about each other. We have full trust in each other which allows freedom in our daily life. Respect is a very big problem if you don't have any in your marriage. If you don't respect each other when you have children, they won't respect you either. It is important to have compromise in your marriage. Decisions can't always be one-sided. This is why communication is so important. A couple should work together daily to make decisions that are needed.

Sarah identified the following factors as significant contributions to her marriage stability and satisfaction: "Our differences create balance, empathy for feelings, communication." She elaborated:

- We are different people and that helps us to support each other and balance our needs

- Feeling what the other person is feeling helps to lend support to each other

- Talking about all the parts of our life brings us closer and helps to avoid conflict or resolves conflict.

Pathological jealousy

Olivia discussed jealousy, based on her personal and professional experience and training. She shared the following reflections regarding jealousy and integrated maturity.

They say some jealousy is good. In the Bible, Jeremiah describes God as a jealous. In some cases, jealousy may help people show they card and are committed to the relationship and are motivated to protect the marriage and mutual respect, allowing people to trust their instincts. However, when people become controlling, humiliating the other and doubting the other's honesty, becoming wrongfully accusatory they may be projecting their limitations on the other. They doubt themselves and question the satisfaction of the other person in terms of sex and money.

Other people may do things that provoke a spouse's jealousy, for instance by provocative dressing and being more emotionally expressive with people other than with their spouse.

It may help to have open and honest conversations with one's partner about the topic of jealousy. It also helps to identify if it is caused by one's own projections, insecurities or past experiences. Other ways of resolving jealousy is to question one's irrational thoughts and behaviors. It also helps to work on improving one's self-esteem.

Stress in marriage

Olivia also discussed stress and anxiety in marriage. She pointed out that there is good stress and anxiety in marriage when they motivate people to move forward and get things done. However, excessive stress and anxiety need to be controlled with exercise and therapy. It helps to identify the stresses and causes of anxiety. Understanding the impact of stress and anxiety within a broader spectrum may help people to talk about preventative measures, seek treatment before it is too late. It is important to be aware of one's feeling of love, self-esteem, loneliness, anger, projecting blame, sadness and workaholics. It is also important to see help from programs related to job loss, caring for family members, death in the family, financial challenges and other intra/external challenges.

Mature people also tend to know how to let go of stress and anxiety, unrealistic expectations, and people with toxic ideas. Mature people are also capable of not playing the roles of martyr, victim, savior and God almighty.

My experience

Based on what you have read in this session, reflect on your own personal experience.

1. How am I preparing myself to live without what I greatly miss from my family of origin?

   _____

2. Who are the people I consider to be significant in my life as I prepare to marry or remarry?

   _____

3. What unique role does each of these people play in my life and why do I perceive that person to be uniquely important?

   _____

4. Who are the people in my life that I can turn to when I need various kinds of help (e.g., emotional, spiritual, financial, social, parenting and/or finding meaning in life)?

   _____

5. Mark off all of the following that impacted your life the most in-between being single and being married?

   o Significant drop in finances

   o Significant increase in finances and improvement in standard of living

   o Increased suffering and rejection from family members and friends

o Feeling very, very lonely

o Challenges to adjust to maintain a paying job while balancing home responsibilities

o Taking on two jobs to handle financial demands

o Going for further education

o Overdrinking

o Change in interactions with members of family of origin

Keys to integral maturity

As keys are important to open doors, consider the following keys to integral maturity.

- Ability to set realistic expectations about oneself and others

- Having the right motivations for marriage

- Practice of unconditional love

- Companionship in order to overcome loneliness

- Ability to give and receive emotional support

- Fidelity to God's plan for humanity: man was not created to live alone

- Tenderness toward self and significant others

- Patience and wisdom to search for the right and compatible partner

- Getting financial support from future spouse

- Need for a parenting partner and real model for children

- Being in love with the partner

- Getting away from pain in the first marriage

- Search for meaning and happiness in life with a partner

- Ability to start over again, praying and trusting in God so that this time it (marriage) would work

- Taking responsibility for one's actions without projecting blame onto other(s).

Study Session 10

Timeless principles and values in marriage

The participants identified the following values as significant ingredients within each individual, marriage, family and society. Table 5 lists some of the values (qualities or attributes) that the participants referred to as "family values." Although not complete, it serves as an invitation for each individual to start developing and implementing these values.

Table 5. Some Core Family Values

Achieving	Gentle	Objective
Active	Happy	Open
Ambitious	Hardworking	Participatory
Analytical	Healing	Patient
Assertive	Honest	Peace-making
Attentive	Honoring of process	Persevering
Attractive (good hygiene, well groomed)	Hopeful	Prayer (individually and in community)
Brave	Humble	Preparing for eternal life
Calm	Inclusive	Rational
Caring	Independent	Receptive
Committed	Industrious	Relational
Communicative	Interdependent	Respectful
Compassionate	Introspective	Self-controlled
Connective	Intuitive	Self-improving
Cooperative	Joyful	Sensitive
Decisive	Just	Sharing
Dependent	Listening	Spiritual
Emotional	Loving	Trusting
Empowered	Loyal	Truthful
Faithful	Mature	Well-rounded
Flexible	Merciful	Wise
Focused	Modest	
Forgiving	Nurturing	

Values are learned, primarily at home and from other influencing person's in one's life. However, values are basically expressed when they are manifested or tested in specific circumstances. For instance, Lucy cited in her responses a quotation from a less-known author as a key manifest of loyalty. Elaborating on loyalty, Lucy wrote: "A woman's loyalty is tested when her man has nothing. A man's loyalty is tested when he has everything."

Anti-values: pride, rudeness, blaming, humiliating the other (especially in public)

Andy: When asked to identify the principles underlying his marriage stability and satisfaction, he mentioned "not forgetting the foundation" and "the willingness of my wife to carry on." He elaborated:

> It has neither been stable nor completely satisfying. I must say satisfaction is in my mind. Mine, I guess like many others, has definitely not been smooth, nor stable, in fact it has been very rocky at times, but I still say I'm satisfied because I always think back to the reason, I married my spouse. That reason has not changed. The absolute trust I placed in her, the day decided she was the one, hasn't changed. It's like I released my entire being to her then, relinquished control of the home, my things, finance, and kids while I faced other things in life. Work, search for a better life, our place in society, etc. in the beginning I looked for someone I could trust and rely on who wouldn't deceive me and wanted me for me, and that I found in her and have never ever doubted her on this.
>
> I only discovered other things later on, other things about her and about myself, which had I known then, could have been a different story but it's neither her fault nor mine and I see no reason why I should change the past decision or my satisfaction now, just because of new discoveries which were always there and not as a result of dishonesty but which one comes to realize or see with age, experience, knowing more about oneself and life in general. In summary, I would say my satisfaction comes

from not forgetting the original "raison d'être," the original reason.

Rowland

Fairness – Because we had separate roles in our marriage, at different times, we grew to understand how limiting and unfair traditional roles were. Coming to our marriage with individually strong senses of fairness, we further developed fairness as a major criterion for work, household and family duties, child rearing, and our personal relationship. Will this action make you/me a better person? Is it fair to those affected by our choice?

Hard work - We both work hard in all that we do. We learned quickly that marriage is never a 50%-50% proposition. You give what is needed, and that sometimes is 100% each. This is much easier to do when you're confident the other person is pulling just as hard.

High principles – We both trust that the other is working from the best principles possible. When conflicts and problems arose, we did not have to question motives or commitment to the best for everyone. The problem was to better understand their preferences and thinking. There was not competition, or a desire to be the winner, or to teach the other a lesson—but a truly collaborative search for the best way out of whatever difficulty arose.

'Long-lasting' is built one day at a time with this person that you love—always listening, empathizing, trusting, and believing that you mutually want the best for each other. Can you change for/with this person as life washes over you? Marriage itself brings its own spiritual and social supports and provides just a little extra incentive to work through that last friction or sacrifice that might be needed

Albert:

Trust in all aspects that she will do her best in all things.

She supports me when I need it.

209

We continue to have an equal voice and influence on our decisions.

We do the things we have to, but if the other is better at it or prefers the duty then they do it.

We have similar values and expectations.

Andy, elaborating on the advice for other individuals to establish stability and satisfaction in marriage, he noted:

> We (Andy and his wife) are still going through it but I am guessing focusing on what brought you together will make one satisfied. Hopefully it is something deeper than skin deep or physical in nature. Contentment is another factor. You will meet fancier people, you will become more comfortable, your status in society will change, don't forget your roots / humble beginnings.

Doris, when asked to identify three major values which have significantly impacted her marriage stability and satisfaction, she stated: "Respect, support, and love." She elaborated:

- Respect, most important, recognizing that negativity in a marriage such as hurtful remarks, being condescending, being made fun of, could not only hurt that person, but severely hurt the marriage.

- Support, it matters, as this is your best friend, when your best friend is feeling down, you should be the one in his/her corner. Make him/her feel better.

- Love, is speaks for itself, without love in a marriage, there is no stability or satisfaction.

Doris

PERSISTENCE AND PERSEVERANCE. Quitting is not an option. We understand our vows – until death, and take those promises very seriously. This goes along with the "Don't go to bed angry" practice. We are people who don't throw out what we can reuse or recycle, so we expect our relationship to last and grow in value. We were raised to work hard, not to give up, but to figure out a way to resolve our problems. "No return, no surrender!"

Doris added:

> I believe we were lucky, with a matching rock-solid work ethic that we used to manage the heavy lifting of the 90%. That's why my query about compatible work ethic is so important under Question #4 in Study Session 3. Here is where there could have been trouble – if one of us demonstrated an unwillingness to share the grueling load. Earlier I explained that the partnership was sometimes 50/50, sometimes unbalanced. That is not a problem unless one of the partners perceives the other to be slacking, or unfairly dumping work on the other by being unavailable or "sick."

Elaborating on the values which reinforce stability and satisfaction in marriage, Doris added the following:

> COMMON VALUES, BELIEFS, AND WORK ETHIC. I've said a lot about these qualities. They are the *sine qua non* of our stability as a couple. We are on the same page for everything that matters deeply, so are not in conflict with each other.
>
> EDUCATION AND PRIVILEGE AS POWERFUL TRAJECTORIES. We have benefitted from our excellent education and class privilege. Through scholarships and parental financing, we started as a couple with excellent personal credentials and no debt. As professionals, we had access to, and could choose, great jobs. We built our economic nest egg on the basis of our privilege, and pass on the economic advantages to our sons. We never experienced the stress of wanting for anything, being uninsured, systematically excluded because of race, or being unemployed and unable to pay our bills. In short, we had no financial, societal, or cultural obstacles to overcome.

Dedication – a decision to fully devote myself towards building a happy and successful life (and future) with my husband according to the commitment I made when we got married.

Trust and support – I choose to trust in my husband and not second guess his actions. I believe that he wants what is best for me and our family ultimately.

Sincere appreciation of each other while acknowledging our imperfections. Such appreciation may not always mean we have everything we want or the best of everything, even in our marriage, but is a conscious acknowledgment that it could be better or worse. The gratitude we show reflects our commitment to look for the good in each other...starting with the little things, and the big things will follow. Gratitude has been said to turn what we have into enough and a house into a home.

Respect for ourselves, each other and our families in the spirit of do unto others as you would like them to do unto you. The respect that I portray reflects the respect that I expect/would like to receive. Even in instances when it's the last feeling you may be inclined to feel about your spouse, your respectful action is your character

Kindness begets kindness and, in the words of the Dalai Lama ... "Be kind whenever possible. It is always possible". Kindness can disorient an enemy as well illustrated in a children's bedtime story "Coals of Fire" that comes to mind. It is derived from a Bible teaching about "if your enemy is hungry, feed him; and if he is thirsty, give him a drink" and in so doing you burn the meanness out of them. My husband is not my enemy, and if I can feed and give a drink to my enemy, then how much more can I do for my husband.

Study Session 11

25 Therefore, putting away falsehood, speak the truth, each one to his neighbor, for we are members one of another. 26 Be angry but do not sin;u do not let the sun set on your anger, 27 and do not leave room for the devil. 28 The thief must no longer steal, but rather labor, doing honest work with his [own] hands, so that he may have something to share with one in need. 29 No foul language should come out of your mouths, but only such as is good for needed edification, that it may impart grace to those who hear. 30 And do not grieve the holy Spirit of God, with which you were sealed for the day of redemption. 31 All bitterness, fury, anger, shouting, and reviling must be removed from you, along with all malice. 32 [And] be kind to one another, compassionate, forgiving one another as God has forgiven you in Christ. (Ephesians 4: 25 – 32)

Anna mentioned every couple is unique. However, every couple should develop a set of rules or guidelines to live by. Such rules do not have to be necessarily written as a "Couple's Constitution Book" or papers on the fridge, but a combination of common-sense rules and negotiated guidelines which are written in every spouse's heart." For instance, Anna noted that the marriage rules/guidelines which have helped her to embrace stability and satisfaction in her marriage include:

> Put each other first. Put family first. Support one another no matter what. Open lines of   communication. Help one another. Have respect for one another and the children. Be honest. Forgive one another and compromise.

Mike, when asked about the marriage rules/ guidelines which have helped him in his marriage, he mentioned:

A household is not a democracy. We, the parents, must be ready and on the same page when problems arise. I am trying to make you and me the best persons possible. Laughter helps. Especially laughing at yourself. Recognize each other's strengths and listen to their expertise.

In regards to the DO NOTs which couples need to implement to embrace marriage stability and satisfaction, Anna mentioned:

> Do not stay angry at one another. Talk about it, it's usually just a misunderstanding.
>
> Do not put one down or criticize each other in public.
>
> Do not allow others to ruin your marriage with a physical attraction or an inappropriate   friendship.
>
> Do not give up easily on your marriage, it's too easy.
>
> Work together, it's worth it.

Mike emphasized:

> Do not go to bed angry. Do not assume you already understand the other's perspective; listen to their messages. Do not let the inmates run the asylum (re: setting limits for children).

Without further elaboration, Andy mentioned that the rules that helped him in his marriage are:

- Communication

- Trust

- Respect

- Honesty

- Support

- Compromise

- Win/Win

He added, the following DO NOT's that couples need to implement to embrace marriage stability and satisfaction:

- Do not belittle each other

- Do not discount each other's feelings

- Do not allow others to interfere in your marriage

Description of house rules and roles

Several participants mentioned that because of the complexity of remarriage, rules are very important in second marriages. Some of the reasons they gave were that rules help to maintain structure and to establish a sense of discipline and order in the house. All of these participants had joint custody of their children with their former spouses, and they had realized that their children were finding it difficult to figure out what to do and not do in the households of their divorced parents.

Some of these participants had attended a seminar about remarriage in which they were helped to understand the importance of establishing rules and making them clear to the children in their households. One of the phrases which participants reported as effective in helping their children to deal with the differences of guidelines while living in two households was the usage of the phrase: "In this house, the rules are: ..."

Experience of others

Further individual discussions with those parents revealed that the rules which had helped better their children in their second marriage were those that were clear, consistent, flexible, not rigid, and to which defined consequences were attached if not followed.

One of the rules that Elías mentioned was:

> In this house, everybody who is at home during mealtime is expected to collaborate in the washing of the dishes after eating. Otherwise, whoever does not collaborate will have to wash the dishes alone after the next meal.

Some participants mentioned that the parents should make the rules in dialogue with their children, so that the children, especially teenagers and young adults, know what is expected of them. However, a few other participants emphasized that parents should not set the rules for their children exclusively. The parents should make rules or guidelines for themselves and abide by them, too. One of rules that participants suggested for divorced parents was that, as parents, they should not criticize their former spouse in front of the children.

In addition to the house rules, several participants attributed the success of their remarriages to the fact that they made a conscious decision with their respective spouses not to get stuck into a rigid structure of abiding by the traditional gender roles.

Abraham clarified:

> I help my second wife a lot with cooking, washing of the dishes, because I do not think that it is a job exclusively for women. This may sound or be perceived as a small thing by some people

in traditional marriages, but it is a great relief to my wife. She likes it, and it makes me feel supportive of her as we share some of the so-called traditional gender roles. Equally, too, I am not the only breadwinner in the house. We have a joint account, and we share all the expenses. However, there are other roles that we had to define clearly. For example, even if my stepson did not need any disciplinarian action because he grew up well-behaved, just in case any disciplinarian measures had to be taken, his biological parents would be the ones to do that, not me.

Several participants mentioned the need for couples to set a ritual for themselves alone and to schedule it in the form of a rule, so that they can comply by it. Elizabeth referred to that ritual as couple time and described it as a special time for her and her husband alone.

Elizabeth mentioned: "I find myself during the week really crazy, very busy, with no time."

By the same token, she encouraged other married people with tight schedules to follow this suggestion:

Find time [together], let the dishes go, let the laundry go, don't wash the floor. It will be there. It is absolutely true. It will be there. Find some time, even one hour a week, special time to go out to dinner. My husband does not like to go out to dinner, so we made a different special time. It is our Saturday date night. I find it very helpful for us and it keeps us fresh.

House rules and roles are of paramount importance in marriage settings. Some participants identified different house rules (bedtime for children) with a soft and firm tone of voice as a means of establishing order within the family and thereby helping each other to live in harmony. Based on their descriptions of the need for house rules, establishing clear house rules and the attached consequences for not abiding by them was a means to greater freedom within the family system, for dealing with the children, and for keeping clear boundaries with former spouses in order to provide collaborative parenting of the children.

Several participants also made a distinction between traditional gender roles and flexible gender roles. Based on their inputs, it seemed that rigid, traditional gender roles (e.g., men as the sole breadwinners and women as the sole nurturers in a home) were not well suited for people in remarriage settings. Instead, they recommended mutual collaboration in many roles. Typical examples of such mutual sharing of roles, included some of the participants having the same bank account (joint method). This enables both partners to jointly pay the house bills and other expenses.

Another example was the move away from emphasizing the biological parent as the only person responsible for the parenting responsibilities of his or her children from the previous marriage. Some participants mentioned that consulting their second spouses empowered them to become better parents, and they felt supported by the new spouse and more adult in their parenting role, especially those participants who did not have amicable relationships with their former spouses.

Henry's parenting style showed his wisdom. He had arranged with his second wife that he would be the disciplinarian of his children from the first marriage, and his second wife would be the one to reward them. He reported that this style had helped him to learn how to seek consultation from his second wife before disciplining his children. He felt supported by his second wife, put his wife into an active co-parenting role, and removed his wife from the position of being resented by his child and his former wife. Instead, she was well-respected as a stepmother without seeming to take away the mother-figure role from the children's biological mother, with whom the children have regular contact. The children like his wife very much because she reinforces their positive behavior by rewarding them.

Marie:

> Make your home a happy place, as desirable as a warm and welcoming "holiday" destination. Hospitality is an art that is inculcated at an early age. We host houseguests, friends and family with the (unconscious) intention of impressing them by "dancing ourselves lame" in providing our best (dinnerware, drinks and food) and in so doing set a standard or bypass hospitality standards previously set by those we are hosting. We should in the same way make our homes a hospitable environment that we are eager to go to, with no need for anyone to procrastinate about going home.

> Don't be "invulnerable" which can often appear as not needing/can do without your partner. Never take sides against your spouse – you must always have their back, even if it means later sorting out the nitty gritty in private. Don't threaten/prepare to leave as an alternative to seeking avenues of resolving issues. Insofar as possible, try to maintain the same circle of friends to motivate and help one another to grow in life and marriage. Independent circles of friends may contribute to the establishment of separate centers of influence that adversely impact the marriage. Appreciate your financial situation; do not overburden your spouse.

> Limit external influences (friends and family) on your marriage – misery loves company, and the information that we share with others in the name of confiding can end up in the wrong domain

or be used to our disadvantage. As the saying goes "three people can only share a secret if two are dead."

Socialize with family and friends, trying to culture a common circle of friends with similar interests, and endearing yourself to your in-laws in a way that eliminates any misconceptions they may have initially had about you, a virtual stranger. Establish personal "headspace" while striking the fine balance of ensuring it doesn't encroach into time spent together resulting in withdrawal and isolation.

Andy:

We didn't create rules. I wish we had but to be candid we've made them up as we went. if I tell you of rules, it would be an academic exercise, and that you can read from any marriage counselor. One I can say however is my wife once reported me to her parents and it didn't go too well. Since then, I believe one unspoken rule has been to solve our problems ourselves. I also think I commented on our situation with her friend who I thought my wife had spoken to of things in our marriage. I was corrected and corrected the lady telling her to leave our matter alone. The result the case resolved itself. The conclusion 3rd parties do more harm than good, they either listen like news or broadcast bad news.

Albert:

Learn to cooperate and set ground rules as to whose duties are what and be clear about how and why as well as respect the other's opinion.

Jean identified the following marriage rules/guidelines which have helped her in her marriage:

- Loving and caring for each other's feelings (not to intentionally hurt one's feelings)

- Communicating openly to each other

- Respect each other

- Discuss financial handling (how you would want to deal with income/expenditure)

- Discuss clearly how both of you are going to deal with your relatives and friends

- Discuss clearly how both of you are going to parent and discipline your child(ren)

Jean added the following DO NOTs that couples need to implement to embrace marriage stability and satisfaction:

- Do not have a sexual relationship with anyone other than your spouse

- Do not talk badly about your spouse to others

- Do not be too restrictive of each other's moves

- Do not be too extravagant (when one is conservative)

- Do not be lazy. There is no place for laziness for a marriage to succeed

- Do not be dirty/untidy environment (when one is clean)

- Do not overdrink

- Do not be disrespectful of each other's religion or political side

- Do not manifest too much anger

- Do not be disrespectful (thinking one is superior to the other)

George

Pray together. Repent and forgive readily. Put the other person first. Think the best of them; putting the best interpretation on actions they take. Keep going out on dates. (We do weekly.) Go away as a couple to refresh at least once per year. Figure out how your spouse experiences being loved (being present and attentive to them, encouraging them with words of praise and gratitude, giving them gifts, meeting their needs with service, touch that imparts how precious they are to you) and do so often.

Take one day at the time and rely upon the grace God supplies for it.

Don't let the sun go down on your anger. Don't hold grudges or keep score. Don't insist on having things your own way. Don't be dismissive of the other's worth, efforts, needs, wants, ideas.

Ted:

Always try to tell the truth. It's easier to forgive an honest mistake than a deceitful lie. Never go to bed angry. Although there were many times it was very difficult not to.

Don't hold grudges. They become a cancer that can destroy your soul.

Be willing to forgive and forget your partner's mistakes, but you must also encourage and applaud your partner's success.

Always try to love yourself for who you are. I believe that you can't love anybody else if you   don't love yourself first.

Miguel:

> Be honest, be kind, fight fair, leave the past in the past, and do not go to sleep if we are mad at each other. Not going to sleep if we are mad at each other. He added: Do not stop being romantic and detailed; do not focus on secondary aspects more than family; and do not focus on what is not important, focus on the blessings you have.

Anne emphasized:

> Put each other first. Put family first. Support one another no matter what. Open lines of communication. Help one another. Have respect for one another and the children. Be honest. Forgive one another. Compromise. Do not stay angry at one another. Talk about it, it's usually just a misunderstanding. Do not put one down or criticize each other in public. Do not allow others ruin your marriage with a physical attraction or an inappropriate friendship. Do not give up easily on your marriage, it's too easy. Work together, it's worth it.

Mateo:

> "Don't go to bed angry" and "Do not be untrustworthy"

Sarah recommended the following rules and guidelines to people contemplating marriage and those already married: "Communication, Trust, Respect and Honesty."

Sarah identified the following DO NOTs that couples need to implement to embrace marriage stability and satisfaction: "Do not belittle each other; Do not discount each other's feelings, and Do not allow others to interfere in your marriage."

Ted:

Try never to give your spouse a reason to NOT trust you. Holding lies inside of you will eat away at your soul and prevent you from loving your wife.

Rowland:

Do not go to bed angry.

Do not assume you already understand the other's perspective-listen to their messages.

Do not let the inmates run the asylum (re: setting limits for children).

Albert:

Don't break trust, it's hard to fix.

Don't be cruel; say things you can't take back.

Have respect for each other

Rowland:

A household is not a democracy.

We, the parents, must be ready and on the same page when problems arise.

I am trying to make you and me the best persons possible.

Laughter helps. Especially laughing at yourself.

Recognize each other's strengths and listen to their expertise.

Doris identified the following marriage rules/guidelines in your marriage that have helped her marriage

- Teamwork, you are in this together as a pair.

- If there is a disagreement, and you find you are at fault, apologize.

- Make time for yourselves, don't smother yourself in work, see a movie, take a short vacation, go out to dinner, "date nights" are a good thing.

- respect is important. Treat each other with respect

- Have family meetings when needed

- Be flexible, but firm. Rules should be followed, but sometimes need to be negotiated

- Discuss rules for the house with your partner

Regarding the DO NOT's that couples need to implement to embrace marriage stability and satisfaction, Doris mentioned:

Do not disrespect one another, don't stay mad long, make up, there are worst things in life then this disagreement. Do not say negative things about each other's families, one should look in the good of people.

Doris suggest the following list marriage rules/guidelines ("Do's") in marriage:

- Resolve unsettling issues before ending the day. Tell your spouse something is weighing on you, and you want to talk it through.

- Say "thank you "often and sincerely.

- Guard your tongue when tempers are aroused. Count to 10 first, so you can remember that you love this person. or stay quiet until you calm down. Then give an "I" message that your spouse can hear, now that he/she has also calmed down.

- Speak and act toward each other with kindness, consideration, and respect.

- Keep promises and tell the truth.

- Be prepared to say yes to whatever is needed – even the hard stuff. See the need and don't wait to be asked.

- Listen to your spouse's opinion, and comment as a friend and partner rather than an adversary.

- Cooperate, rather than compete with your spouse. You are on the same team.

- Make money matters transparent, and share the resources in a way that respects both spouses.

- Communicate with your spouse before introducing new sexual acts or technique and respect other's like and dislike

- Be flexible and generous.

- Share a meal/day together, with no technology – only conversation.

- Find out what your spouse enjoys when you want to be intimate. Be consensual.

Doris added the following list of "DO NOT" guidelines in marriage

- Do not go to bed angry.

- Do not take your spouse for granted. Say thank you and show you are grateful in small ways. On the flip side, do not demand expensive gifts as a sign or love – or remorse.

- Do not snap an angry response at your spouse, in the heat of the moment. You will regret what comes out of your mouth that can't be put back in....

- Do not lie, act selfishly, or willfully break a commitment.

- Do not refuse to do certain unpleasant but necessary jobs – like changing a poopy diaper.

- Do not interrupt your spouse, or dismiss his/her comments with disrespect or annoyance. Similarly, do not yell or swear at your spouse – or anybody, for that matter.

- Do not compete with your spouse or keep score; just improve yourself (e.g., through further education).

- Do not create pretend to be working nor do unproductive work to avoid work that is harder; instead, focus on good work – like parenting, cleaning the dishes, spending time with children, listening to them, etc.

- Do not hoard money, keep separate bank accounts, or deny money to your spouse because you are the one getting the paycheck. Similarly, do not make large purchases without your spouse's knowledge. Make money decisions together.

- Do not be rigid.

- Do not demand sex or sexual acts that make your partner uncomfortable

- Do not bring technology to meals – at home or in a restaurant.

My experience

Based on what you have read in this session, reflect on your own personal experience in order to facilitate the establishment and maintenance of a stable and satisfactory remarriage that may or may not involve custodial child(ren) of one of the spouses.

1. What do I need to know, do and not do?

   _____

2. What should I tell my and/or my new spouse's children and how?

   _____

Keys to proper establishment and management of house rules and roles in remarriage

As keys are important to open doors, consider the following keys to house rules and roles.

- Above all, respect is important. Treat each other with respect

- Have family meetings when needed

- Be flexible, but firm. Rules should be followed, but sometimes need to be negotiated

- Discuss rules for the house with your partner

Study Session 12

Divorce prevention and timely seeking of professional help

43 Be sure of this: if the master of the house had known the hour of night when the thief was coming, he would have stayed awake and not let his house be broken into. (Mathew 24: 43)

8 Be sober and vigilant. Your opponent the devil is prowling around like a roaring lion looking for [someone] to devour. 9 Resist him, steadfast in faith, knowing that your fellow believers throughout the world undergo the same sufferings. 10 The God of all grace who called you to his eternal glory through Christ [Jesus] will himself restore, confirm, strengthen, and establish you after you have suffered a little. 11 To him be dominion forever. Amen. (1 Peter 5: 8 – 11)

Description of professional help

Professional help may be described as the services one receives from a competent person trained in a specific field in order to nurture one's growth, to get advice, assessment, and treatment, and/or to obtain guidelines for addressing a given problem(s). Some of the different types of professionals whose counsel may be sought in regard to marriage include: spiritual and religious leaders, marriage and family therapists, psychologists, psychiatrists, medical doctors, financial experts and/ or social workers.

Experience of others

Some of the participants stated that, even if they did not seek professional help before they married, they acknowledged that their marriages would have been a little easier if they had received some guidance and counseling from competent personnel before remarriage. They indicated that, because of the complexity of remarriage and its challenges, pre-remarriage counseling is important. Henry stated:

> Looking back at my remarriage journey and what I have heard other remarried people experience in my profession as a family attorney, I would recommend that remarrying people should consult religious ministers to understand the importance of the third Person, namely, God in the relationship. Consult social workers to impress reasonable expectations upon you. Um, you know, women don't wake up with make-up on every day. Sometimes they don't look attractive as others and the guys sometimes don't shave for three days in a row.

Many participants acknowledged that, if they had not received professional help from excellent marriage and family therapists after they remarried, their remarriages would most probably have ended in another divorce. Additionally, several female and male participants attributed their stability and satisfaction in remarriage to having consulted their religious ministers after they remarried, but they emphasized that it would have been better if they had received this help before remarriage.

Several male and female participants suggested consulting financial accountants, especially to establish prenuptial agreements. Five female and three male participants suggested seeking help from social workers, especially those who are competent and interested in working with divorced persons, remarried parents, and children in stepfamilies. One of the participants (Abraham), a clinical psychologist and researcher, expressed his appreciation of the work done by family therapists, psychologists, and social workers in their efforts to help parents and children in remarriage settings. Accordingly, Abraham stated:

Based on what I have gone through in my life as a married man in both marriages, I think there is need for specialized training of professionals working with the divorced and people living in remarriage contexts and stepfamilies. I say this because most of the traditional psychologists that I know, including myself, we were trained to work with individuals, not stepfamilies. Based on my literature reviews, I have realized that there are very few specialized remarriage professionals working with people in stepfamilies.

Olivia mentioned:

Many professionals work hard to help people yet the truth is that not every marriage can be saved. Sometimes, divorce counseling is the better choice for parties involved.

My experience

Based on what you have read in this session, reflect on your own personal experience.

1. Have I ever sought professional help related to my marriage, divorce and/or remarriage?

   _____

2. If yes? What were the reasons for seeking help?

   _____

3. If not, what hindered me from doing so?

4. Other than for marriage, divorce and/or remarriage, what other type(s) of professional help have I ever sought and when?

5. What were the reasons for seeking help (e.g., alcohol, drugs, gambling, promiscuous behavior, or mental health issues)?

6. Which problems were resolved as a result of seeking professional help and which ones were not resolved?

7. What has been my experience regarding each type of professional help I have sought?

8. Whenever the need arises, what may hinder me from seeking professional help before or during my marriage?

9. What is my experience of seeking professional help?

10. What types of resources do I need in order to seek professional help now or in the near future?

11. Do I have the needed resources to seek professional help?

12. If not, what am I going to do so as not to miss this opportunity?

13. Has my partner ever sought professional help?

_____

14. If so, what were the reasons for seeking help?

_____

15. What was his/her experience regarding professional help?

_____

16. What are his/her attitudes and level of willingness to seek professional help in regard to our marriage stability and satisfaction?

_____

17. What are his/her attitudes and level of willingness to seek professional help in regard to other related problems?

_____

———————————◆ ◆ ◆◆◆ ◆ ◆———————————

Keys to seeking and making use of professional help

As keys are important to open doors, consider the following keys to professional help.

- Develop a positive attitude toward seeking professional help

- Be aware of the social stigmas and/or personal biases regarding the seeking of help for problems related to mental health

- Be humble and overcome the pride, stereotype and negative experiences attached to seeking professional help

- Determine and clarify the types of problems you want resolved

- Find a licensed and competent professional who specializes in the area of your interest (e.g., remarriage counseling, marriage enrichment, divorce mediation, remarriage preparation, conflict resolution skills, self-esteem, domestic violence, stepfamilies, filing taxes as a couple, marital spirituality, sexual abuse, financial management, pornography, setting clear boundaries, writing one's will, etc.)

- Be honest when speaking with a chosen professional

- Set realistic expectations about seeking professional help

- Seek professional help with the awareness that professionals provide guidelines, not answers, to your problems. They do not live your life for you. Therefore, take responsibility for your decisions and actions while seeking professional help and be consistently committed to making the needed changes

- Seek professional help before it is too late ("Prevention is better than cure.")

- Admit your problems, take responsibility for them and stop blaming yourself by seeking the necessary professional help

- Seek professional help if, on your own, you cannot resolve your problems (e.g., perpetuation of unnecessary guilt, pathological jealousy and/or unresolved problems from the past)

- Seek professional help if you have a tendency to blame yourself for other people's problems (including those of your current partner or former spouse). Know that nobody is perfect. It cannot always be your own fault or the other person's fault. Each person has some "dirty laundry" or unfinished business that may call for professional help

- If you do not have the money and/or the other necessary resources to receive the needed professional services, ask for help from charitable agencies. Ask a friend if you need help (e.g., for transportation or babysitting). Pursue all available means to get professional help

Study Session 13

Attentiveness to physical and mental health challenges before marriage
and after

Mental and physical health plays a significant role in all aspects of our lives. Personality disorders (e.g., narcissistic, antisocial, schizoid, paranoid, dependent and avoidant) are likely to have a significant impact on marriage stability and satisfaction.

Marriage is put at a great risk with an individual or between individuals with a severe mental disorder. These include: severe mood disorders, unresolved traumas, alcohol- and other sub- stance-related disorders, pathological jealousy, communication disorders, eating disorders, gender identity disorders, sexual disorders, sexual dysfunctions and/or other mental disorders due to medical conditions.

All in all, mental disorders and/or physical dysfunction need to be diagnosed because they play a significant role in every individual's relational life. Seeking professional help is highly recommended whenever there is any damage to the human brain (Amen, 2008) before and after remarriage. Become aware of the contributing factors to divorce in first marriages and remarriages. Minuchin and Nichols (1993) emphasized that the failure to identify and resolve the contributing factors (possible causes) of divorce in the first marriage creates serious consequences, because remarrying spouses usually reenact the dynamics of the first marriage in their second or subsequent marriages (Ganong & Coleman, 1989; Gottman, 1994b). Clinical findings in reference to some of the causes of divorce indicated 80 % of the clients reported the lack of in-depth communication as the main contributing factor to divorce (Berger, 1998; Gottman, Notarius, Gonso & Markman, 1976).

Other factors cited as contributing to divorce include personality incompatibility between spouses, un- realistic expectations about marriage and/or unrealistic idealization of one's partner (especially during courtship), marital infidelity, personality abnormality, constant social pressures that create stress, lack of mutual prayer and spiritual life, cultural values that condone violence, domestic violence, conflictive relationships with in-laws, pathological jealousy, money used as a power source to control one's partner, lack of open communication and negotiation about money, use of drugs and alcohol (Carter & McGoldrick, 1998; Gottman, 1994a; Kaslow, 1996; Rutter, 1998; Treadway, 1989).

Working on past and present problems

Remarrying and already remarried spouses, as well as people in stepfamilies are constrained not only by present problems but also by problems lingering from divorce and previous relationships. Therefore, custodial parents are encouraged to seek professional advice, if needed, so that a professional may help them to mourn the losses from a previous relationship. The professional may also be able to show the custodial parent how the new family structure is being affected by those feelings (Berger, 1998; McCulullough, Spence & Worthington, 1994). Similarly, seeking professional help before it is too late may serve as an excellent preventative approach. Consequently, remarrying partners may receive a comprehensive assessment of their integral lives before remarriage in order to explore, anticipate and address future problems before they occur (LeBey, 2004).

Elaborating on compatibility in marriage, Linda mentioned:
"Sometimes no matter how much you want a piece of a puzzle to fit another, it doesn't have the right shape to fit together."

Mateo:

> In addition to physical appearance and beauty, physical health is very important to consider before marriage. I was attracted to my wife because she looked so beautiful and she continues to be. I found in her and still do: attractive, beautiful, goodness, and above all with 'a healthy mind in a healthy body.' Her smiling face, her dimples, her appearance and on-going self-care keep her very attractive and they reflect the beauty of her mental health as well.

Lea:

> Physical health is so important to marriage life. If you are not healthy it adds another level of stress. When I am experiencing fibromyalgia pain, it is hard for me to get around and be productive. It then adds stress to him to make sure I feel OK, but also get done everything I didn't do and that he also has to do prior.

Marie:

> My husband has OCD (tendency toward excessive orderliness, perfectionism and great attention to detail). I did not realize how bad it was until we were living together. I had to adjust my lifestyle to bring peace. It made me a better organized person in the end.

————————◆————————

Study Session 14

Communication

According to Yalom (1995), "We cannot not communicate." In other words, as humans in any relationship with another human being, we are in continuous communication. For instance, even silence is a means of communication. However, many spouses expressed great concerns about the lack of communication. Such concerns call for a description of the meaning of communication, different means of communication, strategies of constructive communication, knowing what to do and what not to do in regard to communication as well identifying the content and process of communication.

Most participants mentioned that communication in remarriages is important because it facilitates relationship building, especially because of the diverse numbers of people involved in a stepfamily. These people include one's children, one's spouse, the former spouse, ex-in-laws, current in-laws, the ex-spouse of one's current spouse and stepchildren. Hilda stated that miscommunication of any kind of contributes to the emotional hurting of the people involved. The flow of information among these members of the extended family can get out of one's control. By the time it reaches the fourth or fifth person, a given message may not match the meaning of what the first speaker wanted to say.

Many participants emphasized that in order to avoid higher risks of miscommunication in stepfamily settings, remarried spouses should learn better communication skills and create time for themselves as a couple. In this way, they can dialogue about the diverse topics that need to be resolved.

Experience of others

According to Beatrice, some of those conversations may revolve around step parenting and how to ask the current spouse to be supportive for the partner's children if their other biological parent does not respond to their emotional needs. Elaborating on the importance of the need for communication in regard to remarriage stability and satisfaction, Felicia mentioned that learning when to keep her mouth shut and when to open it had helped her to improve the relationship with her second spouse.

Based on her experience, Felicia revealed that words can hurt people and affect the relationships of the people one cares about. She emphasized that even if one can offer an apology, what has been said cannot be taken back. Felicia described communication at length as follows:

> Communication involves trust and mutual respect because, even if both spouses see things differently, they can still communicate and influence each other's views. I think that, in a marriage, you learn a lot from your spouse, but at the end, your spouse also learns a lot from you. So you learn to, I would say, adjust. And I would say that behind every good man there is a good woman, and behind every good woman there is a good man. And not being always the same, I think that is a good thing. Being flexible and being different is OK because my husband and I are like day and night. I never always see things the way he sees them. However, when we sit together and I tell him what I think and he tells me what he thinks, we negotiate our differences and come to conclusions.

> Sometimes I will hold back things just to keep the peace in the family. Sometimes I am not happy with decisions, but I hold back. At the end it works. At the end it is for the better because I am too quick at judgment. And I find that, if I hold back and think about things, I am better off.

> So you withhold your judgment, you think through things, and eventually things work out. For the sake of peace sometimes

240

you just stay quiet. For the sake of peace sometimes you should swallow your pride and holds things back. Not always.

Elaborating on the theme of communication, all the participants' input could be put into two major categories, informal communication and in-depth communication. The informal communication is focused on the casual conversations that help people to start interacting with one another, and these conversations need to be maintained throughout the remarriage. Examples of these conversations include topics that are less emotionally charged and they do not tend to be personal. Catherine referred to these kinds of talks as icebreakers that might help in creating an environment of mutual trust so that people may feel comfortable to speak about their personal lives. On the other hand, Beatrice highlighted:

> Even if casual conversations are important, remarrying spouses should go beyond the romantic talks, discussing their ex-spouses, discussing politics, or the weather, and focus on the topics that are more relevant to the establishment of successful remarriages for the partners and their significant others.

The other kind of communication, which encompassed the opinions of all the participants and their perceptions, is the need for in-depth communication between the partners. According to all the participants, in-depth communication consists of taking the risk to discuss emotionally charged topics that most remarrying parents feel insecure to bring up into open discussions with their partners, and the issues remain unresolved. Examples of such issues that all the participants mentioned included money in second marriages, religion, sexuality, relationships with in-laws, unresolved issues from the previous marriage, stepparenting, relationship with their former spouses, pending credit debts, and death. Hilda added that it is also important for divorced parents contemplating remarriage to discuss any histories of mental illness, sub- stance abuse, and domestic violence.

In agreement with the reviewed literature, the participants expressed the need for a validating and interactive process in contrast to avoidant and volatile communication (Burleson & Denton, 1997; Gottman, 1994b;

241

Johnson & Greenberg, 1994). Communication is one the most important ingredients of marital success (Gottman, 1994a; Kiura, 2004; LeBey, 2004; Nichols, 1996). The participants identified communication as one of the primary factors of remarriage stability and satisfaction.

According to Yalom (1985), communication is an on-going process in relationships because people keep on communicating (Kiura, 2004). Likewise, five participants who reported that they were still angry at their former spouses said that even if they tried their best to have no face-to-face interactions with their ex-spouses, the efforts they were making to maintain the silence had become for them like another means of keeping the communication in place with ex-spouses. In light of this, divorced parents contemplating remarriage and those who are already in remarriages should be aware of their constant communication with their significant others, with special regard to the risk of prolonged silences, especially if there are ongoing conflicts and separations within their family systems (Papernow, 1998).

In order to reinforce communication between married spouses, and/or significant others, they need to know some of the major skills of effective communication and to be able to express themselves to their partners. Additionally, Charles emphasized that the perception of good communication requires:

> Every spouse's willingness to be a good listener and ability to learn how to communicate effectively, honestly, constructively, timely, in an appropriate space, in the right manner, with empathy and reduced risk of jumping to conclusions

These observations are also mentioned in the literature about marital communication (Gottman et al., 1976; Kiura, 2004; LeBey, 2004). Kiura (2004) observed: "Couples can injure each other in the vain attempt to resolve conflicts. When this happens, matters become worse while the problem precipitating the conflict remains unresolved."

The participants identified the couple's abilities to resolve conflicts as one of the factors influencing stability and satisfaction in marriage. Some of the skills that the participants recommended after having found them helpful in their marriages included knowing how to channel anger constructively, discerning when to speak and when to keep one's mouth shut, being respectful of one another – even in the midst of strong differences of opinion, and the courage to deal with the problem in a timely fashion without attacking the other person or projecting all the blame onto oneself.

Jean made the following recommendation:

> Communication; be able to adopt to each other's lifestyle; be willing to compromise, be tolerant of one another (no one is perfect); listen, have faith in God; and respect each other.

George:

> Because my wife and I agreed on our destination, we could pull together in the same direction, although how we wanted to get there needed discussion and working out. We spent a good amount of time communicating, back and forth. We strove to listen to each other, paying attention, wanting to understand and value what the other was saying, and not to come up with a counterargument. It was more important for us to find the truth than for one of us to "win" in making decisions. Agreeing that growing in Christian character was important, we put caring for one another and our children ahead of "getting ahead" financially. Self-sacrifice was an essential ingredient for manifesting love to each other, bearing a cost personally to benefit the other. So was mercy.

While it wasn't major in the sense of putting our marriage in jeopardy, I did cause my wife significant distress in two areas. One was saying she could be more attractive to me if she lost weight after bearing our children. I had put my desire for a physically attractive wife before my wife's need to know that I found her attractive, with the confidence and security that would give her. I repented; she forgave. I am much better at complimenting her, but the hurt of the past still lingers in her soul. I can hear it in her voice when she recounts it. A second area was the way I allowed anger to dictate how I treated and disciplined our children. I was not about to spoil my children by sparing the rod. Here too, I repented and changed my behavior, and gradually they came to see that the change was real, and they forgave.

Doris:

GENUINE APPRECIATION: We express genuine appreciation for the other daily. Our most common exchange is NOT "I love you." Rather, it is "Thank you." We try never to take the other   person for granted, and acknowledge simple as well as extraordinary contributions and kindnesses.

PROMPT RESOLUTION OF DISAGREEMENTS: We don't go to bed angry. Now and then, something is said that feels hurtful, or something does not happen as one of us feels it should. We work hard not to let bad feelings fester, and try to clear the air before sleep – sometimes when lights are   out and we don't have to make eye contact. We try to give "I" messages when explaining the upset: "When you said _____,   I   felt   _____,   because _____."

By focusing on how we felt in the situation, we take responsibility for our own reaction, and allow our partner to enter and see our perspective without feeling attacked. It is still hard to hear, but putting things on the table in this way allows us to talk it through and resolve – sometimes with an apology, and sometimes with a promise to take some necessary action to right the wrong. Nothing gets a pass. We deal with issues and move on, trusting that the partner has listened in a caring way, and will be more careful/considerate next time. And time has proven the trust to be well-founded. We don't let each other down.

Lea:

Quality communication. Talking about what we need, when we need it by and how we plan to get it. If you do not voice your concerns or project ahead, it can build that anxiety of never getting anything accomplished. If you are feeling like you're accomplishing things together, you feel more confident in your relationship.

Anne:

Definitely communication, I would say that is number 1. It is necessary to talk things through, to understand one another, and sometimes to compromise. Even after being married for 38 years there are still misunderstandings. I often respond "I thought you knew me better than that", but I still have to clarify comments, responses, and my actions sometimes. Being friends is important and working together. A good marriage is an effort; you always have to work at it, putting the other person first before yourself. Keep each other a priority, and maintain respect for one another. It's always fun to do things with someone else, and a commitment of marriage gives you that reassurance.

Albert:

- Don't say anything you can't take back

- Stand up for yourself but consider your spouse and her feelings

- Your part of the marriage is yours to uphold no one else is responsible but you

- You don't have to win (all the time)

- Stick it out, not all arguments are the end

Miguel, when asked to identify what helps him to avoid the risk of his marriage relationship to become a boring routine, he responded: "Catching up, creating spaces for communication, being intentional to dedicate time for family."

My experience

Based on what you have read in this session, reflect on your own personal experience.

1. What communication skills have I been able to implement and which have helped me and others to get the needed win-win results?

   _____

2. Which communication skills do I want to learn and implement in dialogues and/or conversations in order to improve my communication with the significant people in my life?

   _____

3. What are the advantages of communication in life and specifically in marriage?

   _____

4. Which factors of marriage stability and satisfaction identified in this book do I need to communicate about in greater detail with my partner and/or other significant people in my life?

   _____

5. What are the specifics of each factor that need to be resolved?

   _____

6. How can I engage in difficult conversations and say what I mean without making enemies in the process?

   _____

7. What benefits have I realized by asking more questions than making commands / demands when communicating with others?

   _____

8. What strategies am I going to use in marriage to maintain face-to-face communication other than relying primarily on technological means (e.g., e-mails, telephone and texting)?

   _____

9. What do I need to do to help the other(s) hear clearly and understand what I am saying?

   _____

10. What are my set ways of listening, attitudes and/or behavior patterns that I portray to help the other person know that I am hearing and understanding what he/she is saying?

   _____

11. What makes me think/feel that I am communicating with my partner effectively?

_____

12. What do I need to listen and understand what the other(s) is/are saying?

_____

13. How can I determine that my partner is showing mutual respect?

_____

14. Am I more of a talker or a listener?

_____

15. What do I need to become more of?

_____

16. What areas mentioned in this book and/or occurring in our marriage relationship do my partner and I need to discuss, resolve or negotiate before it is too late?

_____

17. How are we going to arrange our schedules in order to set aside quality time each day to speak with each other without other distractions (e.g., TV, cell phones, sports and computers)?

_____

———————◆•◆•◆•◆•◆———————

Keys to communication

As keys are important to open doors, consider the following keys to communication.

- Values and opportunities for informal and in-depth communication

- In case of on-going conflicts with ex-spouse, avoid the risk of getting children caught up in the midst of those conflicts

- Each partner should know that he or she may have the right answers or words, but may have to hold back to avoid the risk of speaking with anger

- Listen and learn from another person's point of view

- Be aware and accept that every marriage involves some level of conflict

- Learn some conflict resolution skills and practice them (e.g., be patient, give yourself time to think through the issues)

- Establish clear boundaries and guidelines with your children so that they do not break your remarriage in the dream of getting you together with your former spouse.

- Take into account the child's age while communicating about your marriage arrangements

- Be aware of the challenges in marriage related to children (e.g., children with special needs as they create a lot of stress on a marriage)

- Avoid behaviors that influence your children to live in conflict of loyalty situations between you and your spouse (e.g., putting children in the middle of your on-going / unresolved conflicts with your spouse)

- Timely communication of feelings (e.g., if one is hurt by the other spouse, the hurt party should let the other person know that he or she has been hurt in less than 48 hours)

- Complexity of marriage is important to know about before marriage

- Dating while simultaneously parenting may be difficult and emotionally charged

- Difficulty in finding a name to address the stepparent, his or her title, and roles

- Communicate clearly with your spouse about how to discipline and reward children (and stepchildren)

- Keep in contact with the other biological parent and decide how to celebrate future events

Gottman et al. (1976) observed that communication between spouses was a very fundamental ingredient in marital stability. Its absence and the lack of communication skills created a real danger to marital stability, dialogue, and decision-making. Gottman and collaborators drew a general hypothesis that couples who have poor communication may not be able to work collaboratively and they tend to send contradictory messages to their children (Richmond, 1995; Russell-Chapin et al., 2001).

Non-dialoguing spouses are likely to find it more difficult to maintain harmonious relationships, to negotiate about money, friends, religion, sexual expression, work, relaxation time, and parenting roles than dialoguing spouses (Gottman et al., 1976; Nichols, 1996). Likewise, depressed individuals who know communication skills but lack motivation are inclined to communicate negative information (Burleson & Denton, 1997; Gottman & Silver, 1999).

- Usefulness of flexibility: Becoming attentive listeners

Partners need to make a paradigm shift which involves a consistent practice of empathic listening and understanding what the other is really saying. According to Covey (1989) most people typically seek first to be understood by the person or people they are talking to but it is difficult for them to listen with an equivalent amount of intent to understand what the speaker is saying. That is, while the other person is speaking, most people listen with the intent to reply. Most often, during a conversation, these kinds of people are either speaking or preparing to speak. Hence, there is a need for learning and practicing basic communication skills.

Many people apparently seem to be listening, but in actuality they are filtering everything through their own paradigms and reading their autobiographies into other people's lives (Covey, 1989; Ferch, 2001). Therefore, exploring some of the realities and challenges experienced by currently married parents may provide some pathways to improve marriage stability and satisfaction.

Study Session 15

Domestic violence prevention and treatment

31 Do to others as you would have them do to you. (Luke 6:31)

In order for the marriage to be both stable and satisfactory, domestic violence has to be prevented and wherever applicable be treated. Before continuing with this study session, it is important to recall and/or reread what Paul (one of the participants) mentioned about the domestic violence his mother suffered at the hands of his father and how in his first years of marriage he was violent to his wife. Paul is credited for mentioning one of the difficult challenges in many families but which sometimes remains hidden to others and most likely is perpetuated from one generation to another generation within families. Sometimes, two or more family members gang-up against another family. Domestic violence is not genetic. It is a learned behavior and as such, it can be prevented and unlearned.

Domestic violence may briefly be described as an intentional infliction of pain by one or more members to another family member or other within the same household. There are diverse categories of DV. These include but not limited to physical, verbal, emotional, sexual, financial, food deprivation, and spiritual abuse. The one who inflicts the pain is referred to here as the perpetuator and the one who suffers is referred to as the victim.

Paul's revelation of domestic violence manifests the long-standing tradition whereby men have been the perpetuators and women as the victims. However, most recent research studies also indicate that there is an increasing number of men as the domestic violence victims and the women as the perpetrators (Thureau, et al., 2015). Results based on research studies indicate that the prevalence rates of domestic violence, including physical violence, against men by women in heterosexual relationships. Some of these men were abused or maltreated in their childhood and/or adolescence. as children. Additional factors which influence the prevalence of domestic violence include, but not limited to: alcohol use, substance use, pathological jealousy, mental disorders, emotional problems as well as physical impairment. alcohol and/or illegal drugs (Muelleman & Burgess, 1998).

Paul highlighted also that his father was more violent to his mother while his father was under the influence of alcohol. This also reflects the findings that DV tends to be heightened by perpetrators who are abusers of alcohol and/or addicted to other illegal substances (Muelleman & Burgess, 1998).

Consequently, one of the ways of preventing DV is by partners and other family members avoiding addiction to alcohol, drugs, power and control. Treatment of domestic violence in such cases involves the treatment of the addictions, participation in anger management programs and psychotherapy for the perpetrators and victims. Establishing a safety plan is very important for the victims (e.g., focused on self-esteem, empathy and incarceration of the perpetuators.

Study Session 16

5 … clothe yourselves with humility in your dealings with one another, for:

"God opposes the proud

but bestows favor on the humble.

6 So humble yourselves under the mighty hand of God, that he may exalt you in due time. (1 Peter 5: 5 – 6)

Description of conflict resolution

Partners in intimate relationships, especially in remarriage settings, need to understand and accept that given the complexity of remarriage as described in this book conflicts are likely to arise in stepfamilies. Some of the causes, risks and importance of conflict and an exploration of how it may be resolved will be considered in this section. Conflict is an interpersonal antagonism that occurs whenever one's values, actions, behaviors, desires, expectations, customs, points of view, traditions, priorities, interests, rules, power struggle and/or other interaction dynamics interfere with those of another person or group of people. Consequently, if the interference is not resolved using adequate means and in a timely fashion, the conflict may lead one or more people in a remarriage situation experiencing psychological pain and misunderstanding. This may eventually escalate into withdrawal, open verbal attacks, depression, anger outbursts, domestic violence, separation, physical/ emotional abuse, divorce and/or death.

Therefore, it is important that partners in remarriage settings and other close family members plan on how they can reduce the risks of entering into conflict and do their best to resolve each conflict before it is too late. Some of the significant strategies they may use to achieve these goals may include, but are not limited to, setting ground rules of how to handle conflict (e.g., avoid attacking each other), learning some conflict resolution skills (e.g., deal with one issue at a time at an appropriate time), and being committed to finding a solution to the conflict. It is important to reach a consensus that enables the two partners or the individuals involved within a remarriage setting to process their available options, to choose the one(s) which they can mutually agree on, and then to be bound to follow through. All in all, conflict resolution requires the establishment of middle ground and a win-win situation for the parties involved.

Experience of others

Lee mentioned:

> There are many man-made problems which are rooted in arrogance, superiority complex, power struggle, dominance, pride, ignorance, dishonesty, inferiority complex and other vices which have a very detrimental effect in interpersonal interactions, including between people in marital and family situations. Some problems and conflicts can be prevented but most often than not people seek help when it is too late. Therefore, married partners and family members need to acquire the skills for prevention,

solve them in a spirit of humility, as well as learn how to cope with those which cannot be completely resolved.

Several participants stated that some conflict was inevitable and necessary to stay happily remarried. Felicia clarified:

My [second] husband is a very peaceful gentleman, and both of us communicate very well. Nevertheless, however much we love one another, it is hard for us to live together without some moments of conflict between us. Once in a while, we have our arguments, but even then, we respect one another.

Elaborating on conflict in his remarriage, Henry said:

Although it is sometimes very hard for my wife and I to maintain personal integrity during moments of conflict, whenever we resolve any given conflict, I feel good about myself, and we end up hugging one another. In a special way, I give credit to my wife because I have learned   from her better skills of handling and resolving conflicts than I used to do in the past. I used to scream and nag at my wife, children, and coworkers.

I have learned to slow down, try to control my anger, keep my mouth shut as I think through the issues; not speak in self-defense, nor project blame on my wife because sometimes no one is to blame. In fact, sometimes conflicts arise out of misunderstandings, so to put the blame constantly on the other person or to make myself guilty for something I am not responsible for is not healthy. Additionally, as I force myself to slow down and delay passing judgment, I start to feel more comfortable to listen to my wife's perspective and put into context the motivations that might have contributed to what she thinks, feels, says, does, does not say, or decides not to do. Currently, I have also learned the importance of practicing the conflict resolution skills I have learned. Otherwise, without practicing them, I would not be any better at all than before.

With a smile on her face, Dora mentioned:

The conflicts I had in my first marriage have helped me to believe that nothing bad happens without some good coming out of it. I also noticed that some conflicts have strengthened my relationship with my spouse. My experience of conflict in marital relationships is that, if conflict does not escalate into the death of one or both spouses, it can influence those involved to make decisions and take actions that lead to positive change. Looking back on my life, even if the conflicts I suffered in my first marriage brought me a lot pain and humiliation, they prepared me to become more tolerant and persevering in life, especially during the divorce process and as a single mother of five children.

Beatrice said:

I have realized that taking the time to understand the source or sources of our conflicts has helped me to learn better ways of how to handle and resolve conflicts with my husband. I have learned not to minimize conflicts because in every conflict someone feels hurt. I also learned in my remarriage not to turn every minor conflict into a big issue. In a special way, I recall the night when I screamed at my husband for coming home delayed for two hours later than usual. He did not call me to inform me that he would be late nor inform me by phone that something had happened to him. I got mad at him, started thinking and imagining things that I cannot tell you now.

Beatrice added that when he [her husband] came home:

I screamed at him, and I left him in the sitting room. I told him to go to another bedroom. To cut the long story short, he told me that he was stuck in traffic for over an hour after a deadly accident had occurred in front of him. He did not have his cell phone that day because he had forgotten it in his other coat. When I read about that fatal accident in the newspapers the next day, I felt very bad. Not so much about the victims, whom I did not know, but because of the guilt I was feeling for having been unkind to my husband without knowing the cause of his delay and lack of communication.

Two participants (a man and a woman) mentioned that they lacked competency in handling conflict, especially in their first marriages and in the first five years of their second marriages. They were interested in learning some conflict resolution skills and how to control their anger during moments of conflict, especially with their former spouses and stepchildren.

Daniel revealed:

Although I had learned the hard way how to handle conflict more effectively than when I was in my first marriage and during the first five years of remarriage, I eventually learned how to choose my battles and to express my feelings without intentionally hurting my ex-spouse and/or second spouse.

Three participants suggested that if the conflict escalates in frequency and/or anger becomes intensely uncontrollable by one or both spouses, adequate measures must be taken before people seriously hurt one another. In retrospect, thinking over what had helped them in some moments of conflict, those three participants suggested that they found it very helpful to seek professional help because they managed to control their anger by attending anger management programs and through timely communication of their feelings.

Based on personal experience, Felicia suggested: "Each spouse should know that he or she may have the right answers or words, but may have to hold back to avoid the risk of speaking with anger."

Dora also suggested: "In the case of ongoing conflicts with the ex-spouse, the biological parents should avoid the risk of getting children caught up into those conflicts."

Four participants mentioned the likelihood of conflict and/or ongoing expressions of abuse (i.e., physical, emotional, or verbal) in remarriage triad settings. However, one of the main problems highlighted by the participants is the lack of knowing the skills for resolving conflict and the ability to put them into practice during the moment of conflict.

Kiura (2004) observed: "Couples can injure each other in the vain attempt to resolve conflicts. When this happens, matters become worse while the problem precipitating the conflict remains unresolved."

When asked to identify some of the challenges/difficulties he faced at the beginning of his marriage, Miguel mentioned: "Lack of communication and not giving in; hard headed, not being able to understand the partner's perspective."

Miguel identified the following influencing factors for the stability and satisfaction he experiences in his marriage:

- Communication: Rather than keeping feelings and thoughts bottled, we have agreed to talk about an issue that produces disagreement or tension, no matter how hard it may be.
- Acceptance / Tolerance: We have learned to accept each other with our virtues and weaknesses instead of trying to change each other.

259

- Forgiveness: We cannot hold grudges toward each other because we would live resentful

Ted discussed some of the challenges he faced in his married life and how they worked together to resolve them.

My wife's mother refused to give us her blessing for marriage. We were ostracized from most family functions. My wife chose me over her family. I knew that was not easy for her to do. We were unable to have biological children of our own.

I lost my job of twenty-two years when I turned forty. I was an emotional wreck. My spouse, who was a full-time mom, immediately called her old boss and went back to work full-time. I started my own business, while my wife supported me. She never complained or judged me.

Our daughter became pregnant at 15. She delivered our first grandchild at 16. It's easy to be Pro-Life when it's someone else's baby. Not so easy when it's your teenage daughter. We both were happy that my daughter decided to keep the baby. She knew she was adopted and didn't want to do that to her daughter. My spouse immediately quit her job and stayed home so my daughter could complete her high school education. Finances were tough for a while, but we got through it.

Albert identified the following challenges in his marriage and how they were resolved:

My wife's need for control was difficult in the beginning but worked itself out as we grew together.

The birth of a son having disabilities. We did most aspects of learning together and supported each other. We handled each challenge specifically and we each did what we could.

Charles

The difficult times we both experienced were the 8 years we spent childless; we did everything we could possibly do to have a child, but nothing was happening! We coped with that situation and it was beginning to create a problem but as a result of our continued prayers, God answered our prayers by showing us another way we could handle our problem, and that way worked very perfectly and as a result our son was born.

Anne mentioned:

It was hard to make time for each other since we were so busy with the kids, but then again, we formed a close family unit because we believed in raising them ourselves; family was priority. We did things with friends, but most of the time we did things with just our immediate family.

Post-wedding surprises

Problem solving should also include strategies for resolving post-wedding surprises and challenges. Jean described the following post-wedding surprise and challenging experiences, which she encountered after the wedding:

My sexual life became hard when after a year of marriage my husband had to go away in boarding school for further studies for two years. That was hard time but my relatives kept visiting with me and kept me company. He finished school and we enjoyed each other for one year. Then he pursued studies abroad. That was hard again. This time his siblings sent me kids to keep me company. One year after heading abroad for studies he had an accident that left him paralyzed and had to use a wheelchair. That was hard and put a close on sexual life. I longed on having children but the accident seemed to have put an end to that hope. Acting as a maid rather than a wife was hard but had to be done due to the love we both had for each other before the accident. I can say prayers and my family support sustained the marriage.

Ted

Most of her family rejected us. It made it easier at holidays. We always went to my family functions. After 25 years, he phoned his daughter (my wife) and said can we have your mom's 70th birthday party at our house because it was a surprise and his house wasn't big enough. She hadn't spoken to her mother for over 25 years, (here's where the "not holding a grudge thing" comes into play), my wife immediately said yes, knowing that I would support any decision she made. The party went off without a hitch. Later, we were to find out that my wife's father had come down with cancer and was dying. My wife, a nurse, was able to be with him as he died. That brought great comfort to be with him.

My experience

Based on what you have read in this session, reflect on your own personal experience.

1. In what areas do I have difficulty handling conflict?

   _____

2. Whom do I have most conflicts with and what do we argue about?

   _____

3. What types of conflicts do I tend to minimize and do they eventually turn into greater problems within myself and/or with others?

   _____

4. What types of conflict resolution skills do I usually use and are they really effective without hurting myself and others?

   _____

5. What are the conflict resolution skills I have learned from the participants and other sources that I am going to implement in my life and interactions with others?

6. What surprises have you experienced in your marriage and how have you resolved them?

   _____

———————◆•◆•◆•◆•◆———————

Keys to conflict Resolution

As keys are important to open doors, consider the following keys to conflict resolution.

- Stop minimizing conflicts

- Resolve conflict from a win-win stance

- Avoid a superiority or inferiority stance while resolving conflict

- Learn to use "I" statements

- Focus on the problem and how to resolve it without attacking the other or blaming oneself or the other

- Take responsibility for actions, feelings and behaviors

- Learn to negotiate with tact and respect

Study Session 17

This is the "One" I am going to marry

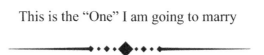

Some of the participants shared with the author some of the difficulties they encountered in deciding on the specific person to marry.

Christine mentioned:

> Deep within my heart I knew I wanted to become married but the unresolved question was: Married with whom? This question bothered me so much after listening to some of the stories of my friends who were married and were not happy living with their choice of spouse. Surprisingly, one day, I thought of the emotional investment I had put into buying my new car and that inspired me to invest my efforts into choosing the man I would like to be my husband and the father of my children. It is not my intention to compare buying a car to searching for a spouse. This analogy may not work for other people, but it worked for me.

> Me being me, I know what I need and what I don't. I knew which model of car I wanted and why as well as the ones which I did not want and why. Consequently, I did my kind of 'shopping list' for the qualities I would like in a man, I divided it into the negotiables and the non-negotiables. Again, some of my negotiables may be non-negotiables for another person and vice versa. For instance, becoming a mother, if God and nature allow it, is unnegotiable for me. However, the height of the man, though it may be good that he is a bit taller than me, it is negotiable and both of us agree with each other's non-negotiables.

Therefore, after making my list, I started to search and gave the same list to a few trusted friends to help me find the qualities I was looking for in man. Six months later, a friend recommended someone to me. I told my friend to ask the recommended person to write a list of his negotiables and non-negotiables before arranging for us to meet. Thanks to God, I have to say, he wrote it and in two months we starting dating. Two years later, we celebrated our wedding and we are happily married. I also know that some people change and/or reveal their true colors after marriage, but I also believe that putting in writing our individual 'shopping lists' and discussing them together made things easier and more effective for us, and our 'match-maker.'

On the other hand, Eric was one of the participants who mentioned that as soon as he saw Maggie (fictitious name) in a supermarket, he instantaneously said to himself: "This is the woman I'm going to marry."

Likewise, Raquel mentioned that she felt the strong conviction and peace of mind as soon as she first saw Willy (fictitious name) at the university. She elaborated: "Beyond reasonable doubt, as soon as I saw, Willy, I knew in my own heart that he was the 'One' for me."

Both Eric and Raquel expressed their joy of the "instant chemistry" they felt at meeting their respective spouses. Both participants informed the author that their love at first sight was accompanied by experiences of inner peace, trust, conviction and hope for the best. Each immediately did his /her best to get the telephone number of the person who had attracted his/her attention. By the time the author asked Eric and Raquel to participate in responding to his questionnaire for this book, Eric and Maggie had just celebrated their forty-fifth wedding anniversary while Raquel and Willy had just celebrated their twelfth wedding anniversary.

On the other hand, participants like Doris, took a lot of time to discern the qualities of their respective future spouses. For example, when asked to describe the factors which helped Doris to become convinced that "Jack" was the person with whom she should get married to, she gave a detailed list of what contributed to her final conviction and resultant decision to get married with Jack. Doris mentioned:

From my observations, and our many discussions, I knew, he (Jack):

- Respected women. He was always very polite and a gentleman. I remember thinking that I would like his mother when we first met. She had taught him well

- Expected me to have and pursue my own work

- Was smart, curious, fun to be with, interesting, and able to make me laugh in unexpected ways

- Was not afraid to work hard and expected to succeed

- Was calm, balanced, fair, and a good problem-solver in a difficult situation

- Spent his money carefully, and took care of his things

- Liked children (lots of beach time with my little neighborhood friends in Atlantic City) and could talk and play creatively with them. They liked him too

- Wanted a family

- Was able to call me out (nicely) on silly comments or behaviors – when he did this the first time, I decided this was almost enough reason to marry the man. It really impressed me that he cared enough to tell me I could do better, and that he did it in such a kind way

- Was largely uncomplicated. He said what he meant, and kept his word and commitments.

- Could hold his own in any intellectual conversation without being offensive

- Liked to sing, go camping, and spend time outdoors

- Had good friends whom I also liked

- Could fix things that were broken, and build things

- Was relaxed with my parents, siblings, and extended family. He was easy socially, and liked people

- Came from a nice family and extended family that welcomed me immediately and graciously, as soon as they saw we were getting serious

- Was interested in growing as a Catholic in a post-Vatican 2 world

- Liked Boston culture, music, museums, sports teams, and would be happy to stay there.

- Liked travel. Peace Corps exposed him to the world, and all kinds of food. He was respectful and appreciative of people from different races and cultures. He was a humble, rather than ugly American

- Was a considerate lover who had not had multiple partners (back to respecting women)

- Would never make me worry about how he presented himself, what he said or did, such that I would always be able to be proud of him. When I articulated this to myself, and recognized its importance.

Study Session 18

Religion, spirituality and faith in God

14 "Now, therefore, fear the LORD and serve him completely and sincerely. Cast out the gods your ancestors served beyond the River and in Egypt, and serve the LORD.

15 If it is displeasing to you to serve the LORD, choose today whom you will serve, the gods your ancestors served beyond the River or the gods of the Amorites in whose country you are dwelling. As for me and my household, we will serve the LORD."

16 But the people answered, "Far be it from us to forsake the LORD to serve other gods.

17 For it was the LORD, our God, who brought us and our ancestors up out of the land of Egypt, out of the house of slavery. He performed those great signs before our very eyes and protected us along our entire journey and among all the peoples through whom we passed.

18 At our approach the LORD drove out all the peoples, including the Amorites who dwelt in the land. Therefore we also will serve the LORD, for he is our God." (Joshua 24: 14 – 18)

Jean stated that her religious and spiritual background has impacted her in many positive ways in her marriage: For instance, she mentioned:

My religious background has helped me keep the marriage going. Focusing on (Life After Death), facing God and wanting to be in heaven with my fore family members keep me in line and I pray daily.

George identified practices that he thought are important:

- Having a common vision and faith

- Communicating well and often with each other

- Being willing to work hard, and to serve the other

- Taking the other person seriously, and oneself not so much

- Agreement for wife to stay home to care for the children, and so to live frugally on one salary

- Having fun together

- Enjoying just being in the other's presence. Neither of us was absent to the other due to overbearing outside interests

- Humility to repent when I've done something wrong or hurt another, and graciousness to forgive readily

- Coming to realize that mercy is a necessary component of justice

- Responding with a sense of humor when things get difficult, but not being flippant or dismissive

Description of spirituality in marital situations

As keys are important to open doors, consider the following keys to spirituality.

- Acknowledgment of the existence of God as Almighty, Creator, Loving, a Spiritual Being, who is interested in the lives of all people as one family and as individuals

- Ability to enter freely into a relationship with God, especially through prayer and spiritual reading, hymns and songs of praise, spending time in adoration, contemplation and meditation

- Commitment to a communal and/or personal spiritual experience and journey of faith

- Acknowledging the religious traditions in family of origin, praying together as a family, participating in religious ceremonies and entrusting our lives to God

- Making use of spiritual values within the religion that one is affiliated with and passing those values on to the next generation

- Turning to God who heals the broken hearted and offers forgiveness

- Understanding the impact of divorce and remarriage on devout Catholics

- Searching for God's blessing on the couple's wedding date and asking for God's continued graces daily

- Giving thanks to God for small and big things in our lives

All participants reported that painful experiences in their divorce had brought them closer to God, especially during those moments when they had to make their hardest decisions as to whether or not to divorce. All the participants (including the two males who had denied belonging to any formalized religion) stated that spirituality played a great role in their remarriage stability and satisfaction.

Elaborating on marital spirituality, Kiura (2004) noted: "Marriage is a relationship of love... The spirituality of marriage will therefore be as good as the personal spirituality of the individual spouses... The first neighbor in a marriage relationship is one's spouse... It is impossible to love God without loving the neighbor... Basic spirituality for a married couple consists in loving God through each other in the hustle and bustle of daily life. This includes forgiving each other here and now for past failures and mistakes…. [and] ending each day by praying together and reading the Scripture. This will provide the couple with resources to handle their human problems with greater insight and understanding."

Experience of others

Elías was a participant who did not identify himself with any religion. He shared his insights on spirituality and religion and how he expressed the influence of spirituality on his remarriage stability and satisfaction. Elías stated:

> Whenever I have to make a decision in my marriage or any other major decision in life, I have to pray first. I give witness that God listens to my prayers whenever I pray…. In my life, I consider spirituality a great inspiration for living an ethical life. I believe that that supernatural power blesses my marriage and family. I perceive this supernatural power to be compassionate, inclusive, transcendent, and infinite.

Even if Elías reported not belonging to any formalized religion, he made the following remark:

> Having no church to go to is a bad thing. Any religion, if well understood and practiced by its believers in the right way, can be a profound source of faith, solidarity, unity for its members, improvement of peoples' lives in their marriages and family life. Religions are good sources of hope and meaning to people, especially if they do not become breeding grounds for dirty politics. Religions are a means of transmitting God's mercy, love and forgiveness, compassion, and hope for eternal life with God.

Most of the Catholics who participated in this study expressed that faith in God had played a significant role in their remarriages. It had empowered them in many ways, especially during the most painful moments of their lives, during the process of divorce, and its aftermath. On the other hand, to illustrate how spirituality was a significant factor in the lives of the Catholic participants, many did not seek annulments from the Catholic Church before they remarried. Consequently, they went to ask for God's blessing for their marriages in front of a religious minister of another religious denomination.

A typical example of a couple's remarriage celebrated by a minister of another religion was that of Charles and his wife Julia. Charles stated that God had a very profound place in his life. He described Julia as a very spiritual woman. According to Charles, he and his wife did all that was possible to have their marriage blessed by a Catholic minister before they started living together. Both of them were divorced Catholics and it was very difficult for them to remarry in the Catholic Church before receiving an annulment from their previous marriages. They tried to get the annulments, but they could not get them by the time of their anticipated marriage.

In pain and frustration of not being able to get married in the Catholic Church, Charles agreed with his wife-to-be to seek God's blessing from an Episcopalian minister. Five years later, they received the annulments. Their marriage was then validated in the Catholic Church. This made them very happy, and since then they became actively involved in their church and have conducted pre-remarriage talks for 10 years to divorced Catholics preparing for remarriage.

According to many participants, spirituality was described as a resource that had contributed in one way or another to their remarriage stability and satisfaction. It has helped them to find meaning and purpose and has kept them in close connection with a Transcendent Being whom they identified as God. All participants expressed their belief in the spirit of God empowering them to live by their marriage commitments, learning to love other people, and forgiving those who had hurt them in one way or another, especially their former spouses. Many participants also described how spirituality had motivated them to improve their behavior in their everyday lives. Additionally, spirituality was a resource for them in their remarriages because it was helpful in motivating them to live morally better lives. By the same token, they were able to distinguish between good and bad ways of acting in interpersonal relationships with their family members, community, and society at large.

All female participants and most males stated that God had a very special place in their remarriages. Some of the ways they had been able to strongly experience God's presence included holding onto prayer, hope, searching for forgiveness from God for the mistakes they felt they had committed as wives or husbands, and as parents against their children.

Catherine remarked:

> I owe a lot of thanks to God for the success of my remarriage. I remember waking up at night and kneeling down to ask for God's guidance and strength when my remarriage was going through a very difficult financial situation. My husband started to have misunderstanding with his brothers and their business almost broke down, yet at that time I was not working. Surprisingly, a month later I got a job, and my husband's relationship with his brothers improved. Their business improved from loss to gain.

Many participants mentioned that turning to God and to their church ministers, and/or to the faith community were also resources for them and were bringing them God's solace, particularly during the moments of discouragement and frustration in their second marriages. They also realized that spirituality was affecting them in their decision-making process. In fact, belonging to a religious denomination and being an active member within one's church were reported by many participants to be significant influences on remarriage stability and satisfaction.

Many participants reported that belonging to a church community was beneficial for them. Each one of them acknowledged the social support he or she received. In a special way, most female participants appreciated the community support especially during the divorce process, mourning divorce, financial difficulties, strong feeling of ambiguity about dating again and remarriage.

One of the participants who elaborated on the importance of spirituality and belonging to a supportive religious community was Henry. After his divorce, he continued to go to church and did a lot of volunteer work in the Catholic Church with other parishioners. Three years later, his parish priest and other committee members in the parish started making arrangements for him to work in close contact with a single woman interested in meeting someone to marry. As anticipated, the two of them started dating, got married, and by the time of the interview they had been together for eight years. All in all, Henry spoke with admiration about how a supportive religious community had helped him on his spiritual journey and helped him meet his second wife, whom he described as "very spiritual, community oriented, and very compassionate."

Dora elaborated on the quality of spirituality in remarriage. She was an active member in her church and her faith was evident as she expressed herself during the interview. She stated:

> Spirituality and action are inseparable. That is why I think that any married man who believes in God should also treat his wife with respect. If he makes a mistake, he should learn to apologize. I feel men should learn to say "sorry" or at least should admit their mistakes and talk about them with their wives. I am concerned about the spirituality of many men because men in general do not admit their mistakes and that affects their marriages negatively.

Furthermore, Dora stated that spirituality goes beyond the mere fact of belonging to a formalized religion and going to a religious building for prayers. Dora made this observation:

> Some people go to church and just pray, and some of them are not as good as they are in the church. Outside of the church building, they do the things they are not supposed to do as churchgoers. So I believe, if there is a God, I know He is happy with me because I try to help. I always try to do the best, do the correct thing, … I taught my kids too.

As noted in the reflections of Adams (1980) and Kiura (2004) on spirituality and marital life, all the participants mentioned that spirituality was a very significant factor influencing their remarriage stability and satisfaction. Two participants clarified that, even if they did not belong to any formalized religion, spirituality was one of the greatest sources of empowerment in their remarriages. Based on the input of the other participants who identified their religions as resources contributing to spirituality, as well as the input of the other two, it seems that that spirituality and religion are not mutually exclusive (Miller, 1999). Marital spirituality seemed to go beyond the boundaries and norms within the participants' religions.

The central message that could be derived from the way all the participants described their remarriages was as a covenant or bond with a Supernatural Power (whom they identified as God). The participants were doing their best to integrate some of their experiences of the characteristics they attributed to God into their remarriages and relationships with their significant others.

Two participants, Grace and Geoffrey expressed additional resounding statements based to their spiritual beliefs. Grace stated: "I believe in a God of love, forgiveness, and who wants us to love our neighbors, and to forgive those who have offended us. Inspired by this belief, I forgave my ex-husband."

Geoffrey mentioned: "One of the reasons I remarried was because God said in the Bible that it is not good for man to be alone. So, after my divorce, I did not want to stay alone.

Doris mentioned:

> Marriage is a sacrament, until death do you part. It should be taken seriously, for better or for worse, in sickness and in health. It is a commitment. I don't see it any other way being raised in a devout Catholic home. I had good examples through my parents.

George:

My wife and I are both Roman Catholics and intentional disciples of Jesus Christ. His way of life directs us. I'd say the only problems came from teachings that we accepted that were skewed in some way, or perhaps misinterpreted or misapplied. To the extent that we lived them genuinely, they have been literally a "God-send." Also, knowing God's mercy for each of us personally enables us to extend mercy to others, thus restoring life to a damaged or hurting relationship.

We delight in our common faith as Catholics of the Roman and Apostolic Church; we appreciate one another and we delight in each other. We self-sacrifice to serve the other.

Common vision and faith. Having a common worldview allows us to have goals and priorities that we work toward together. While we may have to work out how to get there, the destination is shared. Appreciation for and delight in the other. Knowing that the world is better having my spouse in it, that my life is better for having him/her by my side. Demonstrating that belief by showing affection, care and gratitude. Self-sacrifice to serve the other. You prove your appreciation by serving the other despite the cost to oneself, understanding that by loving others we most become who we are meant to be, rather than by putting oneself first.

Marie:

God's grace – many women have the same convictions about marriage and their home as I do. Many women have worked hard and yet through no fault of theirs, their marriages ended. I have been with my husband since high school. Anything could have happened along the way. The grace of God has brought us this far. I am not the most prayerful or the most religious, it is the grace of God. The quote "There but for the grace of God go I" comes to mind.

Marriage is based on love for one another – love that should not be defined by how well one can keep house, cook, do laundry and bear children. If God's plan is to bless the marriage with children, then His will shall be done. If God's plan is to bless a couple in other ways with the exception of children, then let us have confidence in God's grace and accept his will and plan for our lives.

Human beings come together because they share common interests. Be it sports and other social activities, academic pursuits, work interests, physical abilities, etc. Marriage is no exception and requires a common understanding, interests, morals, beliefs, faith, etc. A common religious grounding clearly establishes some of the core attributes and characteristics that are desirable in a marriage partnership by setting expected standards through spiritual teachings, moral ethics, the ability to forgive, kindness, inner strength to go through life's challenges by leaning on a Greater Power. The Word of God is the law and sets the behavioral standard that makes it easier to regulate our behavior as a couple.

That said, my husband and I are yet to have a church wedding. However, our Christian upbringing makes us mindful of the instructions of the Bible regarding the roles of the husband and wife in a marriage. My husband has the final say in all decisions he wants to be involved in (as head of the home). We pray together and fast occasionally. When things get tough, we hang onto our faith to pull through together. The word of God gives us comfort and confidence, always.

The power of prayer (and fasting). Prayer changes things and gives us an opportunity to direct call God and unlock His grace and mercy upon us in His time. We often do not immediately see the answer to our prayers which are dispensed according to God's plan, but the deeper connection through prayer brings peace of mind while deepening our understanding and ability to wait for/receive/appreciate God's grace even when the situation seems overwhelming.

Marie and her husband lived apart due to professional obligations. She identified the following event in her marriage life through which she has found her faith in God to be a great resource in saving her marriage:

> My husband and I continue to live apart. My faith in God helps me to know that I am safe in my marriage.

Doris:

CONNECTION TO A SPIRITUAL FAMILY. Membership in our Institute in the Catholic Church in which the laity are associate members with the clergy has been a tremendous support to our marriage. Putting this spirituality at the center of our marriage and lives is a game changer. We are both committed to practice this spirituality, and help each other to improve our practice. We sometimes gently call each other out when we say or do something that strays from the practice.

Doris mentioned that religious and spiritual background impacted marriage stability and satisfaction as follows:

> It has helped enormously that we share a faith tradition. More importantly, however, is the fact that we share a commitment to develop our spiritual selves as part of our total growth and wellness (intellectual, emotional, physical, social, occupational) agenda. Our spiritual wellness matters, and centering our lives on a spiritual base has grounded us in our thinking and our behavior.

Andy mentioned that he realized God's intervention in regard to how he met and knew his wife. In brief he noted: "The good Lord ordered our steps and I rely on that, in the most difficult of times."

Additionally, Andy credits his faith and circumstances as the factors which helped him to became convinced of the person he was to be married to. He clarified:

- Faith: Trusting God for a life partner and I committed it to God in a prayer

- Analysis of my situation at that time

- Circumstances of our meeting and what I saw about her

- Conviction the day I opened my heart totally to her and was convinced I would trust her with my whole being. I didn't look back after that and she hasn't betrayed that trust.

Ellen stated:

> We (my husband and I) are both Catholic with Catholic school backgrounds. We take our marriage vows very serious and live them daily. We pray daily and live our lives trying to do good. We attend Mass weekly and enjoy being together in church.

Anna mentioned:

> Of course, our faith is a major contributor. God is a part of our marriage. We are committed to him and to each other. We wouldn't be where we are without him. We trust in him and follow his commandments. It's what we believe and how we've raised our children. We pray together (although I do more personal prayer), and attend church together. Many things can go unsaid because it's already understood. We were married in the Catholic Church and brought up the kids in the church. We always support our parish both financially and with our active involvement.

Miguel, when asked to describe briefly some of the events in his married life he has found his faith in God to be a great resource in saving your marriage, responded:

Through the loss (death) of some relatives, the Lord has been our strength. He has provided comfort and strength. Also, financially speaking, there have been some challenges. The Lord has been our Provider.

Sarah stated that her religious and spiritual background impacted her marriage stability and satisfaction because: "My religion taught me that you stand by your vows."

Doris:

Faith has nourished our marriage constantly. The marriage was never in jeopardy, however.

Two examples come to mind where the marriage teetered financially. What might have become a crisis, however, was only a wobble – a bump in the road. The first I have already discussed a little. When I lost my job, we quickly realized that we could turn to God and trust that we would be alright. We let go and let God. Similarly, I quit another job (earlier than my firing) and relocated with my family … We essentially went from 2 full salaries to a half salary – and just trusted that we would manage. We also trusted that God would help me find work when I returned.

Mateo:

The marriage is happy and full of love when it is:

- Christ centered marriage (if the marriage is Christ centered the bond will be stronger)

- When there is love for each other (Love means sacrifice for each other)

- Children (when the marriage is blessed with children)

- Our religious and spiritual background has helped us a lot and makes our family stronger with Christ

Mateo emphasized that the three influencing factors for his stability and satisfaction in marriage are:

- God, because being Christ centered marriage make our relationship stronger

- Love, because it makes us survive anything

- Family, because the family helps us (Mateo and his wife) to persevere to make the marriage work

Andy:

Our religion and spirituality have impacted our marriage very much. Although we both have different understanding of how the Christian practice should be carried out, but essentially, we are from the same kind of background and have a deep Christian faith. Talking for myself however, I am convinced in the direction of God. I believe He orchestrated my meeting my wife and in tough situations I question Him in silence but rely on the fact that He is all knowing and since He orchestrated things from the beginning. He is right. So, we move forward.

Andy added:

Believing in God to come to America so that the family can be together, even with less money is one of the events in which my faith in God has been a great resource in saving my marriage. It finally happened and I think the family being together is what has kept the marriage together, though it hasn't been easy.

Rowland:

We both were raised as Catholics, although the style and commitment of our parents' faith practice differed a lot. We had several strong Catholic couples as friends and godparents to our children. We also had close relationships with a few priests. We both wanted a strong parish experience for ourselves and our children and shopped around parishes to find it. This was yet another shared goal that we worked on. In some more traditional Catholic settings, our dual career lifestyle was criticized, our family planning discouraged, and archaic roles suggested as a better path to a successful marriage.

Regretfully, only one of our adult sons has a practicing faith. They are all good people, in stable marriages, and themselves raising good children.

Shared faith experience – we came from Catholic backgrounds and were involved in our parishes, especially around modeling faith for our children. Approaching and in retirement we have found more time to develop our faith.

Ted:

Having God in our life has a calming influence whenever there was a troubling time. Novenas said together helped us tremendously when we were trying to adopt. It also taught us patience. It took eight years to get our baby. We both go to church every Sunday and it seems that if we have a specific problem at the time, the sermon always seems to deal with that matter directly.

Praying Novenas together while trying to get pregnant and later in adoption very consoling.

Albert:

The guidance of my wife is the reason I have entered into and remained in a close relationship with my church. The requirements of my religion are a strong factor in moving on from hurtful situations and remaining married.

I have complete trust in my spouse, including her opinion and her needs, my religious beliefs, the love of my family.

- I trust what she does, what she says, and what she needs. I can count on her at anytime

- My religious beliefs are that we are two that became one person. Our bond is for life, and love is deeper than just how we "feel" about each other.

- My family is more important to me than my own life. All that I do is for them and that gives me joy.

Rowland:

There was never a period where I considered our marriage in such jeopardy as to need "saving". Having a faith in God was more important sometimes than others. The decline and death of parents (my father, my mother-in-law) who were living in our house in hospice care were times when faith was particularly important. We had to confront our own faith and support that of our children facing the unusually intimate death of a grandparent.

Charles:

- commitment to the sacrament of matrimony as instituted by our Lord Jesus Christ

- the love between the two of us

- respect for each other

Anna stated:

> I know that my religious and spiritual background have made our marriage stronger. We (my husband and I) pray for one another and support each other and you want the same thing for your spouse that you have, including your faith. You want to be with each other for eternity, including heaven, so you work at getting your spouse there with you. It's wonderful if you come from similar religious backgrounds, but if you have similar beliefs that can work too. Your parenting style and being a spouse has a lot to do with your beliefs, so that positive impact can only make it stronger and easier.

My experience

Based on what you have read in this session, reflect on your own personal experience.

1. How do I describe God in my own words?

   _____

2. What is spirituality for me?

   _____

3. What is spirituality for my partner?

   _____

4. What is spirituality for my children?

   _____

5. What is the usefulness of spirituality in my life, especially in regard to my divorce experience and/or remarriage?

_____

6. What key beliefs in my religion have helped me to develop a profound spirituality?

_____

7. What are the impediments to my spiritual journey?

_____

8. What are my beliefs about the annulment process in the Catholic Church and in the sight of God?

_____

9. What resources do I have that empower me to grow spiritually together with the people in my household?

_____

10. What are my beliefs about life after death?

_____

Study Session 19

Family of origin influences and resistance from external pressures

1 Now a man of the house of Levi married a Levite woman,

2 and the woman conceived and bore a son. Seeing what a fine child he was, she hid him for three months.

3 But when she could no longer hide him, she took a papyrus basket, daubed it with bitumen and pitch, and putting the child in it, placed it among the reeds on the bank of the Nile.

4 His sister stationed herself at a distance to find out what would happen to him.

5 Then Pharaoh's daughter came down to bathe at the Nile, while her attendants walked along the bank of the Nile. Noticing the basket among the reeds, she sent her handmaid to fetch it.

6 On opening it, she looked, and there was a baby boy crying! She was moved with pity for him and said, "It is one of the Hebrews' children."

7 Then his sister asked Pharaoh's daughter, "Shall I go and summon a Hebrew woman to nurse the child for you?"

8 Pharaoh's daughter answered her, "Go." So the young woman went and called the child's own mother.

9 Pharaoh's daughter said to her, "Take this child and nurse him for me, and I will pay your wages." So the woman took the child and nursed him.

10 When the child grew, she brought him to Pharaoh's daughter, and he became her son. She named him Moses; for she said, "I drew him out of the water." (Exodus 2: 1 – 10)

The phrase "Family of Origin" is used in this book to refer to the family in which one is born and raised, especially during the formative years of childhood, teenage years and young adulthood. Such a family may include one other person or more people who significantly influence one's life. These people maybe one's biological parent(s), sibling(s), grandparent(s), other relative(s), half-sibling(s), and other elders [e.g., adoptive or foster parent(s)].

One may not be aware of the impact of one's family of origin until he/she starts to live with another person. For instance, Lea mentioned:

> My parents divorced when I was two years old and I was raised by a single mother who was so obsessed with living in an 'immaculate house.' She would go to sleep at very late hours in the night because she had to make sure that every part of the house is clean, the dishes ae all washed and in order, and every corner of the house is sanitized. I made a secret wow to myself never to become so obsessed with cleaning the house until I started living with my husband who grew up in a household where cleanness was not observed. He would leave dishes in sink for hours and his shoe and socks were all over the house. Guess what, after two weeks of living together, I grew impatient with him, I thought of divorcing him and we had a very heated argument about his being dirty. As we argued, I was in admiration of my mother's clean house and mine had become a mess. Later on, my husband apologized for the disorder in the house and we made amends by promising each other to keep a very clean house.

Most of the participants attributed their stability and satisfaction in marriage to the lessons they learned from their families of origin and their past romantic experiences.

For instance, Mike recalled the phrase his father recited to him over and over: 'Live within your budget.'

Mike added:

> What we grew up observing in our homes impacts many people in how they see the world. People tend to predict their future based on the family they grew up in. Stable and happy couples tend to value marriage with those they grew up observing. Not everybody replays the family dynamics they grew up in, yet such influences tend to be very powerful in one's life.

Rowland:

> Support of extended families: We lived our professional/family rearing lives in and around Boston. Our parents had stable marriages and supported our marriage and family. A network of friends, mostly from church and professional connections, was also raising families, and provided support, advice, and occasionally child care, to allow us to function better as parents and professionals.

Andy:

> Persistence and resilience in spite of whatever: there are good times and hard times. I've faced financial crisis and work stress. My persistent wife reminds me of God's faithfulness. We have faced times of crisis, when spouses could call it quits but a persistent wife hangs on and prays. An encouraging and persistent wife is a blessing.

> Faith in God, through difficult times: remembering the reason for deciding and using that to increase faith that it is well.

> Cultural background: sometimes I realize there is a pressure to stick together as those around us too have stuck together. Having similar friends and friends in similar situations makes it difficult to pull away from each other. We attend birthdays together,

graduations together, church together and even when there is a crisis the events bring us together.

Sarah identified three major factors that have significantly impacted her marriage stability and satisfaction: namely, "a committed spouse, my children and other examples of strong marriage." She elaborated:

- My husband, because he is the backbone and strength of our family. He keeps me grounded.

- My children, they are the world to me.

- Examples of strong marriage in my family help to guide me.

Jean described the influences from their families of origin as follows:

My husband's adopted family was known as good faithful Catholic family who instilled family values to the children. I was a family lover, so I chose him to be the father of the children God would give us. Catholic teaching didn't believe in dating couples to engage in sexual activity before marriage, we obeyed that rule. I loved him and trusted him to keep the marriage vows.

He was employed and was performing his job very responsibly and had respect by his co-workers. My baby sister, 6 years old then, was living with me and he was willing to let me keep her with us. One of my goals was to assist my siblings get education and he was willing to help me on that goal. He could control time for socializing with his friends and would get home at a reasonable time. He trusted me by letting me socialize with friends.

Doris

SUPPORT OF "FAMILY." At key points, our parents and siblings assisted: with childcare breaks, help with our first mortgage, and sharing in the care of dying parents. Additionally, our "Faith Family" and "Extended Family by Choice" have journeyed with us and helped us through difficult times to become better people, better parents, better colleagues. Community has sustained us. We have never felt alone or abandoned.

Marie

Marriage can be rewarding and beautiful in so many ways. Your spouse (and children, if you wish to have any) will bring you lots of joy and pride that certainly make life worth living. They do not define who you are as marriage is not an achievement. It provides love, support, companionship, stability, protection, a sense of belonging and a natural sounding board. Two heads working to support each other, which brings to mind the saying that the total is greater than the sum of its parts.

My experience

What are the three fundamental qualities I admire from my family of origin?

_____

_____

_____

_____

What are the three things which I did not like in my family of origin?

_____

_____

_____

_____

What measures am I taking to prevent the things I did not want in my family of origin from negatively impacting my adult interpersonal relationships?

_____

_____

_____

_____

What strategies were positively practiced in my family of origin to resolve conflict?

_____

_____

_____

_____

How was money and other symbols of wealth handled in my family of origin?

_____

_____

_____

_____

What positive roles did faith play in my family of origin?

_____

_____

_____

_____

What negative influences from not practicing the faith play in my family of origin?

_____

_____

_____

_____

Study Session 20

Preparation for the wedding and celebration

————————•♦•♦•◆•♦•♦•————————

Preparation for the Wedding

As a Catholic priest of the Roman Rite, I (author of this book) have been involved in the preparing many engaged couples for marriage and also for the celebration of their weddings. Based on this pastoral experience for over twenty-five years, I have realized that many engaged couples spend a lot of time and resources preparing for the wedding and less time preparing for the marriage itself. Therefore, during these preparations, I ask these couples and discuss at length with the following five questions:

1. What is the difference between a wedding and a marriage?

2. What is the difference between preparing for a wedding and a marriage?

3. What is the importance of the wedding?

4. Why is it important to prepare for both the wedding and marriage?

5. What is the connection between the wedding and marriage?

I receive a lot of responses from the mentioned questions as well as different perspectives from men and women in terms of emphasis, who is more entrusted to doing what as well as insights which these couples come to realize only after being asked these questions. Some have reported that almost all their energies and resources were focused on preparing for the wedding: "Our Big Day!" On the other hand, it appears that more women than men come to the wedding preparations more invested than men and they tend to appear on the day of their wedding celebration very exhausted than most men. Could it be that the men are reserving most of their energies for the Honey Moon and/or the women are the ones handling most of the details for the wedding? I do not know.

All in all, it is important to prepare well for the wedding and marriage. The wedding is for one day and marriage is meant to be for a life time. The wedding day is a day to formalize the committed love the engaged man and woman have for one another, the day they officially BECOME HUSBAND AND WIFE, as well as the day they officially start their marriage journey, and the day which marks the constant point of reference for every wedding anniversary. Important as each external detail may be for the wedding preparation and celebration, the intra-personal and interpersonal preparations for each spouse are of paramount importance for the marriage to become stable and satisfactory. Therefore, this book has been designed to be a constant point of reference from the moment of discerning the vocation to marriage, finding a suitable partner and growing together as husband and wife to sharing Eternal Life together in Heaven with God.

Some of the participants cautioned the need for establishing a budget for the wedding and to honor it. Many couples spend a lot of money on the wedding, some with hopes of getting monetary gifts, yet to their surprise they do receive them as expected. Consequently, the couple incurs a lot of debt for the wedding and it is very hard to pay after the wedding.

Additionally, a significant number of participants emphasized the need for the partners to receive counseling before their wedding ceremony. This type of premarital counseling helps many partners to identify the main influencing factors of marriage which the partners have not addressed and/or are avoiding with hopes that by mistakenly believing that they will automatically be resolved after the wedding. It is important to have an objective third party encourage the partners before the wedding and marriage in order to address areas of conflict before it is too late.

Note: regarding how to prepare for the wedding and marriage in the Catholic Church, contact your parish office. You may also refer to the author's book: Stability and Satisfaction in Remarriage (3rd. Ed.) Part III, Role 3. Remarriage preparation in the Catholic Church (pages 224f). Though focused on remarriage, has a lot of insights for marriage preparation as well.

Study Session 21

Sexual education, family planning and sexual intimacy

4 When Sarah's parents left the bedroom and closed the door behind them, Tobiah rose from bed and said to his wife, "My sister, come, let us pray and beg our Lord to grant us mercy and protection."

5 She got up, and they started to pray and beg that they might be protected. He began with these words:

"Blessed are you, O God of our ancestors;

blessed be your name forever and ever!

Let the heavens and all your creation bless you forever.a

6 You made Adam, and you made his wife Eve

to be his helper and support;

and from these two the human race has come.

You said, 'It is not good for the man to be alone;

let us make him a helper like himself.'

7 Now, not with lust,

but with fidelity I take this kinswoman as my wife.

Send down your mercy on me and on her,

and grant that we may grow old together.

Bless us with children."

8 They said together, "Amen, amen!"

9 Then they went to bed for the night. (Tobit 8: 4-9)

Description of sexuality

All the participants highlighted that they entered their remarriages when they were chronologically older in comparison to when they entered their first marriages, and that that age difference had affected the frequency of their sexual expressiveness. Additionally, five participants above the age of 60 years indicated that they had started to struggle with the question of how to keep sexuality alive as a result of advancing in years.

Experience of others

All the participants emphasized that sexuality was one of the aspects that they wanted to continue to keep alive in their second marriages on the part of both partners. Some of the techniques used by the participants to maintain active sexual expressiveness with one another included the following:

Ten participants mentioned that they had developed a habit of dressing well. Accordingly, Elizabeth identified physical attraction as an integral part of marital stability and satisfaction. In fact, Elizabeth was the only participant out of the sixteen who mentioned physical attraction as a factor influencing both re- marriage satisfaction and stability. Elizabeth said:

If ... you are not physically attracted [to him or her], then you shouldn't be with that person. There has to be a reason why you connected to begin with.

Many participants mentioned that taking periodic honeymoons by going to a hotel (at least twice a year), and/or going to a different place by themselves as a couple were excellent ways to reinforce their remarriage stability and satisfaction. Two participants highlighted that watching sexually seductive movies together with their spouses was an influencing experience for them to feel motivated to engage in romantic activities in the privacy of their bedroom.

In regard to maintaining sexual expressiveness, several participants spoke of the practice of being tender with one another, doing activities together with their partners, eating together, sharing opinions, having sex for pleasure, and learning new techniques of how to position themselves during sexual intercourse. According to Daniel, changing such positions was helpful in overcoming the routine of having sex in the same position. Likewise, changing positions was helping him and his partner to improve their communication about which positions were more suitable for their sexual satisfaction. Hilda elaborated:

> Scheduling the time for having intimacy with my spouse has proven very practical. Due to the many activities that go on in our life as a couple, by the time we go to bed, we are very exhausted and have less energy to engage in sex. In fact, it is my experience that without scheduling sexual intercourse, especially for working and aging spouses, it is possible to let it go without intending it. Yet, genital intercourse is a very important activity that you cannot leave to the fate of spontaneity.

Rowland mentioned about comfortable intimacy as follows:

> We enjoy our sexual intimacy and the everyday signs of affection that reinforce our sense of caring for each other. We've always shared the same bed.

Hilda emphasized that sexual intercourse is an expression of mutual love for one another and can serve as a buffer in bad times. Consequently, she referred to "good sex as good glue" in remarriage.

On the other hand, Charles made this statement:

> Good sexual life starts in the kitchen. Good sexuality begins by helping out with the cooking, with the clean-up of the dishes, and helping clean the house. [It involves] listening to each other's needs and trying to be open to taking care of her needs and what she wants out of the marriage, and by supporting her in her desires to grow as a human being. This kind of mutual collaboration keeps us together, and then we feel comfortable to relax in the same bed, with our arms wrapped around one another.

Felicia spoke of the willingness to engage in sexual intercourse as a means of caring for one's partner. She suggested that spouses should think not only about individual sexual satisfaction but also the satisfaction of their partners. Felicia clarified:

> Sometimes, I'm not in the mood to have sex, but when I think of my husband's needs, I motivate myself to have intimacy because, in the end, both of us benefit from the experience.

Felicia added that this kind of self-motivation had significantly contributed to her marriage stability and satisfaction. This was because, before developing this self-motivation, her history of low sexual desire was affecting the couple's sexual satisfaction in her second marriage. In her opinion, the low sexual desire was a result of the abuse she suffered from her first husband.

Several participants reported having engaged in sexual liaisons during the divorce process while experiencing moments of high anxiety. While elaborating on their loneliness after divorce, the participants' stories included themes of anxiety and anger toward their former spouses, especially the stories of those who reported being involved with multiple partners after divorce, and those who started cohabiting with their partners before remarriage. This was congruent with the literature

300

that reported individuals experiencing intense emotions of anxiety, frustration, anger and/or hatred were more likely to experience intense feelings of sexual attraction (Cox, 2002; Dulton & Aron, 1999).

Aging was another factor that several participants expressed as one of the factors hindering their remarriage satisfaction. They reported that aging had negatively affected their frequencies of sexual expressiveness because of the reduced physical energy in their weakening bodies. These observations were congruent with the literature (Kelley & Burg, 2000). Some of the concrete examples that the participants had designed to keep sexuality alive included establishing a ritual or routine for couple time, and/or going periodically to a different place for honeymoon-like experiences to rejuvenate their remarriage experiences.

My experience

Based on what you have read in this session, reflect on your own personal experience.

1. What are my fears and negative experiences regarding sex and intimacy?

   _____

2. What contributes to a strong sexual relationship for me?

   _____

3. What are my positive attitudes and preferences about sexual intimacy?

   _____

4. What skills do I need to learn for a mutually satisfying sexual relationship?

    _____

5. What do I occasionally think and feel before, during and after a sexual relationship?

    _____

6. What past sexual experiences may negatively impact my remarriage experience?

    _____

7. What sexual experiences may positively impact my marriage experience?

    _____

8. What sexual activities make me feel uncomfortable if demanded by my partner?

    _____

9. What sexual activities help me enjoy sex and how do I let my partner know about them?

    _____

10. What will help us as a couple to avoid the risk of using sex to control one another?

    _____

11. What skills do I need to maintain sexual fidelity and yet interact with other people?

    _____

12. What method of family planning are we going to use that protects life by natural means?

_____

13. How will we keep the marriage and sexual relationship alive beyond changes in desire, needs, moods, age, energy, fidelity, health and/or geographical locations?

_____

14. What am I going to do/not do as a parent to help my children and stepchildren develop a positive attitude toward sexual intimacy, marital fidelity and openness to procreation?

_____

Keys to satisfactory sexuality in (re)marriage

As keys are important to open doors, consider the following keys regarding sexuality

- Differences in sexual desire and in dual-career and aging couples

- Reinforce spontaneity for intimacy and/or scheduling time and space for it by very busy couples

- More people are currently entering remarriage when they are chronologically older in comparison to those entering first marriages. Keeping sexuality alive by aging spouses in remarriage is vital, especially as partners advance in age. Participants suggested that they handled this by maintaining a youthful attitude that involved dressing well, staying mentally alert, taking periodic honeymoons, tenderness, doing things together, going places, eating together, sharing opinions, having sex for pleasure, learning techniques for igniting desire and intent in one's partner and/or watching sexually seductive movies together with their partner

- Take into account gender differences and remarriage

More divorced men spend shorter lengths of time between divorce and remarriage than divorced women (Baum, 2003). Rushing into remarriage before resolving the loss and grief associated with divorce is a great threat to remarriage stability and satisfaction (Kelley & Burg, 2000; Lofas & Sova, 1985; Reis, Senchak & Solomon, 1985). Men generally differ from women by how they learn and practice rituals, attitudes and habits that hinder or facilitate the process of mourning a divorce as a result of having grown up in a given culture (Worden, 1991). Such learned practices may be reinforced by expectations and norms that a particular culture sets for people in reference to their gender, age, religious orientation, level of formal education, socio-economic status, and open- ness to seeking professional help during grief (McGoldrick, Giordano & Pearce, 1996; Miller, 1999; Parkes, Laungani & Young, 1997; Tatelbaum, 1980; Staudacher, 1987, 1991).

———————◆•◆•◆•◆•◆———————

Study Session 22

Finances, investment, symbolisms, dual careers and types of accounts

12 I know indeed how to live in humble circumstances; I know also how to live with abundance. In every circumstance and in all things I have learned the secret of being well fed and of going hungry, of living in abundance and of being in need.

13 I have the strength for everything through him who empowers me. (Philippians 4: 12-13)

Each couple is unique in regard to finances. Although none of the participants and his or her current spouse discussed finances with the help of a professional accountant, all participants in their first marriage and those in remarriage highlighted the need for individuals contemplating marriage or remarriage and their prospective partners to consult with an accountant before marriage in order to choose their appropriate financial model(s) in marriage.

Based on the interviews participants who had joint accounts with their spouses reported more trust in their partners, but joint accounts were not the ideal for all participants. Some of the participants were using both joint and separate accounts, while others had completely separate accounts from their spouses. These models were also similar to those reported by participants in remarriage. Hence, the following drawing (Figure 1) is reproduced from the author's book on stability and satisfaction in remarriage.

Three models were used by the participants:

- 1. Joint (or one-pot method) account: Whereby both spouses have mutual trust and commitment that empower them to put all their financial resources together, hold transparent dialogues about how to invest their money and how to spend it. "Marriage is all about sharing."

- 2. Joint (or one-pot method) and separate (or independent) accounts: This method was reported by the participants who used it for the well-being of their children from a previous marriage, safety reasons and emergencies and/or for separate business accounts.

- 3. Separate (or independent) accounts: No sharing of financial resources, each spouse handles his or her personal account.

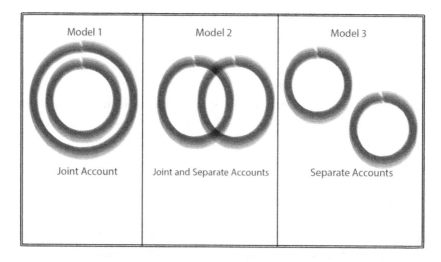

Figure 1. Three models used by married couples in handling their finances.

All participants highlighted that finances are not easy to handle in stepfamilies if they are not negotiated before remarriage. Divorced parents who bring children to second marriages create a situation for the stepparents of their children that may affect the dynamics of the couple and bring about many emotional issues. Many participants mentioned that finances become a difficult topic to handle, especially because there are many people involved within the stepfamily. For instance, Felicia who entered the second marriage with her son reported:

> My second husband [Fausto] was uncomfortable in the first three years to spend money for the well-being of my son. However, I also noticed in him [Fausto] an attitude of ambivalence. This was because I had realized that he wanted to be with me alone [without my son], but how could he do that without paying attention to my dear son?

According to Felicia, once in a while, Fausto would resent spending his money on Felicia's son because Fausto clearly knew that he was not the biological father of her son. Felicia reported that Fausto used to complain to her about her first husband's failure to help her with money for her son. Nevertheless, when he realized that he could not love the mother without caring for her son, he changed his attitude toward the son and started spending money on him. During the interview, Felicia acknowledged with gratitude Fausto's helping her to pay for the college education of her son because her former spouse never spent a penny on her son.

Many participants mentioned that remarried parents, together with their spouses, should have better spending habits. In order to do this, these participants suggested that they needed to know about themselves and how to prioritize their expenses because there are many needs and many people to take care of within a stepfamily setting. Many participants highlighted that each couple is unique with regard to finances. Therefore, they suggested that remarrying partners should have better communication skills about money. If left un-discussed and unclearly negotiated, finances can severely contribute to the disruption of marriage.

Likewise, Grace suggested:

> Remarrying parents should not spend all the money they have, nor spend the money they don't have, especially through use of credit cards.

Although none of the participants discussed finances with a professional accountant before remarriage, all the participants highlighted those parents' contemplating remarriage, together with their prospective spouses, should consult a qualified financial accountant before remarriage. Bernardo mentioned that this kind of consultation is particularly important for remarrying parents who are very rich, have a lot of assets, and/or a lot of valuable properties and/or possessions.

In similar terms, some participants mentioned that prenuptial written agreements are helpful in securing the financial benefits of the remarrying parent and his or her children, just in case the second marriage ends in another divorce or in the death of one of the spouses. Otherwise, the person bringing money into the marriage without a prenuptial agreement might feel insecure financially and not want to risk their money being shared by the children and/or relatives of the other spouse. By the same token, many participants perceived this kind of insecurity as a hindrance to remarriage stability and satisfaction.

When asked how the participants were currently handling their financial arrangements with their spouses, the responses showed three models of accounts: one-pot method, one-pot and independent method, and independent method (Figure 1). Elaborating on these models of accounts, nine participants mentioned that they use the one-pot method. This involves two spouses putting together all their resources into an account and spending together from the same account.

Elías clarified "The pot method has strengthened my marriage and it has helped me to learn that marriage is all about sharing." In specific terms, Bernardo highlighted "Sharing money with the second spouse symbolizes a leap of trust that spouses put in one another, especially for the partner who invests more money and assets into the relationship." Grace emphasized:

> I grew up in poor family and that helped me to learn to value the little we had and to share the little with others. However, irrespective of our poverty, we survived, partly because my parents spent the little money they had prudently, and I used to

hear dialoguing about what item to spend money on. Therefore, I think that when spouses have a joint account, they should not make surprise purchases of more than a hundred dollars without consulting the other spouse, even if the purchase is for the well-being of the other spouse.

I recall that my parents had to make tough choices of removing completely some items from the shopping list because … they did not have the money. They put those items on hold until they got the money for them. My parents also discouraged me and my siblings from borrowing money in order to offer very expensive gifts to one another during the Christmas season.

Several participants reported that they were using the one-pot and independent method. This consists of the two spouses putting together some of their financial resources, especially money, and putting some of their money into a separate account. Hilda was one of the participants who used this method of accounting. Hilda said:

> In my second marriage, we have three accounts. I share one account with my husband, my husband has another one of his own, and I have another account that is mine alone.

When asked for her rationale for maintaining these two separate accounts in addition to the joint account, Hilda replied:

> After divorce, I became a single-mother and I learned how to handle my own money. I started to make all the financial decisions by myself. So, after remarriage, it was not easy for me to give up that autonomy. As a woman, my husband in my first marriage kept me out of all the decisions regarding money. My [second] husband has a separate account also because it is specifically for his business and both of us contribute to the joint account.

Several other participants emphasized the usefulness of having some money that one can spend as he or she likes without the need to be in constant negotiations about money with one's spouse. Two participants out of these had a separate account primarily because they were running businesses that needed different kinds of accounting.

Two participants mentioned that they had independent accounts with their second spouses. When asked about the rationale for separate accounts, Fred mentioned that since his adolescence, he decided not to have a joint account with any future wife because he got tired of hearing fights his parents had over money because they had a joint account.

Another participant, Doris, resolved not to have a joint account based on her experience in her first marriage in which the other spouse spent a lot of money they had in a joint account a few months before their divorce. By the same token, listening to all these stories, it became evident that most of the participants made their financial decisions based on their histories and what they learned from their parents.

Many participants clarified that most of the conflicts surrounding money in the early stages of their remarriages were focused on who pays for what, how much, and why me, as a stepparent, if the children are not mine. However, as the problems surfaced about money, these participants reported that those conflicts helped them to start discussing openly the impact of money on their remarrying. They said it was difficult to speak about the topic of finances. The conversations were emotionally charged at the beginning, but they realized that silence about money would not resolve the problem.

These participants recommended that divorced parents contemplating remarriage should take the risk of discussing money and other financial assets that they bring to the marriage and define in concrete terms (e.g., who is going to pay for the expenses?) Along the same lines, Dora mentioned:

> Informing my second spouse about my elderly parents that I had to take care of has helped my second spouse to understand my financial needs and become supportive by providing more money from his separate account.

Charles narrated his experience as follows:

I grew up in a poor family, whereby being on the breadline affected my attitude toward money. I learned that there are things that my rich neighbors had (for example, swimming pools, nice houses and new cars), and to my surprise the lack of those things influenced me to develop a deeper friendship with the children of our rich neighbors. Detailed conversations and interactions with some of these friends helped me to realize that, although their parents were rich, there were things that their parents could not buy for them, even with all the money that they had. I kept that lesson all through my life and I have not let money take away from me those things that money cannot buy: love, friendship, respect, spirituality, and common sense.

In concluding about finances, Charles emphatically cautioned:

Divorced parents should not focus all their attention on money because there are many important things in second marriages that cannot be bought with money, for instance, winning the trust of the stepchildren.

Salvador mentioned that couples need to work hard to improve their financial situations in marriage. Otherwise, the lack of financial resources in a marriage is likely to contribute to strain on a marriage and on the individual's psychological well-being. This brings with it other kinds of mental problems, selfish attitudes, and behaviors.

Hilda commented that the separation of money should primarily be done for the benefit of the children from the first marriage or relationship(s). This includes the on-going child support and whenever applicable, paying alimony to the ex-spouse. Otherwise, better to have a joint account and maintain open dialogue about money. She added: each individual should know the limits of money and be attentive to resources that money cannot buy. Money is important in life but is not the most important in life.

Albert observed that sharing money also symbolizes a leap of trust that spouses put in one another; especially the partner who invests more money and assets into the relationship. Neighborhood (e.g., living in a suburban neighborhood due to the expected high standard of living, thus creating financial pressure on the couple and family struggling to fit in.)

Using money as a means of control

Ellen elaborated:

> I have the greatest respect for my dad, even after his death because of all the love and sufferings he went through to make sure that we got good education and the basics of life. However, I realized that he had a way of using money to control my mother. He was the only one in the family who kept the money. We grew up in the village, the nearest bank was 70 miles away from home and that meant a full day trip by using public transportation of the only bus, which used to stop in a small town, 7 miles from my home. Mom had to beg him for money, even for an equivalent of twenty cents to buy a matchbox to make fire.

> Ever since, I resolved to study hard and get a paying job as a woman and even if we have a joint account with my husband, we both agreed to have some petty cash in the house which we can both use without questions asked. We do not want to use money to control one another, but we both have a way of controlling our spending.

Ambrose emphasized the importance of establishing a budget as a couple and to do whatever it takes to abide by the established budget. He used the following format:

Budget: Income

Sources of couple's income	Amount of daily income	Amount of monthly income	Amount of annual income
Inheritance			
Husband's job(s)			
Wife's job(s)			
Total			

Budget: Expenses

Examples of expense list	Amount of daily expense	Amount of monthly expense	Amount of annual expenses
Household expenses (e.g., food groceries)			
Mortgage			
Insurance			
Cars			
Payment of school loans			
Investments			
Retirement			
Vacation			
Church donations			
Caring for elderly parents			
Charity			
Medical			
Education			
Total			

Marie:

My husband and I had lengthy discussions about money and investments. My husband and I have separate bank accounts (bear in mind that we live separately so have unique individual costs). We know how much each earns and contribute equally towards expenses for our home and daughter.

The financial resource side has enabled us to better achieve some of our partnership investment goals while supporting our families where required. Happy families place less strain on the marriage as it eliminates the hostility associated with cases where married individuals are no longer able to financially support their extended families to the extent they did before marriage, often perceived as the spouse controlling/finishing their son/daughter/brother/sister's money.

Ellen:

I didn't have any school loans. I had a scholarship. My husband did have loans and we just paid them off. It had no impact on our marriage. It was part of life that had to be dealt with.

Lea:

Equal contribution. Both of us work full-time jobs as well as additional side jobs. We both contribute to all of the bills and the work around the house. The more even the split, the less resentment there can be to build.

Ted:

We had one loan. 120 payments all paid on time. By the time when we finished these payments, we thought we were old people. From day one, we had a common checking account. Since we were both breadwinners, we each contributed. Of course, we had different ideas of how we should spend our money. Sometimes we would fight about it but we always compromised and worked things out.

Albert:

> We made sure all financial decisions were understood to each person's ability.

Charles:

> Some of the main challenges men face in marriage within my society is being unemployed and consequently have no adequate financial resources to support the family. The solution I would suggest for any man in order to hold to his marriage is to have a good paying job and hold on to this job permanently. But after said that, besides having a enough income to feed his family, the man must exhibit the love and the care towards his wife in order to maintain a lasting marriage relationship.

Miguel:

> We are preparing to adjust our budget to pay off our student loans, planning is essential.

Andy:

> No student loans. Praise God. But it is not difficult from other life stresses. Everyone has his or   her   own luggage/baggage I believe.

> We have other loans but they are just that. Living in faith and pay them down regularly. No   extravagance. I credit my wife for this. She isn't extravagant and a wise spender. I may not tell her as often or as much so she doesn't change but aside from some particular influences she   doesn't realize, I have 100% trust she is free to spend and I trust her choices. I sometimes ask but that's just to know that the expenditures are hers and she isn't unduly influenced by others   who may want to take advantage of her.   She has carried this responsibility with extreme prudency.

Andy added:

The fact that we faced an uncertain future financially was a huge challenge plus our start off was not a regular one. I travelled out of the country immediately after our wedding, and we were separated for a year and half full of uncertainty, but we faced it together while being physically apart I've never discussed this part with her but I would ask her now how she felt during those years. For me I was focused on it as my own challenge of providing for my wife and she didn't know what I was going through. Possibly the fact that we were, was a challenge maybe the challenge of facing the battle together in faith, strengthened us. Then our unusual start made us comfortable with being different from everyone. There wasn't undue pressure to get into debt of weddings and honeymoon, and we haven't strained ourselves to fit into society.

Rowland:

Student loans were thankfully not a problem. We had scholarships and family support as undergraduates. Grad school was budgeted into our household and covered by research fellowships or work benefits. However, our first mortgage was a loan-related source of regret. It was held by my wife's father, but at an implied cost: he lobbied for a suburban location and house style that he liked, rather than an urban house and setting that appealed to us. We had our first son in the suburbs, and the commuting and house care were especially burdensome as we started our work-school-child care lives. We decided to sell the house (at a small loss), close the mortgage with family, and move in town to a rental apartment closer to friends and similar couples. It was also closer to work and grad schools. While the family pressure (to be more conventional) was destabilizing, the decision to move back to the city was satisfying. It confirmed that we were committed to our plans and intended to do things on our own.

In these and all subsequent household expense negotiations, we always considered all income and resources to be "ours", not

317

"his" and "hers". While we got separate credit cards for building credit reputations, we have always had one checking account for the household. Financial information has been entirely open, including passwords, safety deposit access, and recently on-line records.

It would have been unfair to manage money separately—creating instability and false accountability. This was true at first, and even more true later when, in most years, my wife had higher pay than I.

Mateo:

Financial challenges, and were resolved by working harder to earn more and be stable financially.

My experience

Based on what you have read in this session, reflect on your own personal experience.

Annual family income	Annual family income in my family of origin (before my first marriage)	Annual family income in my first marriage	Annual income after my divorce and before my second marriage	Annual family income in my second marriage
Below $15,000				
$15,000 – 25,000				
$25,000 – 35,000				
$35,000 – 45,000				
$45,000 – 55,000				
$55,000 – 65,000				
$65,000 – 75,000				
$75,000 – 90,000				
$90,000 – 130,000				
Over $130,000				

Identify the number of all the people dependent on my annual income:

Before my first marriage:
In my first marriage:
In my second marriage:
Currently:

My current home neighborhood may be categorized as:

o   Inner-city

o   Urban

o   Suburban

What are our considerations and conclusions in regard establishing a prenuptial agreement or not?

_____

Keys to financial security and management

As keys are important to open doors, consider the following keys to finance.
-   Each couple is unique in regard to finances. Although none of the participants and his or her current spouse discussed finances with the help of a professional accountant, all participants highlighted the need for parents contemplating remarriage and their prospective spouses to consult with an accountant before

remarriage in order to choose their appropriate financial model(s) in marriage. Three models were used by the participants:

- One pot method - whereby both spouses have mutual trust and commitment that empower them to put all their financial resources together, hold transparent dialogues about how to invest their money and how to spend it. "Marriage is all about sharing."

- Independent accounts – No sharing of financial resources, each spouse handles his or her personal account

- One pot method and independent accounts – this method was reported by the participants who used it for the well-being of their children from a previous marriage, safety reasons and emergencies and/or for separate business accounts

- Lack of financial resources in a marriage may contribute to strain on a marriage and on the individual's psychological well-being, thereby bringing about other kinds of mental problems, selfish attitudes, and behaviors. For instance, being on the breadline could affect people's mental health

- Separation of money should primarily be done for the benefit of the children from the first marriage

- Know the limits of money and be attentive to resources that money cannot buy

- Sharing money also symbolizes a leap of trust that spouses put in one another; especially the partner who invests more money and assets into the relationship

- On-going child support and whenever applicable, paying alimony to the ex-spouse

- Neighborhood (e.g., living in a suburban neighborhood – due to the expected high standard of living, thus creating financial pressure on the couple and family struggling to fit in).

Study Session 23

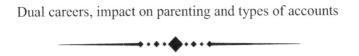

Dual careers, impact on parenting and types of accounts

When the participants were asked to identify the strategies which they have successfully used to have a career and to raise their children, Rowland responded:

> I wanted work that was important and could also accommodate family choices. I pursued a career that allowed me to set much of my own schedule. Though I worked hard, it could happen early or late leaving flexibility around children's needs. Interestingly, going to work with children sometimes was greeted positively, maybe more so for a man than for a woman. Women colleagues appreciated my recognizing family responsibilities; many men also respected my efforts, regretting that their careers had not allowed such roles, or that they had chosen not to participate in family as much.

I had modest goals. I worked to be effective, but not necessarily to be the best and biggest person in the organization. I knew such ambitions would eventually grow and consume all my time. Money was not the sole measure of my success. Similarly, we stayed in the same geographical area professionally, and avoided uprooting the family to a permanent new or bigger home. This allowed us to develop better networks of friends and colleagues who formed a backup for our own needs.

We consciously cultivated self-sufficiency in our children, so they could be fine without us. And when we were with them, we worked to be there 100%. They understood they were important to us and loved by us. But they were not the absolute center of our universe all the time.

Ellen stated the following challenges at beginning of her marriage and how it was resolved:

> I am a nurse and had to work different shifts. My husband wasn't happy, but we talked it out and I explained this is part of my job.

Lea:

> Sometimes it is hard when your hours don't line up and you are not seeing each other for more than 4 hours a day, but if you plan time together into your week you can make it work.

Miguel:

> Each of us is supportive to each other in our individual careers and studies. However, being a full-time dual-career couple, managing time for various roles can be challenging

Marie

> Absence makes the heart grow fonder. The employment related "temporary separations" unconsciously conditioned us to be on our best behavior when we got together. Each time felt like a date and we could not afford to waste time by disagreeing too much during the short breaks!

> Because we were not co-located, the absence of that instant gratification or relief of knowing I am going home to my husband/my wingman was a little challenging. Some issues cannot be effectively addressed on phone ... Sometimes when the going gets tough, one just needs a reassuring hug to know that someone's got your back – and there is no equivalent for this over the phone or video call.

Doris stated:

> Being a dual-career couple was challenging, especially when we had children to raise. However, it made our marriage stable because each of us were able to be flexible with our schedule. We worked with each other to make it work not only for us, but for our children. Sacrifices were made in the workweek, but when the weekends came, we found it all worth it. It helped us financially and we always made sure to take time out in the summer for that all important family   vacation. Time well spent.

Doris added:

> The only negative thing that came from being a dual-career couple was not having more time   with each other. After I had my children, I went back to work for a major airline working 4 pm to midnight, while my husband worked days at the time. We had a lot of family support which   made   it possible to do. Eventually, I became a stay-at-home mom till my children were older, then went back to work. Without the family support, it would have been a struggle financially and perhaps would have impacted our marriage differently.

Jean mentioned that being a dual-career couple positively impacted her marriage stability and satisfaction as follows:

> Working helped keep finances manageable and that eases the pressure of paying the bills. Day- care was affordable

Ellen mentioned:

> We both have very different jobs but still have stress from our jobs. Every night we talk about our day and try and help each other to release stress. We also encourage each other to enjoy what we do at work.

Sarah mentioned that being a dual-career couple has positively impacted her marriage stability and satisfaction because: "Financially it has benefitted us." However, Sarah noted that being a dual-career couple has negatively impacted her marriage stability and satisfaction due to the "stress of child care and household responsibilities and balancing out life. Bringing the stress of work home."

Charles:

> Being a career couple has impacted our marriage positively due to the fact that at the end of each day, we are able to share different experiences we have encountered each day. Based on my personal experience, being a dual-career couple has not negatively impacted our marriage stability and satisfaction and instead, it has increased its stability because of different experiences we bring back home each end of the day and share to each other those experiences.

Andy elaborated on the positive aspects of his dual-career household as follows:

> My case wasn't always dual-career. My wife stayed at home for a long time. But recently when the dual career household started, we have had to adjust like we've always done. The positive impact is the better income, but it brings its downside. The positive part is both individuals better value each other as contributing to the household. I've seen my wife brighten up on contributing financially even though she has not been asked to. She is happier, has a better sense of self-worth I believe and I also value her contributions that I have not asked for.

> Further reinforcing my original belief and trust in her that she would do what is right for the household. Her excitement in sharing her daily work experiences make for interesting

conversations and I am just thrilled to see a new life in her. For me, another positive aspect is there is less time for fighting since both have gone to work and expended energies at work.

When asked about the negative aspect of his dual-career household Andy mentioned: "The downside of being a dual-career couple is there is less time for the family. "

Rowland

Satisfying professional work – we both had work we believed was important. Each gave the other the space to pursue their aspirations. Our jobs allowed a level of financial security for the family. Flexibility at work allowed us to share and trade off breadwinning, childcare, community service, etc.

Shared childcare and household responsibilities –we worked out and shared the roles of breadwinner, at-home parent, financial manager, house cleaner. The roles shifted, especially when the family was younger. We tried to discern who needed something (job change, moving, education) most, in both short and long term.

Rowland added:

Hard work – we both have strong work ethics such that we never feel there is an unfair effort by one or the other. Such feelings could be toxic and reduce cooperativeness and common purpose.

Ted:

We stayed together because we loved each other. We both knew that we could each survive without the others financial support.

When my wife went back to work, I became Mr. Mom to a seven-year-old. Of course, we didn't agree on what a seven-year-old should be allowed and not allowed to do.

Both Independent breadwinners: From the start, we were both financially independent. We both had good jobs. That reduced the number of fights we had concerning financial decisions. We both knew that we were together because we loved each other, not because we needed someone to provide us with financial help.

Rowland

We both have believed in the intrinsic goodness of the other's professional work. It was worth encouraging and even sacrificing to make the other successful. Our work also paid well enough that we could be free of major financial worry, educate our children well, and plan for retirement. Having these goals outside one's individual ambitions was helpful in weathering professional up and downs. Seeing our partner initiating good changes in society was very satisfying and worth personal sacrifices or delays in goals.

Juggling two careers was often only possible with sacrifice by one or both of us, or by our children (although they were largely unaware). We often were able to "take turns" in a sense, as needed. Sacrifice meant delaying goals, taking lower-paying positions to do the right kind of work, suffering through job uncertainty and loss, and constantly fighting social conventions that defined narrow roles for men and women. One-sided sacrifice could breed instability and resentment, especially if the benefits are unclear or transitory. We avoided these by constantly talking through what was needed and what we could accomplish. We also thought we were waging small battles that would make it easier for the next couple (or our children's generation) to avoid our constraints. Sadly, this has more often not been the case. Systems and attitudes that we slightly pried apart to make room for our family, slid quickly back into place once we were gone. A new generation is still facing many of the same battles.

Albert:

The dual-career part is a problem. It interferes in our personal contact terribly but I suppose we grew used to it. WE live in this mode …looking at life now, but it is not forever.

Study Session 24

Dealing with infertility and some alternative options

5 In the days of Herod, King of Judea, there was a priest named Zechariah of the priestly division of Abijah; his wife was from the daughters of Aaron, and her name was Elizabeth.

6 Both were righteous in the eyes of God, observing all the commandments and ordinances of the Lord blamelessly.

7 But they had no child, because Elizabeth was barren and both were advanced in years. (Luke 1: 5 – 7)

3 Blessed be the God and Father of our Lord Jesus Christ, the Father of compassion and God of all encouragement,*

4 who encourages us in our every affliction, so that we may be able to encourage those who are in any affliction with the encouragement with which we ourselves are encouraged by God. (2 Corinthians 1: 3 – 4)

All the participants expressed their desire of wanting to become parents of biological children. It was easy for some, yet others had difficulty at the beginning but later become parents, while for others, it was completely not possible. Each participant's story had its unique circumstances and challenges. For instance, Doris mentioned:

We (Doris and her husband) didn't become parents until nine years into our marriage, however, not by choice. We were dealing with infertility and had trouble to conceive. Fortunately, we were blessed with two children and made our marriage more whole. It by far was God's greatest gifts to us. Having children never impacted our marriage negatively. We always wanted a family.

Doris added:

Going through infertility is stressful, heartbreaking, and seemingly hopeless when you don't conceive after going through so much treatment. We decided that if all treatments for infertility failed, our next step would be adoption. During infertility, the couple must support each other, regardless who is the one having the difficultly. Discuss alternatives, adoption, foster care, working with children.

Jean described how not becoming parents in the early years of her marriage impacted her stability and satisfaction as follows:

It was the hardest in my marriage, just held on by prayers and family encouragement. Much as both of you desired to have children, briefly describe what helped you to deal with the realization that one of you or both cannot successfully contribute to the life of a baby?

That was the hardest thought in our life. Having relatives around (nieces, nephews), visiting priests and friends helped a lot.

Jean's situation of not conceiving a biological child was a result of the accident her husband suffered. He was left paralyzed below the waist; this was finally resolved with the medical doctors' interventions. The doctors managed to extract semen directly from her husband and with the available technology inserted the extracted semen into her and successfully conceived. Consequently, Jean advised other people in similar situations to consult with their doctors. She noted: "Doctors have solutions to this issue, so use their advice."

Marie:

> However, I am aware of cases of childless friends and some who really struggled before they got a child. The greatest pressure comes from the in-laws who aspire for a continuation of the family name. They expect results nine months after the wedding; failing which, they would be all too ready to get their son/brother a fertile wife to produce them an heir!

> In one case, my friend conceived triplets at a relatively advanced age through in vitro fertilization after 10 years of marriage and multiple miscarriages/failed IVF attempts. She still wasn't spared the patriarchal narrative of "no one to continue the family name" as the triplets were all girls.

A young couple I know got married in 2014 and by 2016 the guy was under a lot of pressure from his family to find another wife! I have had to talk to them periodically to remind the gentleman he married her because he loved her, and that children are a bonus that should not be a deal breaker since they can also adopt. Although they are still together and seemingly happy, one can sense the discomfort.

Doris:

> Even though this (infertility) is not my experience, I have family members where this has been the case. If the fertile partner is female and REALLY wants to bear a child, this can still be an option. My family members have successfully pursued these great alternatives: in vitro fertilization and surrogate (sperm bank) insemination. And the families I know that have chosen adoption feel so lucky and happy to have found each other! Realistically, however, these routes can be costly. Both partners need to be comfortable and committed to pull off any of these alternatives.

Doris elaborated:

An inability to have a child in the usual way is a major life disappointment. Grieving needs to take place about what may not be. I suggest that couples seek help/counseling to work through their grieving. With time and support, they can emerge stronger as a team, and be open to explore other options.

If the couple decides not to have children, satisfaction and joy can come from their active support of each other's professional and personal pursuits. I want to reiterate that most of my married life I have spent without children, so all couples need to learn how to be together and satisfied without the distraction and preoccupation with children.

If a couple wants to have special relationships with children, there are ways to do that too, through extended family, volunteer work, foster parenting, leadership of student organizations (like Girl Scouts or Youth Groups). I believe we can choose our extended family, and not have to rely on the people in our family tree. I encourage childless couples to do this, if they want a special relationship.

Ellen stated the following major challenge in her marriage and how they handled it:

We did eight years of fertility work without success. It was stressful. We never blamed each other for not being able to conceive. It brought us closer together. Then, after many prayers, God brought a baby girl through adoption. When she was a teenager, her behavior was troublesome. My husband felt it was Ok and she would outgrow it. We started to argue about her on a daily basis. We went for marriage counseling which reminded us to work together and how much we loved each other.

Charles:

The difficult moment we were having for almost eight years after our wedding was not having a child. Nonetheless, afterwards, when our son was born, the bond between me and my wife was made stronger. Our son acted as a chain that connected us together, and it definitely created our marriage stability and satisfaction to this day.

Ted:

We had numerous nephews and nieces that we were and are very close to. We are very special to them. When we finally were able to adopt a baby girl, they became her adopted siblings. To this day, they are all still very close even though some are separated by thousands of miles.

Ted's advice:

Just remember that you married each other because of love. You didn't marry a "wished for" baby. Adopt a baby; "adopt" your siblings' baby. It gives great satisfaction to be able to help some else. It worked for us.

Ted:

My wife was, and is still family oriented. Her mother was her best friend. My wife had to leave her home for me. I promised myself that I would never make her regret that decision. After several operations, my wife was still unable to get pregnant. After eight unsuccessful years of trying to get pregnant, we were lucky to be able to adopt a beautiful baby girl. When I lost my job, my wife immediately said I will go back to work full-time for as long as it takes to get back on our feet. She was happy to support me because we always looked at each other as a team.

Andy expressed a profound sense of his children. He elaborated:

Hmmmm, I don't want to contemplate what could have been. I am extremely grateful to God for what is. Very simple. Again,

I don't want to contemplate what could have been. I am extremely grateful to God for what is. I can't begin to fathom what others go through, but I pray God provides each of us the grace to carry our burdens. From our culture, it would have been difficult for either of us.

Study Session 25

Co-parenting skills and stress management

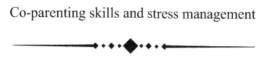

The following are some of the responses from the participants regarding how becoming parents impacted them as individuals and as a couple:

Andy:

> It gave both of us something else to focus on. Raising and caring for the children became the focus of our life. I can say it became that way for much of our adult lives. I can't say it was a negative thing because had it not been for the kids, I don't know what would have happened. It's the only life I know of and I'm not willing to change or contemplate what could have been. I am extremely happy and satisfied with the kids in our life.

Anna noted:

> Sharing and working together helped us become good parents because raising a family is hard work, but it's easier when done with someone else. It helped us get through the difficult times. When one was weak, the other was strong. We all have good and bad days, different strengths and weaknesses, and busy and quieter times within our extended family. You learn from one another since everyone comes from different backgrounds. Our strengths come out when we share in responsibilities.

When Rowland was asked about becoming a parent in the first five years of his marriage, he positively discussed the resultant impact on the couple's marriage stability and satisfaction; he responded:

Having a baby gave us a newer, constant focus for all our efforts. His presence also forced difficult discussions about roles and responsibilities because we immediately faced full-time work for me and full-time graduate study for my wife, who took our baby to the university. By working through those problems, we built a deeper trust than we had as relatively carefree young professionals. I especially had to get rid of deliberate and unconsciously ingrained ideas about who did what in a household, laying groundwork that helped address harder problems as more children arrived. Our son was a healthy and easy child, who adapted to our ambitious schedule. The grandparents thought we were trying to do too much. This resistance added to our stability as it focused our sense that we were together going to show them it would work.

A long discussion around a second child ensued, at which point we swapped roles. I returned to grad school with the second baby, while my wife returned to work supporting the family. We developed a much more balanced understanding of these traditional roles by living them. We also decided to move back closer to grad school and child care and nearer similar families trying to support dual careers. Our discussions about roles worked out because we had already developed a keen sense of loyalty, trust and fairness, and saw how hard the other was working to reach our mutual goals.

Rowland also mentioned that becoming parents in the first five years of his marriage somehow negatively impact their marriage stability and satisfaction in ways which they also managed to resolve. He elaborated:

Learning to be a parent is always demanding, exhausting work. Our ambitious schedule combining work, school, and child care only added to the baseline stress and exhaustion. It was a more unstable time in that the whole arrangement could have collapsed in disappointment, despite our intentions. Satisfaction was threatened by others telling us we were too ambitious, unfair to our children, on a fool's errand, etc.

Marie mentioned that parents need make a conscious effort to avoid the risk of insinuating sibling rivalries due to one parent or both playing favorites intentionally or subconsciously with their children. She elaborated:

> My dad was a good man but he had a bad habit of playing favorites. He used to compare me to my brother by saying that he is very smarter than me and that my brother was the one who would choose where we could go for vacation. Much as I loved and respected my father for all the good things he did for the family, his favoritism of my brother intensified the existing low-key sibling rivalry between me and my brother.

Referring to the Bible story of Joseph in the Book of Genesis, Marie quoted the following passage, which illustrates how Israel (the father) provoked a sibling rivalry between Joseph and his brothers:

> 'Israel loved Joseph best of all his sons, for he was a child of his old age; and he made him a long tunic. When his brothers saw that their father loved him best of all his sons, they hated him so much that they would not even greet him. One day ... they plotted to kill him ... When Reuben heard this, he tried to save him ... they sold Joseph to the Ishmaelites (going to Egypt) for twenty pieces of silver.' (Genesis 37: 3 – 28).

Ellen stated that being able to adjust her hours at work helped her successfully have a career and to raise her adopted child. She clarified:

> I was lucky being a nurse. I could make my hours around when my husband was home with our daughter, so I never had to worry.

Miguel was asked to identify the strategies he has successfully used to have a career and to raise children. He responded:

Time management is essential. Prioritizing what is important and what is foundational; identify needs versus wants.

Lee added that not every emergency is important.

Sarah was asked to identify a very difficult moment in her marriage and she mentioned: "It is a struggle having a child with a disability."

Doris:
> A difficult time in our marriage was having my husband work steady nights and raising two small children ages 2 and 4 years old. I felt a heavy burden when he left for work, having no help with simple household chores, raising the children. Even though he was home during the day, working nights, he would need his rest and sleep till late morning, early afternoon. Eventually, I adjusted. I had to. He was the breadwinner and when he had the free time, he showed what a good husband, father, and provider he was. That is how I overcame this challenge, he showed he loved me and his family by the time well spent with us when he could.

Doris identified the following strategies, which they have successfully used as a dual-career couple and to raise their children:

> Since we worked full-time and had evening commitments every week (teaching for him and community meetings for me), we needed to be highly organized:
>
> o To produce meals that were nutritious and practical
> o To manage household tasks. The boys understood we were trying to juggle a lot, and as members of the household, they needed to help. From an early age, they had serious chores, from helping with meal and lunch prep, food planning and shopping, sweeping common areas, and folding clothes. As they got older, they got their own laundry baskets

(in 7th grade) and managed their own laundry. They also helped with dinner prep/cooking tasks.

- o To make sure one parent was fully present for dinner, homework help, sports events, and sick days, bedtime, and later, curfew times. My husband and I carefully worked over our schedules to accommodate family needs. Being fully present meant more than being at home. It meant being completely available to our sons during these times – no multi-tasking. My husband was great at this, as I described earlier. I took longer to get there, but was inspired by his example and success with the boys.
- o To schedule and cover doctor's appointments – planned and emergency.
- o To schedule and participate in parent-teacher conferences (both of us participated) and school presentations.
- o To assure that our house had basic provisions for school projects (markers, poster boards, etc.).

Marie:

Childbirth is often considered to be the culmination of a marriage and earns one the final "seal of approval" from family and friends, especially the in-laws! There is also a strengthening of the bonds of love when you have a baby, that physical representation of a little bit of both of you that is the product of your love …

Our daughter gave me a new purpose in life, part of which includes being a role model in an endeavor to be the best mum that I can be.

A husband is a wife's "No.1" and used to getting all her affection and attention! Babies are so small, helpless and demanding – often requiring Mummy's undivided attention. This unfortunately results in a reorganization of the priority list, relegating husband to "No.2." The perceived decline in affection and attention can result in the man feeling neglected, ignored or no longer relevant. In my case however, my husband was rarely around and when he did come, he would dote on our daughter, so it did not have a significant negative effect on the marriage.

I have a friend who, unable to deal any more with the emerging jealousy and accusations of neglect told her husband he was not her relative, but the baby was, and that equal treatment would have to start with diaper changes for both him and the baby!

Marie suggested the following strategy for having a successful career and raising children:

> Good planning and accepting help from others. We only have a child at the moment, so it is manageable.

Jean mentioned:

> Since we had our child late in our age, we had other people around who could help and also used day-care most of the time. Outside work had to be done in order to keep finances under control.

Doris elaborated as follows in regard to how becoming parents in the first five years of her marriage positively impact her marriage stability and satisfaction.

> It made us re-evaluate our communication. Now there was real stress in our lives, and as the new mom who was also a full-time graduate student, I felt the weight of the 24-hour-ness of a baby that I couldn't get away from, and relentless course deadlines. I surprised myself by experiencing post-partum depression (something I had not believed in previously). I was overwhelmed, but knew I couldn't wallow there, so I trusted our friendship and told my husband how badly I felt – about the

baby and about him. It was not his fault, but I had no one else to lash out against.

He (my husband) was so relieved when I was finally able to articulate my anger. He hadn't known what to do to make me feel better, and felt guilty and upset about how my silence and depression had shut him out. We both confessed! That broke the ice that had formed between us. Before this, for the first three years of marriage, we thought of ourselves as a team. Now that we had a tiny adversary, we needed to become a team in earnest. During the next two years, we talked openly and made adjustments so I could get real breaks, and not be the default (go to) parent when both of us were at home on weekends. I had to call him on his habit of burying his head behind a newspaper, such that our son would look around for someone to help him and, seeing only one head, would come to me. To raise my husband's consciousness, I developed a schedule with two-hour blocks that identified which parent was "on" if our son needed something – from a diaper change to a playmate.

My husband stepped up, paid attention to our son when it was "his" time, and learned how to parent. In fact, he learned to devote himself to our son when he was "on," and not to multi-task. I later followed his example. Each of us helped the other. Forced scheduling was no longer necessary. We were both tuned in to respond to our son, and we were fair about sharing time with him and making time for our own work.

When it was time to consider a second child, I was not interested, but my husband persisted. That was year 5 of our marriage. By then we had re-established good communication skills under stress, so he negotiated with arguments like: It's not good for a child to be a single child. I was unmoved. Something could happen to one child, and we would be without any. Still unmoved.

Finally, he said: I REALLY want a second child, and if you won't cooperate with me on this, it can't happen! I heard this plea, and softened, on condition that he would be responsible for the early care of this child. He agreed, and was good on his word. I knew I could count on him, because he had embraced the care of our first son, and was very competent in his parenting. Two weeks after our second son arrived, I started full-time work. My husband got up during the night to feed the new baby while I slept through. He then dropped our first son off at a day-care center and bundled the baby off to his graduate school classes.

Our first son was the catalyst that helped us negotiate the terms of our parenting partnership, but my husband's follow through with the second son told me everything I needed to know about his commitment. We were not getting much sleep, but our dual course (work and parenting) was set. We were stable and satisfied.

Additionally, Doris described a negative impact of becoming parents in the first five years of her marriage as follows:

We (my husband and I) experienced a communication setback as we adjusted to new feelings and expectations. But because we were committed to the enterprise and to each other … we addressed the issues, found solutions, and emerged with a real sense of partnership and teamwork.

Doris cautioned:

Having a baby is NOT the way to improve a marriage that is rocky. It is highly stressful, with lots of potential to impact a marriage negatively.

Charles:

I want to definitely say that becoming parents has never negatively impacted our marriage stability and satisfaction but instead it created a strong bond between us to this day.

Sarah mentioned that becoming parents in the first five years of her marriage negatively impacted her marriage insofar as "It interfered with alone time."

Sarah mentioned that becoming parents in the first five years of her marriage positively impacted her marriage stability and satisfaction: "It brought us closer together, because we had to work together for someone greater than us."

Mateo said becoming parents in the first five years of marriage positively impact his marriage stability and satisfaction because: "The children make our marriage cohesive." When asked how it negatively impacted marriage stability and satisfaction, he mentioned: "It affects us financially."

Albert:

> Parenting was a natural thing to us, and the surprise of starting right out of the gate was a joyful one. We are planners and we were prepared for the needs of a family. The task of parenting allowed us to work very close together in raising our child.

Miguel commented on becoming parents in the first five years of marriage:

> "we were both focused on caring for our child, we shared knowledge and interests, as well as concerns. We had someone else to look out for. However, the challenge I experienced was not being the primary focus of attention of my partner, having to share time together and reduced sense of attention toward her.

Ted:

> Share responsibilities. Forgive mistakes

Rowland:

I viewed certain efforts as "helping" on tasks that were naturally and solely my spouse's (e.g. child care). This assumption caused resentment because I would "help" when convenient, but the default responsibility was hers. Eventually we decided/I understood that all tasks were ours together in our relationship. Who bore which responsibilities, and at what point in our relationship, depended on circumstances and experience.

In our first house, we made mistakes in choosing where to live and in what circumstances. We persevered until we could change housing and rebuff family pressures.

We faced some family health crises with one parent. With the help of siblings and the advice of friends and colleagues we participated in an intervention that was not successful. This experience brought into strong relief the problems caused by poor communications and hardened attitudes.

My experience

Based on what you have read in this session, reflect on your own personal experience.

1. How am I preparing myself to become a good and collaborative parent with my spouse?

_____

2. How am I preparing myself to become a good stepparent if my prospective spouse is a custodial parent to his/her children from the first marriage?

Keys to collaborative parenting

As keys are important to open doors, consider the following keys to collaborative parenting

Set house rules that state clearly how you want things to be (e.g., in this house, nobody has the right to badmouth one's ex-spouse in front of the children; table manners must be respected, including the positioning of the forks, knives, and saucers

- Keep clear boundaries with significant others, especially with your ex-spouse, children, and the impact of society on your life and remarriage

- Avoid unnecessary resentment of your prospective spouse by your biological children

- Develop and put into practice the guidelines for parenting and stepparenting

- Understand that divorce ends a marriage, not a family

- Reduce your children's risk of feeling responsible and/or guilty for your divorce by verbally informing them it was not their fault

- Overcome frustration and/or guilt from your first marriage, and if necessary, use professional help

- Be aware that joint physical custody that involves very short-term alternations of residences (e.g., on a weekly, weekend or monthly basis) enables the children to be with both parents, but it leaves the children lacking a place to call home

- For the greater benefit of your children, avoid the risk of bringing anybody you are dating to your home until both of you really feel committed to one another

- Prevent and/or reduce the risk of another divorce by maintaining marital fidelity. Avoiding an extramarital affair is crucial to marital trust. It is not easy to forgive an affair. Even if one does, there will always remain a doubt in one's mind: "Can I trust my ex-spouse again? No."

- Seek counseling if necessary to address your unresolved issues related to the previous marriage (e.g., unresolved pain, anger, and/or frustration).

Study Session 26

Relationships with in-laws and precautions

———◆•◆•◆•◆•◆———

1 There is an appointed time for everything,

and a time for every affair under the heavens.

2 A time to give birth, and a time to die;

a time to plant, and a time to uproot the plant.

3 A time to kill, and a time to heal;

a time to tear down, and a time to build.

4 A time to weep, and a time to laugh;

a time to mourn, and a time to dance. (Ecclesiastes 3: 1 – 4).

Marie mentioned:

Marriage is a learning process that brings two independents together to forge a common life during which they learn more and new things about each other and make compromises to accommodate their differences in strengthening their unity. It is in the same way that building a relationship with in-laws requires the investment of time socializing with them, learning more about them as they too learn about you, and in so doing making the necessary accommodations and compromises required to build the lifetime relationship established by our marriage.

Marriage is also a lot of work, and depending on one's cultural background, the roles are generally pre-established. You must constantly be mindful of the needs of another, but the greater burden of sustaining the marriage generally rests with the woman. There may be some truth in the statement that "the man may be the head of the house, but the woman is the neck" and can/should turn the head accordingly.

Everyone's marriage is different and there is no one-size-fits-all solution to challenges which are part of a normal marriage. What works in one marriage may not work in another, and the kind showed on soap opera and love movies is fiction for entertainment value.

Settle down with someone you are comfortable with and someone you know has your best interest at heart. Listen to the person; watch his actions, reactions and relationships.

Maintaining the relationship with friends and family after marriage had to be managed. We each were very attached to our siblings, and my husband to his parents as well (I lost my mother before marriage). As discussed above, I came to a realization that my husband needs his family as much as I needed mine. It helped very much that my in-laws are reasonable and independent people, who genuinely want to see our marriage succeed.

The need to have more children put a pressure on our relationship, especially as in-laws and family members became involved. This brought us closer together as we had to, as one front, deflect the pressure and resolve not to be bothered by it.

Jean clarified that she had no problem adjusting to her in-laws. She emphasized:

My in-laws were very nice to me and visited briefly just to see how we were doing. My in-laws were never a problem for me.

Doris

Interestingly, there were negatives within my extended family. My father predicted publicly that our marriage would not last, when he saw my husband dealing with two cranky children as he tried to change diapers, while I was busy doing something else. Obviously, this arrangement of sharing professional work and family work would not have suited him (my mother was a stay- at home Mom). Armed with a fresh PhD, my husband accepted a job in academia at a salary that was much less than he could have earned in the electronics industry/private sector, and this also was cause for concern. My mother criticized his decision as one that would force me to have to go to work, instead of staying at home (as a mother should...). I informed her that it was our joint decision – one that enabled EACH of us to work and to parent. Being an academic would give him the flexibility to do that. So, despite their warnings, we grew in stability and satisfaction.

Doris added:

I had the good fortune to meet my future in-laws when my husband and I were in our early stages of friendship, so there was no pressure to be the "girlfriend." On my days off from my waitressing job, I often took the bus to their home and helped with jobs (like painting the garage doors) in exchange for dinner and a ride back to my rented room. I got to "hang out" with them without my husband being around. We developed a nice relationship that just got better once we were married. My in-laws were very respectful of our marriage decisions, and unlike my parents, did not interfere or criticize what we were doing and how we were doing it. Their feedback was completely positive and supportive.

It helps that we were able to spend 6 years in our slow courtship. The luxury of this time made it possible for all of us to develop genuine relationships. I suspect that, if I hadn't married my husband, I still would have kept in touch with his parents.

When asked what helped him to adjust to his in-laws, Rowland mentioned:

> They were happy to give me a chance. I had been a good student, worked hard, was starting a good career. I was clean-cut and Catholic. What became difficult was when we decided to mix grad school with starting a family. While they complained to their daughter that I could be making more in a different job, allowing her to stay home, they did not directly criticize me. Our adjustment was to politely go our own way, saying only that these dual careers were what we felt called to be doing. The childcare was going to work out with the two of us and one baby—we'd be OK. When the second child came, and I took him to my grad school work, they were even more concerned.
>
> Again, we stuck to our plans and showed them that our children were healthy and happy. With the arrival of the third, they asked, "so who will take care of this one?" Our cheerful reply was "All of us!" As with dealing with our children, we planned for criticisms from in-laws, got ourselves both on the same page, and nicely went our own way. As the years passed, we had a good relationship although they always suspected we might be ruining our children or our own marriage.
>
> Practically, we honored them at holidays and family gatherings, kept them up-to-date with family news, and lived 200 miles away so that there were no surprise visits or easy meddling. A few aunts and uncles strongly spoke on our behalf too.

Andy, when asked what had helped him to adjust to his in-laws, he replied: "Nothing." Then he elaborated:

> I wasn't prepared for that but I quickly realized they will always be on the side of their child. They don't know what you face or where you are coming from. Respect them for who they are and having raised your spouse to marry you. Irrespective, give them their dues as you would your parents. As for the siblings of your spouse, it will vary on how you are received. If you flow well, flow with them. If you don't, it wasn't meant to be. Be cordial,

but you don't have to be best of friends; neither do you need enemies. That philosophy has helped me now, but it took me time.

Ted mentioned that it took 25 years to start relating amicably with his in-laws: "but in the end, it worked out. Have patience; it's worth waiting for."

Andy:

- As a guy, leave the house when provoked.

- Do not touch the core button of each other. Core button is where hurts the other person the most. It is a no-go-zone. Leave it alone no matter how much you are provoked.

- Leave your families outside your fights.

When asked about what helped him to adjust to his in-laws, Miguel responded: "having good communication with them."

Study Session 27

Forgiveness, on-going forgiveness and reconciliation

—————————◆•◆•◆•◆•◆————————

8 If we say, "We are without sin," we deceive ourselves, and the truth is not in us.

9 If we acknowledge our sins, he is faithful and just and will forgive our sins and cleanse us from every wrongdoing. (1 John 1: 8-9)

Andy:

There have been many difficult moments. In fact, too numerous to count, but for the major ones, many were my fault. How do we resolve them? Well sometimes through apologies, sometimes allowing time to heal things, and I must say many times, the willingness of my spouse to carry on. For me I have left countless times but been back due to her humility, and it is just the way we have been able to carry on. Some of the issues are still not resolved and maybe they will never be resolved, but we carry on in spite of them. One day at a time.

Marie

Forgive each other – to err is human, and we are both human. Forgiveness frees us to move forward instead of dwelling/getting stuck in the past. Do not look back and keep bringing up the past. Let bygones be bygones. Don't "let go" of yourself (appearance and grooming) while taking it for granted that you're already married anyway. Always pay the same kind of attention to grooming as you did when you started dating.

Intra- and interpersonal healing: Dangers of projection based on past relationship(s)

Lea:

> The in-laws are awesome – that has healed the healing process and I went into the marriage without the conscious effort to fight the temptation the stereotype which has been perpetuated for centuries that mothers-in-law are bad people toward their daughters-in-law. This positive attitude toward her has help me a lot to accept her and appreciate her as a mother figure to me as well. She has also accepted me in kind.

> This has brought a lot of mutual understand and I don't put my husband against his mother nor does he say or do things which would put me in a confrontation situation with her. I have realized that, as human beings, we tend to believe in stereotypes and myths about a certain group of people without searching for the facts. Yes, like in every society there are bad and good people. The fact is that some mothers-in-law are very mean toward their daughters-in-law and vice versa, that does not mean that ALL mothers-in-law and daughters-in-law are bad people toward one another.

Hilda mentioned that before her divorce she maintained a very cordial relationship with her mother-in-law and even after the divorce her first husband, she still had a good relationship with her ex-mother-in-law.

Ellen elaborated:

> I met my mother-in law when I was 13 years old. Bob and I were friends and we all hung out together. My mother-in-law was like

every one's mom in our crowd. She was very happy when my husband and I got together. We weren't even engaged and she bought us pots and pans. We were good friends before we got engaged.

Based on these observations, both Hilda and Lea encourage other women to be more civil with their respective mothers-in-law and avoid the risk of stereotyping all mothers-in-law as bad. Additionally, they cautioned the mothers-in-law to also be more welcoming, supportive and less critical of their respective daughters-in-law.

Hilda cited with great admiration how her ex-mother-in-law with sincere objectivity expressed how her son's limitations (Hilda's ex-husband) were the major contributing factor to the divorce as follows: "Even if he is my son, I hold him responsible for the things which he did and did not do, which no other woman should ever have to bear within a marriage."

Study Session 28

Celebrating small and big anniversaries in marriage

Nine participants emphasized the importance and advantages of celebrating wedding anniversaries.

Teresa mentioned that every year she celebrates with her husband their wedding anniversary because every anniversary day brings her memories of that day in which her life was changed forever. She added: "I hope it did the same for my husband as well. Celebrating every anniversary has helped us to prioritize our marriage bond."

Lorenzo stated:

> I grew up without seeing my parents celebrating their wedding anniversaries. However, after the religious minister who prepared us for our wedding and marriage suggested that we celebrate every year our wedding anniversary. He was right. We have been doing it every year and every year we get an opportunity to reflect on how we have changed, grown, improved ourselves, set new goals for the next year and evaluate how being married and faithful to one another has empowered us to become more stable and satisfied in our marriage. Thanks to my wife who constantly reminds that our wedding anniversary is coming up in a few days.

Eight participants mentioned that celebrating every year their wedding anniversaries was an opportunity for them to be together with their spouses and recall the significant events that have happened in their marriage journey. Special focus was on the joyful moments, the birth of their children, the challenges they have overcome and how celebrating each anniversary has helped to strengthen their stability and satisfaction in marriage. Ellen elaborated:

> My husband and I decided early on in our first year of marriage to celebrate every anniversary. Even if people are accustomed to celebrating the 10th, 25th, the 50th, 60th,75th, both of us agreed to celebrate each wedding anniversary in almost the same way we each other's birthday in thanksgiving for the gift of life.

Doris emphasized:

> Each wedding annual celebration does not have to be so elaborate, in a hotel, with many people and extraordinary expenses. Every anniversary has to be celebrated as another significant milestone in marriage, especially in these days when divorce seems not to take a break!!! It was as simple and yet profoundly meaningful as: sharing a special hug, a simple breakfast, lunch or dinner, a glass of wine in honor of the anniversary, and/or for those with a religious background, to offer together a prayer of thanks to God. My husband and I agreed on attending Mass together on the day of our wedding anniversary.

Miguel:

It is important to celebrate anniversaries. For instance, the renewal of wedding vows and focus on their values. Celebrating the wedding anniversary for my wife and I is not about being spending too much money, but the value of acknowledging one another, thanking God for another year as a married couple, renewing our commitment to one another and plan on how to continue moving forward together.

Marie

> Make a special effort to remember birthdays, anniversaries and other milestone dates, including sad ones like the death of family members and close family friends.

Study Session 29

Permanent sites for professional marriage and remarriage services

———————◆•◆•◆•◆•◆———————

Some of the participants mentioned that it was very hard for them to know whom to turn to and where to receive comprehensive preparation for marriage or remarriage. Some churches offer some preparations but they tend to be very brief and generally just scratch the surface of the areas which need to be explored and mastered. Currently, there are so many institutions where people are trained to become well-equipped and others profession but when it comes to marriage, there is still a great need for permanent sites where interested individuals and partners may turn for training and preparation for marriage.

This may help them to get a better sense of what they are getting into before making a final commitment to one another and afterward as they make the challenging adjustments to married life. Most of the participants the author interviewed for this book and all the participants in his study about stability and satisfaction in remarriage mentioned that they needed guidance about preparation for marriage within an environment that is conducive to healing, reflection, prayer, and learning.

The site(s) for marriage and remarriage services should be permanently located so that interested people know where they could be referred and/or come back for professional help whenever needed in the near and/or distant future. The directors and the other personnel working in such buildings are cautioned not to stigmatize people who experience divorce. An atmosphere of hospitality and respect for the dignity of every person needs be held to the highest standards.

Five participants recalled having attended, in a costly hotel, a weekend preparation course that was organized by three remarried couples and a priest. All five participants described that weekend experience as very inspiring, very loaded, expensive, and without an opportunity for any follow-up session, even if needed, because the directors admitted that they were not professionals, and there was no place to meet afterward.

Alicia stated:

> I have heard of many places where different types of training are offered (e.g., computer training centers, nursing schools, police training centers, sports centers, and schools for foreign languages). However, I have never heard of a training center exclusively dedicated to the training of people for marriage and/or remarriage. That bothers me a lot. I remember pronouncing my vows before the municipal judge the day I married for the first time and the second time, but I did not receive any training about marriage or remarriage. Above all, I really needed it before my remarriage because I did not want to run into the same problems without knowing how to address them.

Alicia clarified:

> The Pentecostal Church I go to does not offer pre-remarriage training. In my local church and county there is no established site for remarrying parents where they can go and receive pre-remarriage counseling. To the best of my knowledge, I think only the Catholic Church is the one that has started to offer that kind of training, and I hear that it is only for Catholics who are widowed or divorced who have received their annulments from the previous marriage.

Daniel (a resident of a county other than Alicia's) mentioned:

> I haven't seen nor heard of any permanent building or center offering remarriage counseling in my local county. However, it is heartbreaking to see my close friends divorcing, remarrying within six months or so, and then re-divorcing. I wish I knew

where to send them to seek guidance before they continue hurting their children also by those changes.

When asked if he thought his friends would go there to seek remarriage services, Daniel replied:

> I am not certainly sure. Probably, let me answer your question by referring to the people who go to the medical clinics. I do not go to my doctor unless I am sick or if he recommends me for a medical check-up. Honestly, who goes to the medical doctor without being sick? However, the good news is that, whenever you get sick, you can go to the hospital because it is there for you. You know where it is, or someone else takes you there. Therefore, it is my educated guess and heartfelt desire that people in need of remarriage services will have greater chances of going there, especially if they are accessible, with safe parking lots, financially affordable for people with low income, and if the confidentiality is ensured.

Geoffrey said:

> Based on personal experience, most remarriage problems became more explicit after I started living with my second wife, not during our courtship, and yet I did not know where to seek help when I most needed it. I am not sure whether I had idealized so much my wife while we were dating, and I felt I did not need any professional help before remarriage. However, I think that, if I had known of any established buildings with qualified personnel (particularly for remarried spouses), I would probably have sought post-remarriage counseling to address the problems which we faced in the first five years of remarriage.

Eight participants (four males and four females) expressed that they had observed increasing numbers of divorces, remarriages, and second divorces in their neighborhoods. All of them made the suggestion regarding an urgent need for establishing permanent buildings where people can receive remarriage services. Those participants also suggested that the buildings should be geographically accessible, within safe neighborhoods, with parking spaces, and where people can be referred for help at an affordable cost for the professional services they receive.

Fred stated:

> There is a school almost for everything, for example, driving schools, agriculture and seminaries where religious ministers are trained. However, the government has almost nothing set in place to help the people prepare themselves for marriage or remarriage. The marriages in civil courts are primarily focused on paperwork and writing signatures. Beyond that, there is no preparation at all for married life.
>
> I do not know of any other church, apart from the Catholic Church, where a selected number of Catholics, those whose marriages have been annulled, are offered a one-day or one-weekend pre-remarriage preparation workshop. I hear the content is good, but the workshop is too rushed, with limited numbers of participants, and very costly.

Fred added:

> Based on my marital experience of twenty-five years in both marriages, I have realized that I have made many mistakes because of my ignorance about first marriages and the complexity of remarriage. Hopefully, I would have avoided some of those mistakes if I had participated in a comprehensive premarital preparation program within a formalized institution.

The participants highlighted that some of the workshops that professionals could offer would include those focused on how to help couples communicate better, to learn and practice different skills. Examples of such skills include: problem-solving and/or conflict resolution skills, open and mutual negotiation dialogues about finances, sexuality, parenting and step-parenting skills and setting clear boundaries with in-laws. Couples should also be counseled on how to attain a level of acceptance that some aspects of life cannot be changed and how to stop attempting to change one another.

Based on the consulted literature, remarrying parents may be helped in such workshops to learn about how to maintain a significant level of shared spirituality and prayer time, to learn to forgive oneself and the other, to constantly recall the purpose(s) of their marriage, to learn to negotiate differences of opinion, and, whenever necessary, to join a support group and to seek professional help before the problems escalate (Ahrons, 2004; Ganong & Coleman, 1989; Kerr & Bowen, 1988; O'Leary et al., 1998).

My experience

Based on what you have read in this session, reflect on your own personal experience.

1. What self-help books, training programs, or other resources have I found helpful in regard to:

    o   Preparation for marriage

    o   Marriage enrichment

    o   Parenting in marriage

2. What are the main ideas that have impacted me in each of the self-help books, training programs, or other resources that I have identified in question 1?

_____

3. Which of the ideas in each the self-help books, training programs, other resources have I found least helpful and why?

4. Which of the self-help books, training programs, or other resources
    can I recommend to somebody based on his or her situation?

Study Session 30

On-going education and mutual empowerment in marriage

————————◆•◆•◆•◆————————

Annette asked:

> As a woman who went to school, with two degrees, did I really
> go to school just to become a stay-home mom? I also want to
> develop my potential and all the training I got for my career.

Both Rowland and his wife value education and they both encouraged
each other study, supported each other in raising their children so that
each could accomplish his/her desired career. Based on personal
experience Rowland mentioned that being a dual-career couple
positively impacted your marriage stability and satisfaction. He
elaborated:

> We both have believed in the intrinsic goodness of the other's
> professional work. It was worth encouraging and even
> sacrificing to make the other successful. Our work also paid
> well enough that we could be free of major financial worry,
> educate our children well, and plan for retirement. Having these
> goals outside one's individual ambitions was helpful in
> weathering professional up and downs. Seeing our partner
> initiating good changes in society was very satisfying and worth
> personal sacrifices or delays in goals. Balancing dual careers
> provided opportunities to demonstrate our real commitment to
> making the other the best person they could be.

On the other hand, Rowland also observed that being a dual-career
couple somehow negatively impacted their marriage stability and
satisfaction but managed to move forward. He clarified:

365

Juggling two careers was often only possible with sacrifice by one or both of us, or by our children (although they were largely unaware). We often were able to "take turns" in a sense, as needed. Sacrifice meant delaying goals, taking lower-paying positions to do the right kind of work, suffering through job uncertainty and loss, and constantly fighting social conventions that defined narrow roles for men and women. One-sided sacrifice could breed instability and resentment, especially if the benefits are unclear or transitory. We avoided these by constantly talking through what was needed and what we could accomplish. We also thought we were waging small battles that would make it easier for the next couple (or our children's generation) to avoid our constraints. Sadly, this has more often not been the case. Systems and attitudes that we slightly pried apart to make room for our family slid quickly back into place once we were gone. A new generation is still facing many of the same battles.

Additional recommendations to individuals and couples to embrace marriage stability and satisfaction are presented

Rowland:

> Expect change. Practice on achieving harmonious little changes to be ready for the blockbusters that life will present.

> Talk with "I" messages, rather than with "you" messages. E.g., "I feel overwhelmed by deadlines and getting kids to sports" versus "You should figure out how to drive the kids—it's your problem".

> Avoid criticism and complaint.

> Be a peacemaker with your spouse, family, children, everyone you meet. It's a good habit.

> Seek help when you suspect it is needed. It's a hard job, and we don't arrive with all the answers.

Anne made the following recommendations to individuals and couples to embrace marriage stability and satisfaction:

> Talk with others that are in a strong marriage. Learn from them and model your life after them. Keep God in your marriage. Work at it, it's worth going through life together!

Ellen remarked:

> Marriage is the most wonderful relationship with love you can have in a lifetime. I would let them know it is a daily job to keep a marriage going strong but worth the work.

Lea emphasized the following rules/guidelines which have helped her and her spouse in their marriage:

- always be honest

- make sure we spend one full day together each weekend

- compromise

- try and listen to the other when their angry and revisit it when you are calm

- be each other's best friend

- always tell the truth

- be patient

Sarah made the following recommendations: "Communication, talk it out! And, don't be afraid to ask for help."

Doris started her recommendation to individuals and couples to embrace marriage stability and satisfaction by quoting Saint Pope John XXIII to captures the essence of a stable and satisfying marriage:

> 'In essentials unity;
> in non-essentials liberty;

and in all things charity.'
(Pope John XXIII, 1961)

Marriage has predictable and unpredictable dimensions that make the institution move forward in a healthy way. The process is jazz. You begin with a solid base in friendship, etc. (the attributes under Question #1 that unify, and that you can predictably count on). Then one partner leads with a melody, and the other riffs off it, with deep understanding of the person and what informs this new direction. Sometimes the other partner takes the lead. Listening carefully and being present with and for the other person makes something fresh happen – over and over, as a sophisticated and nuanced piece of music evolves for each person (liberty) and for the couple itself. Kindness and consideration matter 24/7 (charity). The result is a marriage that is stable, satisfying, and unique. It's an amazing experience – the ultimate life journey.

Lea added the following DO NOT's that couples need to implement to embrace marriage stability and satisfaction:

- Do not hold grudges

- Do not blame each other

- Do not talk negatively about each other to one another

Sarah: "Communicate with each other and be open and honest to foster trust"

Ellen stated and then cautioned:

Marriage stability and satisfaction is important but not everything you need in a marriage. You need to work together daily to have a successful marriage. You can make it a fun time for both of you. We never go to bed mad at each other. If we have a disagreement, we talk it out and compromise a settlement before bed. We kiss "hello, good bye and good night" always. We also kiss spontaneously for no reason.

You need to say you are sorry if you make a mistake.

Don't let pride get in your way.

Do not disrespect your spouse.

Do not argue with your spouse in front of children or visitors.

Do not get mad or angry at your spouse if you want something and they don't. Talk it out.

Study Session 31

Using divorcee prevention strategies and seeking professional help
before it is too late

Miguel, when asked about some insights or advice he would like to
recommend to individuals and couples to embrace marriage stability and
satisfaction, he mentioned:

> To seek mentors or counseling when needed. There is nothing
> wrong with asking for help. It is wrong not to ask for help when
> it is needed. Ask for help before it is too late.

Mateo's advice to those interested in marriage and those already
married: "persevere and make your family Christ-centered."

Doris provided the following insights or advice as recommendations to
individuals and couples to embrace stability and satisfaction marriage:

> If there is a struggle once married and things seem hopeless to
> stay together, try a marriage encounter, speak to a priest, go for
> counseling, and pray for God's help.

Doris described in detail as follows some of the things which help her
(and her husband) to avoid the risk of marriage becoming a boring
routine:

> We entered the marriage as hopeful and curious individuals who
> enjoy continuous learning and development. Being bored is not
> part of our reality, so it doesn't enter our marriage.
>
> Marriage has enriched our hopefulness and curiosity. Learning
> together is a joyful gift, as we seek to engage each other as
> friends who know one another well and can anticipate what our

partner would find interesting. We see life as rich and full of new things to learn and experience. And since we see our relationship as also growing, there is always new territory to explore together. Nothing is ever "routine."

We enjoy the hopefulness of each new day, and have remained busy and engaged, such that we are never bored with what we're doing or with each other. We read widely, but often differently (both on paper – books and periodicals, and online), exchange items electronically, and talk about a range of intellectual, philosophical, practical (how to), and spiritual topics over meals or during extended car time together (we have a lot of this time as retirees visiting grandchildren, family and friends around the country).

He may share an interesting news story or analysis that he thinks might appeal to me, while I share interesting human interactions and "news" about neighbors, family, or fictional characters. He loves words and their etymology. Often, he plays with words and makes up a riddle or joke based on a prior but recent conversation. He uses at least one new word (that I have never heard before) every week. He continually surprises me and makes me laugh! I like the poetry of words, and share poetry. We both do a daily meditation with Richard Rohr and share insights, and we try to read a daily scripture passage and also discuss. Now that we are retired, we have time to watch really excellent TV series, and discuss these fictional characters as well. We are never at a loss for meaningful discussion. From my perspective, my husband is the most interesting person I know.

Sometimes we also take on new projects. One person may take the lead, and the other supports. For example, I became a beekeeper several years ago. My husband assembles all the frames and "supers," and I tend the bees and extract honey. We create new learning curves for ourselves, and new topics to research and master.

Study Session 32

Empty nest arrangements and marital bond recommitment

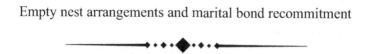

Some of participants whose children had left home stated that the adjustment was not easy for them as individuals and as a couple. Two participants in particular emphasized that after their children went their separate ways, there was an emptiness in their home which could be felt and threatening at times. They had spent most of their time caring for the children, their lives as spouses had been kind of "put on hold" and started to project their frustrations on each other.

Teresa mentioned that she had a lot of arguments with her husband after the children left home. She added: "I had got accustomed to cooking for many people and after all the children left, kept cooking a lot of food, and this upset my husband very much, accusing me of wasting money and food. I became so defensive as I realized that had no idea of the pain I felt after all the children moved out of the house and out of state!!! It was like we (my husband and I) were getting to know each other again."

On the other hand, some of the other participants mentioned that after the adjustment to their children's leaving home, they felt so much relief and enjoyed each other's company as spouses, including but limited to increased sexual intimacies and satisfaction in their marriages. Other participants also shared their experiences of the empty as well as cautioned other couples to prepare well for the empty next and do their best to share life together and recommit to one another and enjoy their hobbies.

Elaborating on the empty nest experience, Doris stated:

> SEXUAL INTIMACY: It is a natural extension of our friendship and partnership. We care for ourselves, try to remain

attractive, take the time to understand each other's needs and preferences, and enjoy this very special way of being together. Like everything else, our intimacy has evolved, and changes as we get older. Surprisingly, some of those changes have been for the better! I would argue that Items A through I (above) constitute a kind of ongoing relational foreplay that is psychologically positive, and makes the sexual encounter meaningful and joyful.

Hobbies and stress reduction strategies (e.g., humor and sports)

Participants were asked about their hobbies and stress reduction strategies as well as what helps each one of them to avoid the risk of their marriage relationship become a boring routine. Examples of some of their responses include the following:

Ted:

> We reserve time ever Friday night to have sit together to discuss the week's problems (not necessarily with each other) and to have someone listen to our venting.
>
> Oh Yea...Don't forget sex. That helps a lot.

Lea:

- We have more flexibility to do things like go on date nights and take trips. This is used as quality time spent together to develop further connection in the relationship.

- Making sure we are doing new things and getting out of the normal routine

- Traveling and experiencing the world together

Ellen

We love to try new things and travel. We try and plan a trip at least every 6 months. It could be going to a Caribbean Island or a driving trip. We read about different things we can do together and introduce new experiences to enjoy.

Doris

COUPLE TIME. We carve out special time for us as a couple. We positioned ourselves as the central players in our family drama – the ones who needed to stay close, strong, connected, and able to endure whatever assailed our family. This meant we needed to take care of each other, and grow our relationship. Children were an intense part of our partnership, but transient. Throughout their childhood, we reserved one weekend each year (our anniversary weekend) to get away and focus on each other. Annually, we asked a trio of grandmother and great aunts to babysit, or swapped weekends with friends who also needed time away from children.

Even before children, we were committed to taking care of our relationship. When we were   married, neither of us could cook, so we invented a ritual called the "Intimate Dinner Party." Taking turns, we prepared a complete meal from scratch and served the other partner a special, candlelit dinner that said "I love you" in a powerful way. Practical benefits were that we adopted especially tasty items to serve when friends came to dinner. We learned to cook while pampering each other in this special way, and we maintain this ritual, even though we are now quite competent in the kitchen.

Beyond these specific events, we paid for or traded babysitting time (when we couldn't find or afford babysitters) so we could go out to dinner occasionally, or to a concert. And we grew curious children who were glad to accompany us on road trips to destinations that interested us as adults. We learned to make special time in and around the children – sometimes when they were asleep.

Doris added:

> LAUGHTER and SINGING. We want to be joyful people, and these help us. My husband makes me laugh every day. Both laughter and music lighten any load and brighten any difficult situation. We have learned from Buddhism that misery is transient, and often self-imposed. We try to let it wash over us and not dwell in it. When something bad happens, we assess the situation as follows: Are we or our children harmed? If the answer is "No," we know we will get through it together.
>
> Music and laughter help us to be tough on the issues but soft or gentle with each other. We go for the satisfaction of the long line – the WHOLE piece of music – not worrying about perfecting each measure. We are not rattled by small bumps or discomforts on the way.
>
> My husband and I also leave home periodically, and go on learning treks – locally, to drivable distant locations, and even to exotic destinations, as we identify new thing to learn by doing. Fortunately, we have some resources to travel. Unlike our family and work lives, in their intensity, our current lives are focused in the present, and specifically, on the present moment. We are enjoying the simplicity and peacefulness of this focus. It is slow enough for us to think, ponder, catch our breath, listen to a bird sing, admire a mated pair as they build a nest, notice a centipede making its way in the grass, and be grateful for each other and all our blessings.

Study Session 33

Retirement planning and participation in community voluntary
activities

When Rowland was asked about what helped him and his wife to
adjust harmoniously to their retirement, Rowland mentioned:

> We both like to keep busy and never defined our deepest selves
> as our work identities. We retired in part because all three sons
> announced that they were expecting within six months. We
> chose to be available to watch and support these new arrivals.
> We also had built a weekend cottage in upstate NY that could
> serve as a retirement home, far from our work sites.
>
> Just before retirement we began working on developing a
> consecrated life within Catholicism. ... [This] provided a good
> focus for growing spirituality. We immediately became
> involved in our small rural parish doing significant volunteer
> work. We have an active outdoors focus on a wooded property
> with many seasonal chores around gardening. In our wider
> community we volunteer for Meals on Wheels and Catskill
> Neighbors (serving shut-ins). Finally, we have traveled often to
> see grandchildren in California, Oregon and New York City.
> We have ventured abroad with friends on "bucket-list" kinds of
> trips about once a year. These efforts are usually collaborative,
> giving us many reasons to work together and continue talking
> about our shared goals.

Rowland made the following recommendations for spouses preparing
for retirement:

It (retirement) can be a momentous change in life's pace, your individual and couple identity, and your circle of friends. Try to view it positively, as an opportunity rather than as a stumbling block. Being prepared financially makes a dramatic difference. Begin early to assess and plan your downsizing a household, finding a place for retirement, and goals like travel or hobbies. Consider how your household will work with both home—what is necessary and fair? Finally, and individually, look for new friendships as well as ways to nurture existing (but possibly neglected) friendships. View it as a new outward-looking adventure, rather than a confining retreat from active life.

Rowland:

We recognized early that the only constant in life is change, such that adaptability and constant growth were needed. We have always had some challenge on our agenda – moving forward with children, work, and now in retirement. Because we work hard, these challenges tend to be ambitious, even a little crazy at first. But most have turned out well enough, giving satisfaction and in a sense, we can think bigger next time. We also have avoided distractions like TV, media, shopping, computer games, that tend to be isolating and ultimately predictable and repetitive. Boredom is an individual's own problem—taking the first step to fight the inertia of boredom can be tiring and challenging. Successes on small adventures lead to bigger ones, and before long you are busy and more energized that you could have imagined.

Study Session 34

Recommendations for spouses preparing for retirement

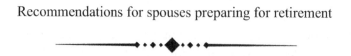

Rowland:

> It can be a momentous change in life's pace, your individual and
> couple identity, and your circle of friends. Try to view it
> positively, as an opportunity rather than as a stumbling block.
> Being prepared financially makes a dramatic difference. Begin
> early to assess and plan your downsizing a household, finding a
> place for retirement, and goals like travel or hobbies. Consider
> how your household will work with both home—what is
> necessary and fair? Finally, and individually, look for new
> friendships as well as ways to nurture existing (but possibly
> neglected) friendships. View it as a new outward-looking
> adventure, rather than a confining retreat from active life.

Jean mentioned that the following strategies have helped her and her
spouse to adjust harmoniously to their retirement:

> We had to change our life style by cutting down on the
> expenditures. Trying to explain those who had been depending
> on us to find other resources to cover them. It was hard on those
> who were accustomed to monthly help. We had to find different
> activities to occupy our time.

Doris elaborated as follows:

> People and financial resources, and the imagination to use them
> creatively. The difference between us as young retirees (we
> were 62) and people who are reluctant to retire is that we
> counted on the strength of our imagination and friendship to

shape a positive experience. We could SEE ourselves as comfortable, happy, and engaged in retirement, and liked what we saw.

We retired with a generous pension to a home we had been building and developing for 10 years before we moved there full-time. Because we had a presence (and family – my sister and her extended family) in this new community, and in the local Catholic Church, where we were lectors and sang with the choir, we arrived as familiar faces – not newcomers. We had instant acceptance and community on the same road where my sister lived and had developed loving friendships with neighbors who extended their good will to us. It was a perfect situation

We did not stop working hard, but the shift to wonderful outdoor work that interested and relaxed us – gardening and landscaping, forest and stream management, building projects – filled our days and kept us happily in the present moment. We did not feel stuck with or "on top of" each other, but rather carved out our own outdoor projects, with lots of alone, quiet time, and came together for meals and rest breaks, and helped each other as needed. For the first time in many years, we had NO night meetings, and enjoyed long hours together making and enjoying meals, etc.

We wanted to continue developing all aspects of our being. For intellectual stimulation, we kept in touch with friends and happenings online, and found luxurious time to read and reflect on our reading. Occupationally, we maintained a link with our professional past by teaching courses online for the first two years. Since we had never watched TV, we only watched an occasional Netflix movie, delivered by mail or rented from the local General Store. I joined book groups, and pursued professional writing and electronic mentoring (Skype is wonderful). We both said yes to volunteer projects and roles in our new community (both church and civic organizations), and developed new friendships and new networks. We had access to great hiking, skiing, swimming, and took advantage as we could to stay healthy.

My husband and I expected to discover new interests and possibilities. As the grandchildren were growing, we invented new rituals, first driving cross-country during the winter for West Coast visits to wonderful communities where our sons lived, and later flying the grandchildren to our home for an intense week of "Cousin Camp" activities and bonding for this new generation. When grandchildren celebrated their 10th birthdays, we planned and accompanied them (two cousins at a time) on an international trip, taking them to places we also wanted to explore. At 15, we organize "coming of age" rituals by the family's multigenerational women (for our granddaughters) and men (for our grandsons). We will continue to invent new rituals.

Jean made the following recommendations for spouses preparing for retirement:

Work as long as you can. Be prepared to reduce you budget to fit the adjusted income. Plan on activities that are not costly. Plan travels ahead of time to get reasonably priced tickets. Be ready to fit your living style in the new budget.

Likewise, Doris mentioned the following recommendations:

- Imagine what you will do and where you will be. If you don't like what you see, you have work to do before you retire.

- Be active in planning your retirement – not passive.

- The idea is not just to stop working, but to shift into other meaningful activities and pursuits – both individually and as a couple

Study Session 35

Legacy of giving back and/or contribution to society

9 Let love be sincere; hate what is evil, hold on to what is good;f

10 love one another with mutual affection; anticipate one another in showing honor.g

11 Do not grow slack in zeal, be fervent in spirit, serve the Lord.h

12 Rejoice in hope, endure in affliction, persevere in prayer.i

13 Contribute to the needs of the holy ones,j exercise hospitality.

14 Bless those who persecute [you],k bless and do not curse them.

15 Rejoice with those who rejoice, weep with those who weep. (Romans 12: 9 – 15).

Give back to the community. Charity begins at home if one of the spouses develops Alzheimer's or other medical conditions, the other spouse should be there for them even if the other person is not aware of who they are. That is not the time for marital infidelity.

Some who have experienced spouses physical and mental breakdown to the point that the other cannot recognize them persevere because they know they know who the person is…in sickness and in health until death do you part.

Study Session 36

Participating in the salvation of each other's soul and hope for eternal life in Heaven

3 Blessed be the God and Father of our Lord Jesus Christ, who in his great mercy gave us a new birth to a living hope through the resurrection of Jesus Christ from the dead,

4 to an inheritance that is imperishable, undefiled, and unfading, kept in heaven for you

5 who by the power of God are safeguarded through faith, to a salvation that is ready to be revealed in the final time.

(1 Peter 1: 3 – 5)

Lucy mentioned:

"I am not a pessimist but a realist. I am convinced that the only certain thing in life is death. As soon as one is conceived in his or her mother's womb, that person is destined to die. This is true for married people as well. As soon as they are married, anything can happen to one or both of them. Therefore, during courtship, and more so after marriage, the spouses should talk about their mortality and put in writing their individual Wills and start preparing to encounter death - as a path way to their final destination in Heaven. All is well that ends well."

Lucy elaborated:

I am a catholic woman and so is my husband. I learned that life can change in a minute after the death of both my parents in automobile accident on the day of my wedding. After the wedding reception, they both died instantly and my husband supported me all the way through and we started talking about the certainty of death. The priest who officiated our wedding was the very one who celebrated the funeral Mass of my parents. In his homily, he mentioned the following words which I have kept ever since in my heart:

'Life is mystery and a gift from God. Your parents made their marriage vows 55 years ago to stay together until death do they part. They parted together in death to Heaven - our True Citizenship is in Heaven.'

Marie

Our individual career progression demands forced my husband and I to live in different countries for close to 10 years. The relatively "independent" lifestyles in a way established different "kingdoms" which initially made it difficult to settle down when we eventually lived together. We clashed often on decisions affecting the running of our home and parenting our daughter. With time, re-adaptation and communication, we got over most of our differences through a mixture of compromise and understanding.

Part 5

Writing the Conclusion

Dear reader, allow me to ask you to write your conclusion to this book. This is also what I asked every reader of my book on embracing stability and satisfaction in marriage.

The Author acknowledges that without the participants' contributions this book would not have come into existence in its current format. Each participant had a significant impact on the author and for that he is most grateful. The author learned from the participants that one must consistently work on marriage stability and satisfaction and that work needs to be done before dating till death do they part., with the eyes always focused on Heaven. In the meantime, whoever contemplates marriage or is married, the author suggests that you should:

- Think stability in marriage, seek it and practice it and work on it every day

- Think satisfaction in marriage, seek it, practice it and work on it every day

- Think Heaven as your destination with your spouse for ever and ever and work every day on becoming a holy person by doing God's will in your life.

Therefore, the conclusion to this book can only be written by "YOU." What have the participants taught you? How do you plan on implementing what you have learned regarding stability and satisfaction in marriage? Now it is time for you to write your own story!

Appendices

Writing dating and marriage check lists to reinforce stability and satisfaction in marriage

Each one of the following appendices is connected to the others. Each may serve as an extra tool for use before dating, during courtship and after the wedding in order to identity the challenges need to be resolved because of their significant impact on the stability and satisfaction in marriage. The following narrative may serve to illustrate the importance of the attached appendices.

I (author) have realized that before many people shop, they take time to write a shopping list. That time spent exploring what needs to be bought and what can wait, or assuring that a certain item is still available, is time well invested and has many benefits. It saves time in the shopping center. It helps to avoid the risk of buying something one wants but does not necessarily need. It helps to stick to the budget and it leaves room for some flexibility while actually shopping.

Similarly, shopping requires self-knowledge. A friend told me (author) that despite spending time writing a shopping list, whenever she goes shopping, she buys things which attract her attention even if she does not really need them. She referred to herself as a "compulsive buyer." She finally made an intervention for herself after realizing that she could not control her "compulsive impulses" to buy things for the sake of buying. The effective intervention she designed for herself involved her writing a shopping list at home, then e-mailing her written list to the shopping center. A designated person would put the needed items in a shopping cart, bring it outside the shopping center, and then complete the transactions. She added: "this intervention has saved me a lot of money and is very effective for me. Ever since, I only buy what I really need and not what attracts my eyes. I shop for what I lack and need."

Based on the above observations, as the time of writing a shopping list and self-knowledge are important as pertains to shopping, analogically, writing a checklist while searching for a suitable marriage partner has many benefits. The author refers to this endeavor as "writing a dating and marriage checklist." It seems many people tend to become romantically attracted to physically attractive people, or at least admire them and somewhat imagine the attractive person is competent, integrated and so forth. Caution has to be taken in regard to whom to date instead of letting oneself start dating or marry someone based solely on attractiveness. Hence the adage: "Not everything that glitters is Gold."

Therefore, the following appendices are included in this book to serve as samples which can be checked and added upon by every person, engaged couple, spouse(s) in order to use time more productively while searching for a prospective spouse, while dating and after marriage. Each sample appendix of checklists is not conclusive and may not apply to every person or couple. However, it is included in this book to serve as a suggestion and an invitation for those interested in dating and making a commitment to marriage to stability and satisfaction in marriage. Therefore, each person and couple should take some time to write checklists for dating, courtship and marriage.

The author suggests, among other things to write for each checklist, it is important to include the identification of challenges to avoid or resolve. In other words, whoever is interested in dating well and making a commitment to establish a stable and satisfactory marriage ought to take the time to write a checklist of specific challenges and explore effective strategies for resolving them. Caution: each person should avoid the risk of thinking that the partner will change automatically for the better after marriage. Secondly, given the core value each person allocates to a specific area in his or her life, each list should be marked as Applicable (A), Negotiable (N) or Unnegotiable (U).

Note: The following items on each samples of check lists have been deduced by the author from some of the contributions of the participants in this book. Others have been modified or elaborated upon by the author with permission from the Tribunal of the Diocese of Metuchen, New Jersey, from the Tribunal's Autobiographic report checklist form.

Appendix 1: Personal characteristics

Key: A = Applicable; N = Negotiable; U = Unnegotiable

Myself				Personal challenges	Partner/Spouse		
A	**N**	**U**	**#**		**A**	**N**	**U**
			1	Struggling with sexual orientation			
			2	Drinking problem / Alcoholism			
			3	Drugs/Substance use (using/used			
			4	Moderate/severe mental disorders			
			5	Mood swings			
			6	Very dependent			
			7	Very independent			
			8	Very demanding/domineering			
			9	Irresponsible with money			
			10	Impulsive			
			11	Self-centered			
			12	Possessive / jealous			
			13	Tendency to lie			
			14	Prone to depression			
			15	Emotional /physical abuse			
			16	Sexual infidelity			
			17	Physical abuse			
			18	Severe economic problems			
			19	Other addictions			
			20	Food * self-starvation			
			21	Food * eating to point of feeling ill			
			22	Food * eating in secret or isolation			
			23	Food* binge eating and purging it			
			24	Gambling			
			25	Pornography			

			#				
			26	Infertility			
			27	Problems with physical health			
			28	Dishonest			
			29	Aggressive assertiveness			
			30	Vindictive			
			31	Belief in superstition and witchcraft			
			32	Religious fanatic			
			33	Struggling with faith/religion			
			34	Inflexible			
			35	Pleaser			
			36				
			37				

Appendix 2: Family Background

Key: A = Applicable; N = Negotiable; U = Unnegotiable

Myself				Family Background	Partner/Spouse		
A	N	U	#		A	N	U
			1	Untimely deaths or illness			
			2	Divorces in the family			
			3	Sexual abuse			
			4	Drinking problems in the home			
			5	Psychological/emotional problems			
			6	Violence			
			7	Trouble with the law			
			8	Drug abuse			
			9	Extremely close family ties			
			10	Severe economic problems			
			11	Sexually transmitted diseases			
			12	Genetic diseases			
			13				
			14				
			15				

			16				
			17				
			18				
			19				
			20				
			21				
			22				
			23				
			24				
			25				
			26				
			27				
			28				
			29				
			30				
			31				
			32				
			33				
			34				
			35				
			36				
			37				

Appendix 3: Problems existing before the wedding

Key: A = Applicable; N = Negotiable; U = Unnegotiable

Myself					Partner/Spouse		
A	N	U	#		A	N	U
			1	**Problems existing before the wedding**			
			2	Family opposition to the wedding			
			3	Opposition to the wedding by friends			
			4	Poor communication			

			5	Long absences / separations			
			6	Irritability /argumentativeness			
			7	Indications of unfaithfulness			
			8	Drug or alcohol use			
			9	Physical abuse			
			10	Internal pressure to get married			
			11	External pressure to get married			
			12	Pregnancy before marriage			
			13	Financial difficulties			
			14	Mixed religions			
			15	Unemployment			
			16	Poor job performance			
			17	Sexual problems			
			18	Lack of attention / affection			
			19	High sensitivity to criticism			
			20	Worrisome			
			21	Procrastinator			
			22	Extreme risk-taker			
			23	Very cautious			
			24	Irreconcilable differences			
			25	Sarcasm			
			26	Avoidance of problems			
			27	Blaming self			
			28	Blaming of others			
			29	Lack of interest in continuing education/ learning			
			30	Lack of agreement on dual career advancement			
			31	Superiority complex			
			32	Inferiority complex			
			33				
			34				
			35				
			36				
			37				

Appendix 4: *At time of the wedding*

Key: A = Applicable; N = Negotiable; U = Unnegotiable

Myself					Partner/Spouse		
A	*N*	*U*	#	*At time of the wedding*	*A*	*N*	*U*
			1	Not mature enough to understand what the marital commitment entails			
			2	Trying to run away from something unpleasant in one's life			
			3	Marry because have been dating for so long			
			4	Serious doubts whether marriage is the right decision			
			5	Experience lack of strong marital bond and happy relationship			
			6	Little or no previous dating experience			
			7	Personal involvement/experience with physical or sexual abuse			
			8	Personal involvement with alcohol or drug abuse			
			9	Receiving counseling for moderate /serious psychological disorder			
			10	Unable to establish stability in a job			
			11	Experience of violence or other antisocial behavior			
			12	Experiencing difficulties with sexual orientation			
			13	Feel that most important thing in life is personal happiness			

			14	Intend to marry as long as spouse is faithful			
			15	Want to back out of the ceremony but cannot do so			
			16	Have no experience of a stable and satisfactory marriage while growing up			
			17	Feel obliged to marry as a means to continue living together			
			18	Never intend to have children			
			19	Intend to delay, limit or exclude children until financially stable			
			20	Never intend to take responsibility for any children			
			21	Believe sexual infidelity is acceptable			
			22	Sexually unfaithful before or shortly after the wedding			
			23	Grew up believing that divorce is acceptable			
			24	Feel divorce is acceptable in certain circumstances			
			25	Intend to only marry as long as both feel fulfilled			
			26	Feel that because of pre-marital pregnancy , there is no other alternative to marry			
			27	Intend to marry because only because parental objections to living together			
			28	Afraid to marry for some reason (Identify such reason[s])			
			29	Do not understand that marriage is a spiritual union (Sacrament) and not only just a civil union			

Myself			#		Partner/Spouse		
			30	Deceiving the other partner about the reason for marrying			
			31	Concealing something to the partner which he or she has a right to know before marrying			
			32				
			33				
			34				
			35				
			36				
			37				

Appendix 5: *After the wedding: invitation to seek professional help before it is too late*

Key: A = Applicable; N = Negotiable; U = Unnegotiable

Myself					Partner/Spouse		
A	N	U	#	*After the wedding*	A	N	U
			1	Marital infidelity			
			2	Infertility			
			3	Moderate/severe mental disorders			
			4	Physical illness			
			5	Lack of employment			
			6	Stress			
			7	Severe economic problems			
			8	Sexually unfaithful before or shortly after the wedding			
			9	Do not want to have sexual relations unless birth control is used			
			10	Lack of parenting skills / mutual collaboration in parenting			
			11	Empty nest syndrome			
			12	Low sexual desire			

			13	Struggles with caring for elderly/sick parents/relatives			
			14	Struggles caring for special needs child/children			
			15	Lack of mutual agreement regarding pets			
			16	Struggling to share the faith and pray together			
			17	Struggling with anger management			
			18	Mood swings and poor communication			
			19	Sexless marriage after having children			
			20				
			21				
			22				
			23				
			24				
			25				
			26				
			27				
			28				
			29				
			30				
			31				
			32				
			33				
			34				
			35				
			36				
			37				

Appendix 6: Empty nest

Key: A = Applicable; N = Negotiable; U = Unnegotiable

Myself				Empty nest	Partner/Spouse		
A	N	U	#		A	N	U
			1	Feeling sad and relief too when the children leave home			
			2	Adjusting to become a couple again, after years of sharing the home with children			
			3	Filling the emptiness/void in the daily routine created by absent children			
			4	Establishing a new kind of relationship with adult children			
			5				
			6				
			7				
			8				
			9				
			10				
			11				
			12				
			13				
			14				
			15				
			16				
			17				
			18				
			19				
			20				
			21				
			22				
			23				
			24				
			25				

			26				
			27				
			28				
			29				
			30				
			31				
			32				
			33				
			34				
			35				
			36				
			37				

Appendix 7: After the Retirement and/or death of a spouse

Key: A = Applicable; N = Negotiable; U = Unnegotiable

Myself			After retirement		Partner/Spouse		
A	N	U	#		A	N	U
			1	Symptoms of Adjustment disorder after retirement			
			2	Poor communication			
			3	Interpersonal emotion regulation			
			4	Coping with boredom:			
			5	Excessive drinking			
			6	Excessive television time			
			7				
			8				
			9				
			10				
			11				
			12				
			13				

			14			
			15			
			16			
			17			
			18			
			19			
			20			
				After Death of a spouse		
			1	Loneliness		
			2	Hope for eternal life		
			3			
			4			
			5			
			6			
			7			
			8			
			9			
			10			
			11			
			12			
			13			
			14			
			15			
			16			

References

Adams, J. (1980). *Marriage, divorce, and remarriage in the Bible: A fresh look at what scripture teaches.* Grand Rapids, MI: Zondervan.

Ahrons, C. (1994). *The good divorce: keeping your family together when your marriage come apart.* New York: HarperCollins.

Ahrons, C. (2004). *We are still family: What grown children have to say about their parents' divorce.* New York: Harper Collins.

Amato, P. R. (1987). Family processes in one-parent, stepparent, and intact families: The child's point-of-view. *Journal of Marriage and Family, 49,* 327 – 337.

Amato, P., & Ochiltree, G. (1987). Child and adolescent competence in intact, one-parent, and stepfamilies: An Australian study. *Journal of Divorce, 10,* 75 – 96.

Amen, D. (1998). *Change your brain - change your life: The breakthrough program for conquering anxiety, depression, obsessiveness, anger and impulsiveness.* New York: Three Rivers Press.

American Association of Marriage and Family Therapy (AAMFT) (1998). *Code of ethics.* Washington, DC.

Anderston, T., & White, G. (1986). An empirical investigation of interaction and relationship. Patterns in functional and dysfunctional nuclear families and stepfamilies. *Family Process*, 407 – 422.

Aponte, H. (1994). *Bread and spirit: Therapy with the new poor, diversity of race, culture, and values.* New York. Norton.

Baum, N. (2003). The male way of mourning divorce: When, what, and how. *Clinical Social Work Journal, 31* (1), 37–50.

Beal, J., Coriden, J., & Green, T. (Eds.). (2000). *New commentary on the code of canon law.* New York: Paulist Press.

Berger, K. (1998). *The developing person through the lifespan* (4th ed.). New York: Worth.

Berger, R. (2000). Remarried families of 2000: Definitions, description, and interventions. In W. Nichols, M. Pace-Nichols, D., Becvar, & A.Napier (Eds.), *Handbook of family development and intervention*, pp. 371 – 390. New York: John Wiley & Sons.

Berry, D. (1998). *The divorce recovery source book.* Los Angeles: NTC/Contemporary Publishing Group.

Billings, A. (1979). Conflict resolution in distressed and nondistressed married couples. *Journal of Consulting and Clinical Psychology, 23*, 362 – 371.

Black, D. (1998). *Smart dating: A guide to starting and keeping a healthy relationship.* New Orleans, LA: Paper Chase Press.

Bohr, D. (1999). *Catholic moral tradition: In Christ, a new Creation.* Huntington, IN: Our Sunday Publishing Division.

Boszomenyi-Nagy & Krasner, B. (1986). *Between give and take: A clinical guide to contextual therapy.* New York: Brunner/Mazel.

Bowlby, J. (1980). *Attachment and loss (Vol. 3).* New York: Basic Books.

Bowen, M. (1972). On the Differentiation of Self. First published anonymously in J. Framo (Ed.), *Family Interaction: A Dialogue Between Family Researchers and Family Therapists*, pp. 111-173. New York: Springer.

Brehm, S. (1992). *Intimate relationships* (2nd ed.). New York: McGraw-Hill.

Breunlin, D., Schwartz, R., & Kune-Karrer, B. (1992). *Metaframeworks: Transcending the models of family therapy.* San Francisco: Jossey-Bass.

Brown, J. (1998). *The self.* Boston: McGraw-Hill.

Brown, S., & Booth, A. (1996). Cohabitation versus marriage: A comparison of relationship quality. *Journal of Marriage and Family, 58*(3), 668 – 679.

Burleson, B., & Denton, W. (1997). The relationship between communication skill and marital satisfaction: Some moderating effects. *Journal of Marriage and Family,* 59, 884–902.

Carter, B., & McGoldrick, M. (1998). *The expanded family life cycle: Individual, family, and social perspectives* (3rd ed.). Boston: Allyn & Bacon.

Catoir, J. (1996). *Where do you stand with the church? The dilemma of divorced Catholics.* New York: Alba House.

Champlin, J. (1997). *Together-for-life.* Notre Dame, IN: Ave Maria Press.

Cherlin, A. (1992). *Marriage, divorce, remarriage (revised and enlarged).* Cambridge, MA: Harvard University Press.

Coleman, M., & Ganong, L. (1985). Remarriage myths: Implications for helping professions. *Journal of Counseling and Development, 64,* 116 – 120.

Covey, S. (1989). *The seven habits of highly effective people: Powerful lessons in personal change.* New York: Simon & Schuster.

Cox, F. (2002). Remarriage: A growing way of American life. In F. Cox (Ed.). *Human intimacy: Marriage, the family, and its meaning,* pp. 513 – 537. Australia: Wadsworth.

Creswell, J. (1998). *Qualitative inquiry and research design: Choosing among five traditions.* Thousand Oaks, CA: Sage.

Cunningha, C., & Foley. W. (1994). The relative stability of remarriages: A cohort approach using vital statistics. *Family Relations, 43* (3), 305 – 311.

Davidson, M. (2003). *The everything divorce book: Know your rights, understand the law, and regain control of your life.* Avon, MA: Adams Media Corporation.

Demo, D., & Acock, A. (1997). Singlehood, marriage, and remarriage: The effects of family structure and family relationships on the mother's well-being. *Journal of Family Issues, 17,* 388-407.

de Shazer, S. (1985). Keys to solution in brief therapy. New York: Norton.

Dulton, D., & Aron, A. (1999). Some evidence of heightened sexual attraction under conditions of high anxiety. In E. Aronson (Ed.), *Readings about the social animal* (8th ed.), pp. 486 – 499. New York: Worth Publishers/W. H. Freeman.

Erera-Weatherley, P. (1996). On becoming a stepparent: Factors associated with the adoption of alternative stepparenting styles. *Journal of Divorce and Remarriage, 25,* 155 – 174.

Erlandson, D., Harris, E., Skipper, B., & Allen, S. (1993). *Doing naturalistic inquiry: A guide to methods.* Newbury Park, CA: Sage.

Falicov, C. J. (1988). *Family transitions: Continuity & change over the life cycle.* New York: The Guilford Press.

Ferch, S. (1998). Intentional forgiving as a counseling intervention. *Journal of Counseling and Development, 76,* 261 – 270.

Ferch, S. (1999). Marital forgiveness: A case study of forgiveness and multiple extra-marital affairs. *Marriage and Family: A Christian Journal, 2,* 169 – 170.

Ferch, S. (2001). Relational conversation: Meaningful communication as a therapeutic intervention. *Journal of Counseling*
and Values, *45* (2), 118 – 138.

Fincham, F., Beach, S., & Davila, J. (2004). Forgiveness and conflict resolution in marriage. *Journal of Family Psychology, 18* (1), 72 – 81.

Fitzpatrick, M. (1990). Models of marital interaction. In H. Giles & W. Robinson (Eds.). *Handbook of language and social psychology, pp. 433 – 451. Chichester*, NY: Wiley.

Fisch, R., Weakland, J., & Segal, L. (1982). *The tactics of change: Doing therapy briefly.* San Francisco: Jossey-Bass.

Fivaz, R. (1991). Thermodynamics of complexity. *Systems Research, 9,* 19-32.

Floyd, F. (1988). Couples' cognitive/affective reactions to communication behaviors. *Journal of Marriage and Family, 50,* 523 – 532.

Framo, M. (1985). Remarried families: Couple's issues. In H. Grunebaum, R. Chasin, & D. Jacobs (Directors of Course Syllabus), *Family therapy – Working with couples*, pp. 29 – 30. Harvard Medical School: Department of Continuing Education, Cambridge, MA

Frankl, V. (1963). *Man's search for meaning.* New York: Washington Press.

Freedman, J., & Combs, G. (1996). *Narrative therapy: The social construction of preferred realities.* New York: Norton.

Ganong, L., & Coleman, M. (1989). Preparing for remarriage: Anticipating the issues, seeking solutions. *Family Relations, 38,* 28 – 33.

Gelso, C., & Fassinger, R. (1992). Personality, development, and counseling psychology: Depth, ambivalence, and actualization. *Journal of Counseling Psychology, 39,* 275 – 298.

Glaser, B. (1992). *Basics of grounded theory analysis.* Mill

Valley, CA: Sociology Press.

Glaser, B., & Strauss, A. (1967). *The discovery of grounded theory: Strategies for qualitative research.* New York: Aldine Hawthorne.

Glick, P., & Norton, A. (1977). Marrying, divorcing and living together in the United States today. *Population Bulletin, 32* (5), 4 – 8.

Gold, B. (2023). Gray divorce stories: The truth about getting divorced over 50 from men and women who've done it. Barry Gold, Middletown, DE.

Gordon, K., Baucom, D., & Snyder, D. (2004). An integrative intervention for promoting recovery from extramarital affairs. *Journal of Marital and Family Therapy, 30* (2), 213 – 231.

Gottman, J. (1991). Predicting the longitudinal course of marriage. *Journal of Marital and Family Therapy, 17*, 3 – 7.

Gottman, J. (1993). A theory of marital dissolution and stability. *Journal of Family Psychology, 7*, 57 – 75.

Gottman, J. (1994a). What predicts divorce? Hillsdale, NJ: Lawrence Erlbaum Associates.

Gottman, J. (1994b). *Why marriages succeed or fail… and how you can make yours last.* New York: Simon & Schuster.

Gottman, J., Coan, J., Carrere.A., & Swanson, C. (1998). Predicting marital happiness and stability from newlywed interactions. *Journal of Marriage and Family, 60* (1), 5 – 23.

Gottman, J., & Levenson, R. (1988). The social psychophysiology of marriage. In P. Noller & M.A. Fitzpatrick (Eds.), *Perspectives on marital integration,* pp.182-199.Clevedon, England: Multilingual Matters.

Gottman, J., Notarius, C., Gonso, J., and Markman, H. (1976) *A couple's guide to communication.* Champaign, IL: Research Press.

Gottman, J., Ryan, K., Carrere, A., Erlay, P. (2001). Toward a

405

scientifically based marital therapy. In H. Liddle, D. Santisteban, R. Levant, & J. Bray (Eds.), *Family psychology: Science-based interventions*, pp. 147 – 174. Washington, DC: American Psychological Association.

Gottman, J., & Silver, N. (1999). *The seven principles for making marriage work: A practical guide from country's foremost relationship expert.* New York: Crown.

Gray, C. (1996). When therapy is not in the client's best interest: Adapting clinical interventions to the stages of divorce. *Journal of Divorce & Remarriage, 26*, 117 – 127.

Groth-Marnat, G. (1999). *Handbook of psychological assessment* (3rd ed.). New York: John Wiley & Sons.

Hackney, H. & Cormier, S. (1994). *Counseling strategies and interventions.* Boston: Allyn & Bacon.

Haley, J. (1984). *Problem solving therapy* (2nd ed.). San Francisco: Jossey-Bass.

Heínisch, P. (1955). *Theology of the Old Testament: Be holy as I Yahweh our God am holy.* Collegeville, MN: The Liturgical Press.

Hendrick, S. (1995). Close relationships research: Application to counseling psychology. *The Counseling Psychologist, 23*, 649 – 665.

Himes, K., & Coriden, J. (1996). Current theology: Pastoral care of the divorced and remarried. *Theological Studies, 57* (1), 97 – 124.

Hollingshead, A. (1975). *Four factor index of social studies.* Unpublished manuscript.

Jacobson, N., & Christensen, A (1996). *Integrative couple therapy: Promoting acceptance and change.* New York: Norton.

James, S., & Johnson, D. (2001). Social interdependence, psychological adjustment, and marital satisfaction in second marriages.
Journal of Social Psychology, 128 (3), 287 – 303.

Johnson, S., & Greenberg, L. (1994). Emotion in intimate interactions: A synthesis. In S. Johnson & L. Greenberg (Eds.), *The heart of the matter: Perspectives on emotion in marital therapy*, pp. 297 – 323. New York: Brunner/Mazel.

Kabali, J. (2017). Embracing remarriage stability and satisfaction. *Dorrance Publishing Co. Pittsburg, PA.*

*Kabali, J. (*2023). Stability and satisfaction in remarriage (3rd ed). Relationship Harmony, Inc. Middletown, DE.

Kaslow, F. (1996). *Handbook of relational diagnosis and dysfunctional family patterns.* New York: John Wiley & Sons.

Kelley, P. (1995). *Developing healthy stepfamilies.* New York: The Harrington Park Press.

Kelley, S., & Burg, D. (2000). Why remarriages succeed. In S. Kelley & D. Burg (Eds.), *The second time around: Everything you need to know to make your marriage happy.* New York: HarperCollins.

Kennedy, T (1995). *Doers of the word: Moral theology for the third millennium.* Liguori (Missouri), Triumph Books.

Kerr, M., & Bowen, M. (1988). *Family evaluation: The role of the family as an emotional unit that governs individual behavior and development.* New York: W. W. Norton.

Kiura, J. (2004). *Success in marriage.* Nairobi, Kenya: Paulines Publications Africa.

Kupisch, S. (1987). Children and stepfamilies. In A. Thomas & J. Grimes (Eds.), *Children's needs: Psychological perspectives.* Washington, DC: National Association of Psychologists.

Kurdek, L. (1994). Conflict resolution styles in gay, lesbian, heterosexual nonparent, and heterosexual parent couples. *Journal of Marriage and Family, 56,* 705 – 722.

Larson, H., & Holman, T. (1994). Premarital predictors of marital quality and stability. *Family Relations, 43,* 228 – 237.

Larson, H., Nowell, K., & Nichols, S (2002). A review of three comprehensive premarital assessment questionnaires.

Journal of Marital & Family Therapy, 28 (2), 233 – 239.

LeBey, B. (2004). *Remarried with children: Ten secrets for successfully blending and extending your family.* New York: Bantam Books.

Levant, R., & Philpot, C. (2002). Conceptualizing gender in marital and family therapy research: The gender role strain paradigm. In H. Liddle, D. Santisteban, R. Levant, & J. Bray (Eds.). *Family psychology: Science-based interventions*, pp. 301 – 329. Washington, DC: American Psychological Association.

Lewis, H. (1980). *All about families: The second time around.* Atlanta, GA: Peachtree.

Lincoln, Y., & Guba, E. (1985). *Naturalistic inquiry.* Beverly Hills, CA: Sage.

Lofas, J., & Sova, D. (1995). Stepparenting: *The real problems. The real solutions* (Revised and updated). New York: MJF Books.

Lofas, J. (1998). *Family Rules: Helping stepfamilies and single parents build happy homes.* New York: Kensington Books.

Lofas, J., & Sova, D. (1985). *The family challenge of the nineties: Stepparenting* (Revised and updated). New York: Kensington Books.

Lutz, P. (1983). The stepfamily: An adolescent perspective. *Family Relations, 32*, 367 – 375.

MacDonald, W., & DeMaris, A. (1995). Remarriage, stepchildren and marital conflict: Challenges to the institutionalization hypothesis. *Journal of Marriage and Family, 57* (2), 387 – 399.

Maslow, A. (1961). Peak experiences as acute identity experiences. American Journal of Psychoanalysis,21, 254-260. Reprinted in A. Combs (Ed.), *Personality theory and counseling practice.* Gainesville, FL: University of Florida Press.

McCulullough, M., Spence, N., & Worthington, E. (1994). Encouraging clients to forgive people who hurt them: Review, critique, and research prospectus. *Journal of Psychology and Theology, 33*, 3 – 20.

McFarland, F. (1992). Counselors teaching peaceful conflict resolution. *Journal of Counseling and Development, 71*, 18 – 22.

McGoldrick, M. (1995). *You can go home again: Reconnecting with your family.* New York: Norton.

McGoldrick, M. (1998). Becoming a couple: In M. McGoldrick & B. Carter (Eds.), *The expanded family life cycle: Individual, family, and social perspectives* (3rd ed.), pp. 231 – 248. Boston: Allyn & Bacon,

McGoldrick, M., & Carter B. (1998). Remarried families: In M. McGoldrick & B. Carter. *The expanded family life cycle: Individual, family, and social perspectives* (3rd ed.), pp. 417 – 435. Boston: Allyn & Bacon.

McGoldrick, M., Gerson, R., & Shellenberger, S. (1999). Genograms: *Assessment and intervention* (2nd ed.). New York: Norton.

McGoldrick, M., Giordano, J., & Pearce, J. (Eds.). (1996). *Ethnicity & family therapy* (2nd ed.). New York: The Guilford Press.

Megan, Z. (1998). *Exploring adolescent happiness: Commitment, purpose, and fulfillment.* Thousand Oaks: Sage.

Mertens, D. (1998). Research methods in education and psychology: Integrating diversity with quantitative and qualitative approaches. Thousand Oaks, CA: Sage.

Miller, A. (1985). Guidelines in stepparenting. *Psychotherapy in Private Practice, 3*, 99 – 109.

Miller, W. (Ed.). (1999). *Integrating spirituality into treatment: Resources for practitioners.* Washington, DC: American Psychological Association.

Minuchin, S. (1974). *Families and family therapy.* Cambridge,

MA: Harvard University Press.

Minuchin , S., & Nichols, M. (1993). *Family healing: Strategies for hope and understanding.* New York: The Free Press.

Morrow, S., Rakhsha, G., & Castaneda, C. (2001). Qualitative research methods for multicultural counseling. In J. Ponterotto, M. Casas, L. Suzuki, & C. Alexander (Eds.), *Handbook of multicultural counseling* (2nd ed.), pp. 575 – 603. Thousand Oaks: Sage.

Myers, J., & Schwiebert, V. (1999). Grandparents and stepgrandparents: Challenges in counseling the extended-blended family. *Adultspan Journal,* 1, 50 – 60.

Muelleman RL, Burgess P. Male victims of domestic violence and their history of perpetrating violence. *Acad Emerg Med.* 1998; 5: 866–870.

Nakonezny, P., & Shull, R. (1995). The effect of no-fault divorce law on the divorce rate across 50 states and its relation to income, education, and religiosity. *Journal of Marriage and Family, 57* (2), 477 – 488.

Nichols, W. (1996). *Treating people in families: An integrative framework.* New York: The Guilford Press.

O'Leary, D., Heyman, R., & Jongsman, A., Jr. (1998). Communication. In D. O'Leary, R. Heyman, & A. Jongsman, Jr. (Eds.). *The couple's psychotherapy treatment planner,* pp. 51 – 59. New York: John Wiley & Sons.

Oyebade, J. (2005). *Love guide: Top secrets for peace of mind, success and happiness in your love-life.* London: Good Publications International.

Papernow, P. (1998). *Becoming a stepfamily: Patterns of development in remarried families.* Cambridge, MA: Gestalt Institute of Cleveland Press.

Parkes, C., Laungani, P., & Young, B. (Eds.). (1997). *Death and bereavement across cultures.* London: Routledge.

Paul VI. (1969). *Evangelii nuntiandii.* Rome: The Vatican Press.

Peck, M. (1997). *Further along the road less traveled: The unending journey toward spiritual growth.* New York: Simon & Schuster.

Pope John XXIII: "'In necessarii unitas, in non necessariis libertas, in omnibus caritas'," Recherches de

science religieuse 49, (1961):552 (549-560).Rafuls, S., & Moon, S. (1996). Grounded theory methodology in family therapy research. In D. Sprenkle & S. Moon (Eds.). *Research methods in family therapy*, pp. 64 – 80. New York: The Guilford Press.

Reis, H., Senchak, M., & Solomon, B. (1985). Gender differences in the intimacy of social interaction: Further examination of potential explanations. *Journal of Personality and Social Psychology, 48*, 1204 – 1217.

Richmond, V. (1995). Amount of communication in marital dyads as a function of dyad and individual marital satisfaction. *Communication Research Reports, 12*, 152 – 159.

Robinson, G. (1984). *Marriage, Divorce & Nullity: A guide to the annulment process in the Catholic Church.* Collegeville, MN: The Liturgical Press.

Russell-Chapin, L., Chapin, T., and Sattler, L. (2001). The relationship of conflict resolution styles and certain marital satisfaction factors to marital distress. *The Family Journal: Counseling and Therapy for Couples and Families, 9* (3), 259 – 264.

Rutter, S. (1998). Lessons from stepfamilies. *Journal of Marriage and Family Therapy 38*, 185 - 190.

Sager, C. (1985). Second marriages: Working with the couple. In H. Grunebaum, R. Chasin, & D. Jacobs (Directors of Course Syllabus): *Family therapy – Working with couples*, pp. 47 – 48. Harvard Medical School: Department of Continuing Education, Cambridge, MA.

Sager, C., Brown, H., Crohn, H., Engel, T., Rodstein, E., & Walker, L. (1983). Treating the remarried family. New York: Brunner/Mazel.

Satir, V., & Baldwin, M. (1983). *Step-by-step: A guide to creating change in families.* Palo Alto, CA: Science and Behavioral Books.

Shlemon, B. (1992). *Healing the wounds of divorce: A spiritual guide to recovery.* Notre Dame, IN: Ave Maria Press.

Skeen, P., Covi, R., & Robinson, B., (1985). Stepfamilies: A review of the literature with suggestions for practitioners. *Journal of Counseling and Development, 64,* 121 – 125.

Smoke, J. (1995). *Growing through divorce.* Eugene, OR: Harvest House.

Spinier, G., & Thompson, L. (1984). *Parting: The aftermath of separation and divorce.* Beverly Hills, CA: Sage.

Sprenkle, D., & Moon, S. (1996). *Research methods in family therapy.* New York: Guildford.

Staudacher, C. (1987). *Beyond grief: A guide for recovering from the death of a loved one.* Oakland, CA: New Harbinger.

Staudacher, C. (1991). *Men & grief: A guide for men surviving the death of a loved one; A resource for caregivers and mental health professionals.* Oakland, CA: New Harbinger.

Stepfamily Foundation (2004). *Stepfamilies.* http:/www.stepfamily.org

Staudacher, C. (1994). *A time to grieve: Meditations for healing after the death of a loved one.* New York: HarperSanFrancisco.

Strauss, A. (1987). *Qualitative analysis for social scientists.* New York: Cambridge University Press.

Strauss, A., & Corbin, J. (1998). *Basics of qualitative research: Techniques and procedures for developing grounded theory* (2nd ed.). Thousand Oaks, CA: Sage.

Subortnik, M., & Harris, G. (1994). *Surviving infidelity: Making decisions, recovering from the pain.* Holbrook, MA: Adams Publishing.

Tatelbaum, J. (1980). *The courage to grieve: Creative living, recovery & growth through grief.* New York: Harper & Row.

Tessman, L. (1978). *Children of parting parents.* New York: Norton.

Thies, J. (1977). Beyond divorce: The impact of remarriage on children. *Journal of Clinical Child Psychology, 6,* 59 – 61.

Thureau S, Le Blanc-Louvry I, Thureau S, Gricourt C, Proust B. Conjugal

violence: a comparison of violence against men by women and women by men. *J Forensic Leg Med.* 2015;31: 42 – 46.

Treadway, D. (1989). *Before it's too late: Working with substance abuse in the family.* New York: Norton.

Tribunal for the Roman Catholic Diocese of Metuchen. Autobiographical Report Checklist Form, Effective December 8, 2015. Piscataway, NJ.

Visher, J. (1994). Stepfamilies: A work in progress. *The American Journal of Family Therapy, 22* (4), 337 – 344.

Wallerstein, J., & Blakeslee, S. (1989). *Second chances: Men, women, and children a decade after divorce.* Boston: Houghton-Mifflin.

Wallerstein, J., & Blakeslee, S. (1995). *The good marriage: How and why love lasts.* New York: Warner Books.

Walsh, F. (1998). *Strengthening family resilience.* New York: Guilford.

Walsh, F. (2002). A family resilience framework: Innovative practice applications. *Family relations, 51,* 130 – 137.

Walsh, W. (1992). Twenty major issues in remarriage families. *Journal of Counseling and Development, 70* (6), 709 – 716.

Wang, H. & Amato, P. (2000). Predictors of divorce adjustment: Stressors, resources, and definitions. *Journal of Marriage and Family, 62* (3), 655 – 669.

White, L. (1990). Determinants of divorce: A review of research in the eighties. *Journal of Marriage and Family, 52,* 904 – 912.

White, M. & Epson, D. (1990). *Narrative means to therapeutic ends.* New York: Norton.

Worden, W. (1991). *Grief counseling and grief therapy: A handbook for mental health practitioner* (2nd ed.). New York: Springer.

Wolcott, I. (1999). Strong families and satisfying marriages. *Family Matters, 53,* 21 – 30.

Yalom, I. (1995). *The theory and practice of group psychotherapy* (4th ed.). New York: Basic Books.

Zwack, J. (1983). *Annulment: Your chance to remarry within the Catholic Church: A step-by-step guide using the New Code of Canon Law.* Cambridge, MA: Harper & Row.

Made in the USA
Columbia, SC
22 August 2024

40920011R00228